# DAVID

# L David.

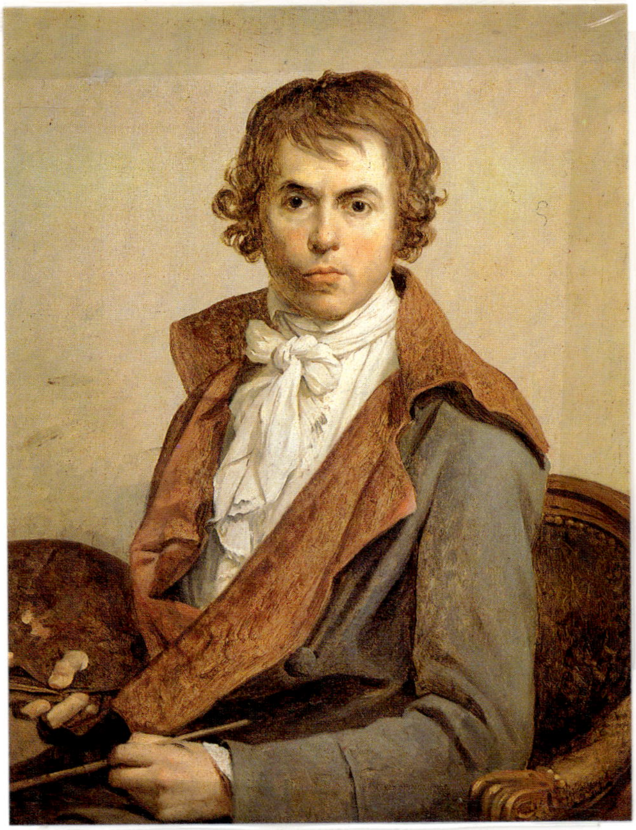

BY BERNARD NOËL

BONFINI PRESS

*Title page*: Self Portrait, 1794
Oil on canvas, 31⅞″ × 25½″ (81 × 64 cm)
Musée du Louvre, Paris

*Series published under the direction of:*
Madeleine Ledivelec-Gloeckner

*Translated from the French by:*
Marie-Hélène Agüeros

Printed in Italy – Industrie Grafiche Cattaneo s. p. a. , Bergamo

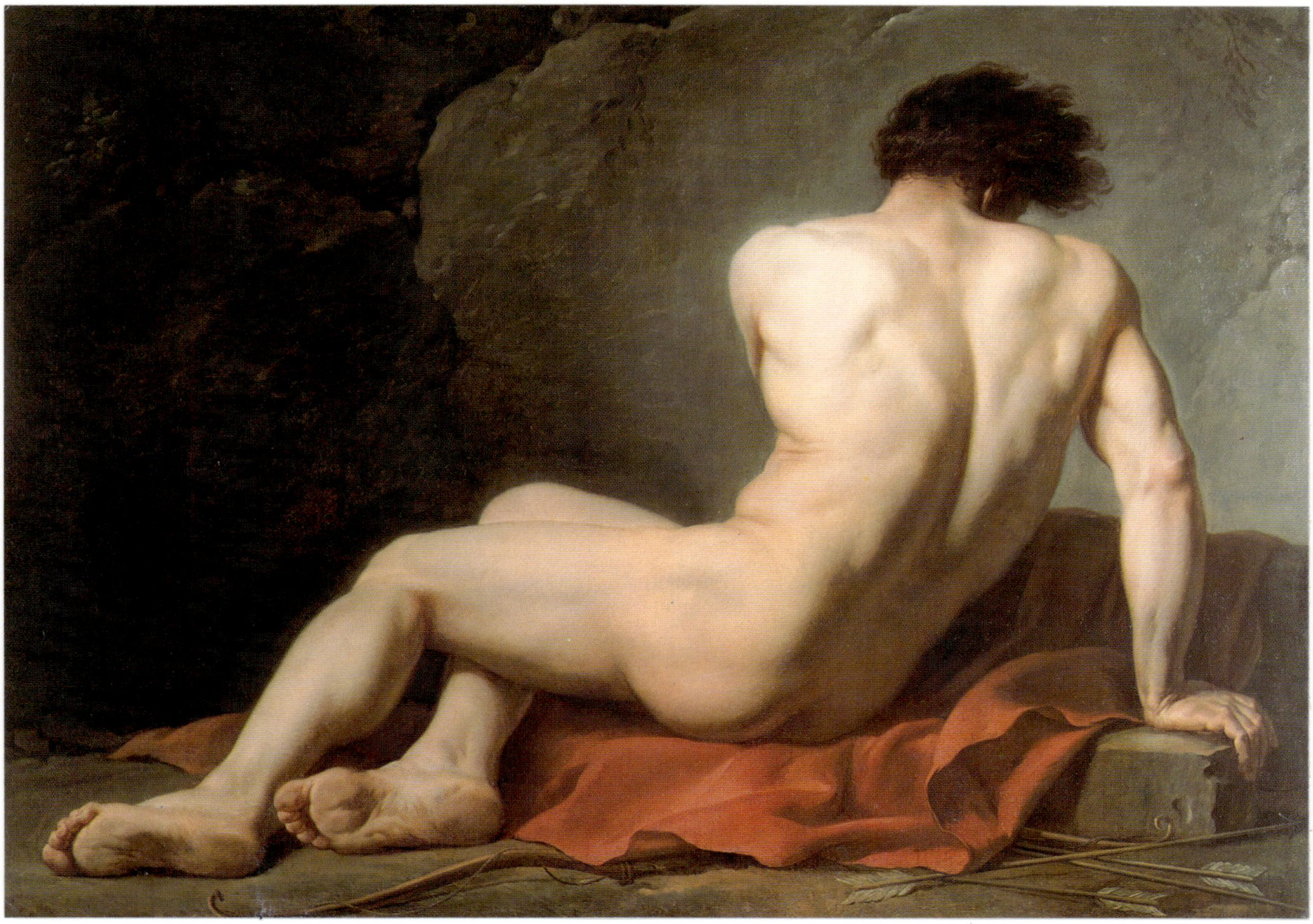

NUDE STUDY (also called PATROCLUS), ca 1780. Oil on canvas, 49¼″ × 36$^{15}/_{16}$″ (125 × 170 cm)
Musée Thomas Henry, Cherbourg, France

Virtue and beauty: In the contemporary world these two words are rarely associated, especially to describe the foundation of the bourgeoisie's politics or ideals. There was a time before and during the French Revolution, however, when the contradiction between change and continuity was resolved. Subsequently, when diverging interests prevailed, this unique moment in time seemed beyond belief, as if it had never happened. Jacques-Louis David's art captures this moment and records its brilliance forever. When the bourgeoisie claimed to speak on behalf of the people, it merely was a vanguard carrying the people's force of protest. It suddenly rushed toward change after having been patient for so long. In the heat of this revolutionary movement the bourgeoisie successfully combined ethics with politics. Reality became a reflection on history, and the present was both the flower of the past and the root of the future. The government had been overthrown, social structures had been changed, everything was beginning anew. Everything, however, also ended. Values were suddenly overturned.

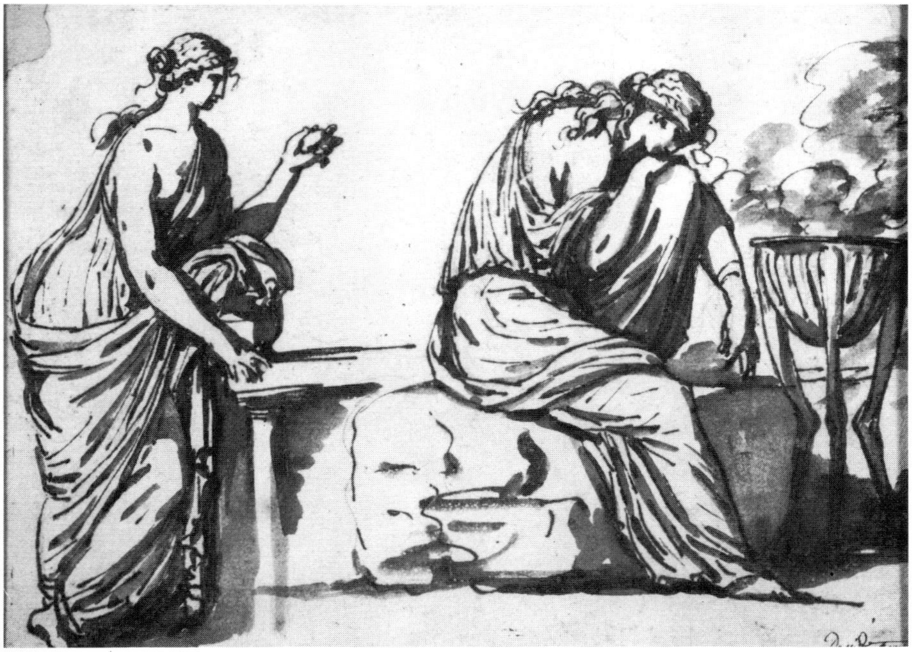

*Two Women, 1775-1780*
*Pen and brown ink*
*and gray wash on*
*white paper, 5¹¹⁄₁₆″ × 7⅞″*
*(14.5 × 20 cm)*
*Smith College Museum*
*of Art, Northampton*
*Massachusetts*

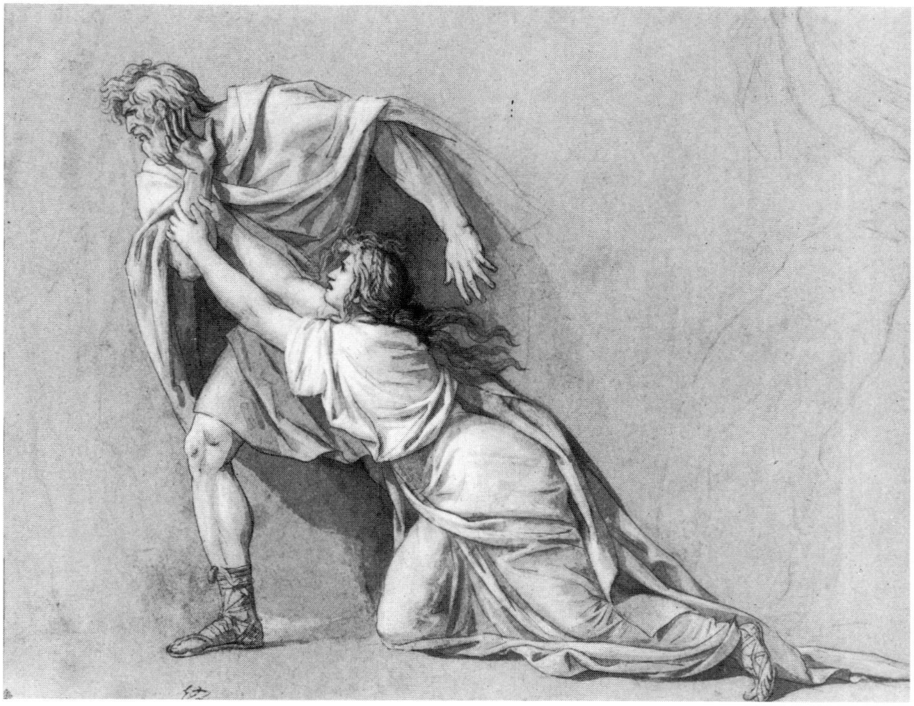

*The Departure of*
*Marcus Attilius Regulus*
*for Carthage, 1785-1786*
*Pen and black ink*
*with brush and gray wash*
*over black chalk*
*heightened*
*with white gouache*
*on gray-blue laid paper*
*12⅜″ × 16″*
*(31.5 × 41.5 cm)*
*The Art Institute of Chicago*
*Clarence Buckingham*
*Collection*

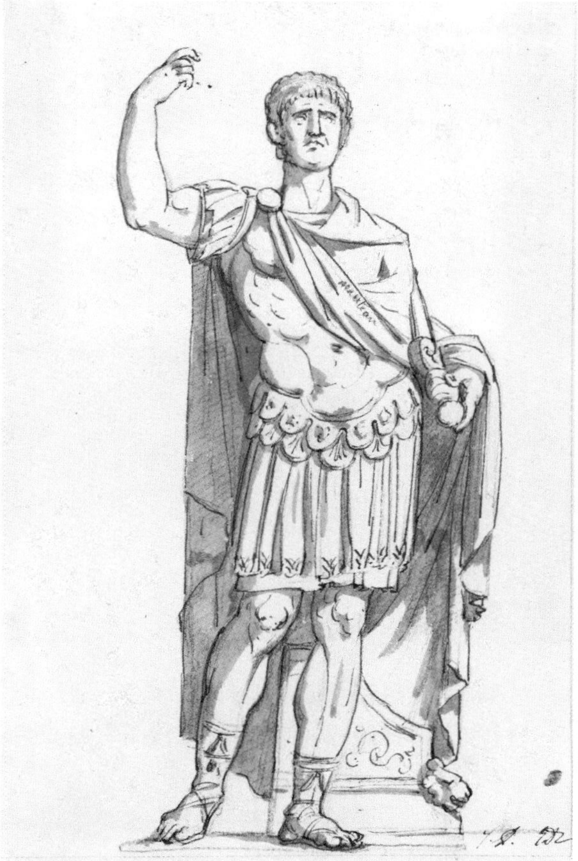

*Augustus, Roman album, p. 3 verso*
*Pen and gray wash over black chalk on white laid paper, 8¼" × 5⁹⁄₁₆" (20.9 × 11.1 cm)*
*The Fogg Art Museum*
*Harvard University, Cambridge, Massachusetts*
*Bequest of Grenville L. Winthrop*

Property became the issue rather than change. New ideas were taken to the gallows, virtue became pot-bellied, politics returned to the palace, and beauty to its illusions. Bourgeois society was not even aware of the fact that it had become the establishment, or that it had remained in power because God was dead and because, from then on, a spade was to be called a spade. This lack of lucidity caused men to be shot in the name of brotherhood, exploited in the name of equality, or outlawed and deported in the name of freedom. The bourgeoisie butchered the Paris Commune of 1870 to preserve the Revolution of 1789.

This evolution took only eighty years. David's life did not span it all and he did not betray his ideals as a good citizen nor his art. His paintings were influenced by his time, but the reactionary backlash to the revolution of 1789 and the Empire had an even greater influence on the opinion held of his work. Therefore, in order to understand his art, it is necessary to go back to his life and time, to do away with layers of subsequent events and interpretation.

Jacques-Louis David was born in Paris in 1748. At a very early age he decided to become an artist, and he was only seventeen when he enrolled as a student at the Académie Royale de Peinture et de Sculpture.[1] A precious style, the great master of which was François Boucher, was fashionable at the time. Also, an artist needed to be awarded a Grand Prix — or Prix de Rome — and to become a member of the Academy to show that he was worthy of a place in the arts. He would then be regarded as more than a craftsman. While some found this sort of competition easier than others, David had a difficult time with it. He attempted to abide by the appearance of fashion without giving in to its spirit. He tried four times before he was awarded the Prix de Rome in 1774, and legend has it that in the process he almost gave up on life.

That same year, 1774, Louis XV died and Louis XVI came to power. This was a time when there seemed to be more past than future. When David arrived in Italy the following year he found, however, that there were different sorts of past. One concept of the past wants to stop time in order to maintain existing privileges, while another accentuates qualities of courage, willpower, and virtue. Instead of shackling the present, this latter concept encourages the present to know itself. This was the past that David discovered in the relics of antiquity: the recently undertaken excavations at Pompeii, and

(1) The Académie Royale de Peinture et de Sculpture was created in 1648 by the painter Charles Lebrun upon his return from Italy. Its seat was at the Louvre and it showed the works of its members at the Galerie d'Apollon. It organized the first Salon de Peinture in 1667 and ran a school. (Note of the translator).

the Roman sculptures. In 1779, when David returned to Rome from Naples, he felt as if "he had just had a cataract removed": He could see as he had never seen before.[1]

The past has a meaning which goes beyond mere chronology. This meaning becomes part of the present and fosters emotions and reflections that change one's view. A true understanding of the values and art of antiquity should not lead the artist to copy them out of admiration but to imitate them in a manner that gives them new life. When David was copying Roman bas-reliefs, he was training in a realism that forced him to draw bodies, scenes, and landscapes. From the art of the past he discovered the anatomy of live bodies; while at the Academy, he had merely drawn classical studies from live nudes. Also, when he gave up depicting pictures to paint flesh and muscle, he switched from artistic to social values and he looked at the world with a Roman's eye, that is to say, a republican eye.

Until then the bourgeois in David had regarded painting as a part of the established institutions. This changed in Italy, when he found that art could shed light on his own condition and social class. Thus David became part of the Enlightenment. He may not have known it at the time, but his art was soon to encounter the thinking of the Parisian philosophers. For the moment, he just enjoyed seeing and painting what he saw.

In 1781 he exhibited a painting he had started in Rome and completed in Paris: a portrait of a man on a horse. The horseman greets the viewer with a wide movement of his right arm, and his eyes stare at a point in space, where the viewer has replaced the artist. In the lower left part of the painting, a dog seems to burst into the picture, barking. The whole scene is carefully constructed. It stands out against a background of even ashlar stones, which leaves little space for the sky appearing between the bases of two columns in the upper part of the painting. There is a feeling of endless movement in spite of the careful construction, and this movement is due to colors and light rather than to attitudes or lines.

While the background is strongly outlined by the realistic depiction of a wall, it defines no connection other than that of the picture itself. The subject is totally contained in the painting. For the first time, an artist played freely with texture and colors, which in turn became shapes and brought them to life. The viewer sees more than royal blue, yellow, and creamy gray tones; he also discovers his own space and the pleasure to enter that space. The painting gains an eternal youth as it springs from an everlasting present. When the viewer tries to find the reason for this vitality, his gaze switches from the yellow trousers to the white folds in the shirt, and it gets lost in the effervescent mane, the wavy stream of the tail, and the long brilliant hair. The *Portrait of Count Potocki* (see page 9) is a portrait as it should be, but it is also more than that, containing all the freshness of the painter's eye.[2]

In the eighteenth century the quality of a painting was not all that mattered. Everything was judged according to a definition of major or minor art. A portrait, however well done, was only minor art, as were landscapes and genre scenes. Only history painting was considered major art. From about 1750, the Bureau of Royal Buildings, which oversaw the arts, tried to rejuvenate the major arts, especially through commissions for the royal castle at Choisy. The Encyclopedists and philosophers, who championed a "moral" art, were pushing in the same direction. Meanwhile, fashion favored a minor

(1) *Fragment autobiographique*, in J.L. Jules David, *Le Peintre Louis David 1748-1825. Souvenirs et documents inédits*. Paris, 1880, 2 vol.

(2) It was said that David took part in a hunting party organized by King Ferdinand IV of Naples, during which Count Potocki tamed a horse. Born in 1757, Stanislas Potocki was a member of one of the richest and most illustrious families in Poland. He later distinguished himself in politics and also translated the works of Winckelmann. (Note of the translator).

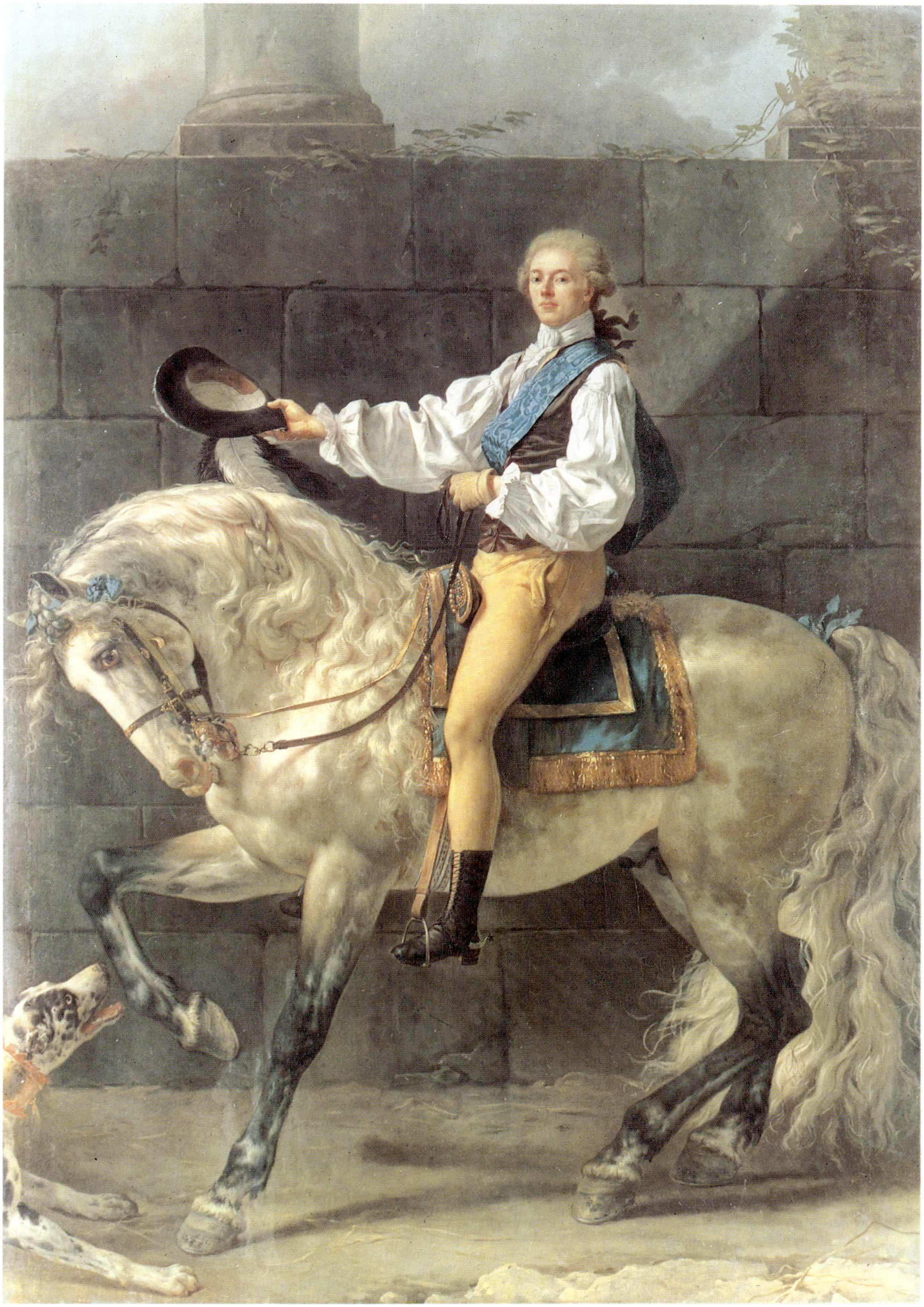

Portrait of Count Stanislas Kos Potocki, 1781
Oil on canvas, 9′11 11/16″ × 7′1 7/8″ (304 × 218 cm). Muzeum Narodowe, Warsaw

Minerva Battling with Mars, 1771
Oil on canvas, 44⅞″ × 55⅛″ (114 × 140 cm)
Musée du Louvre, Paris

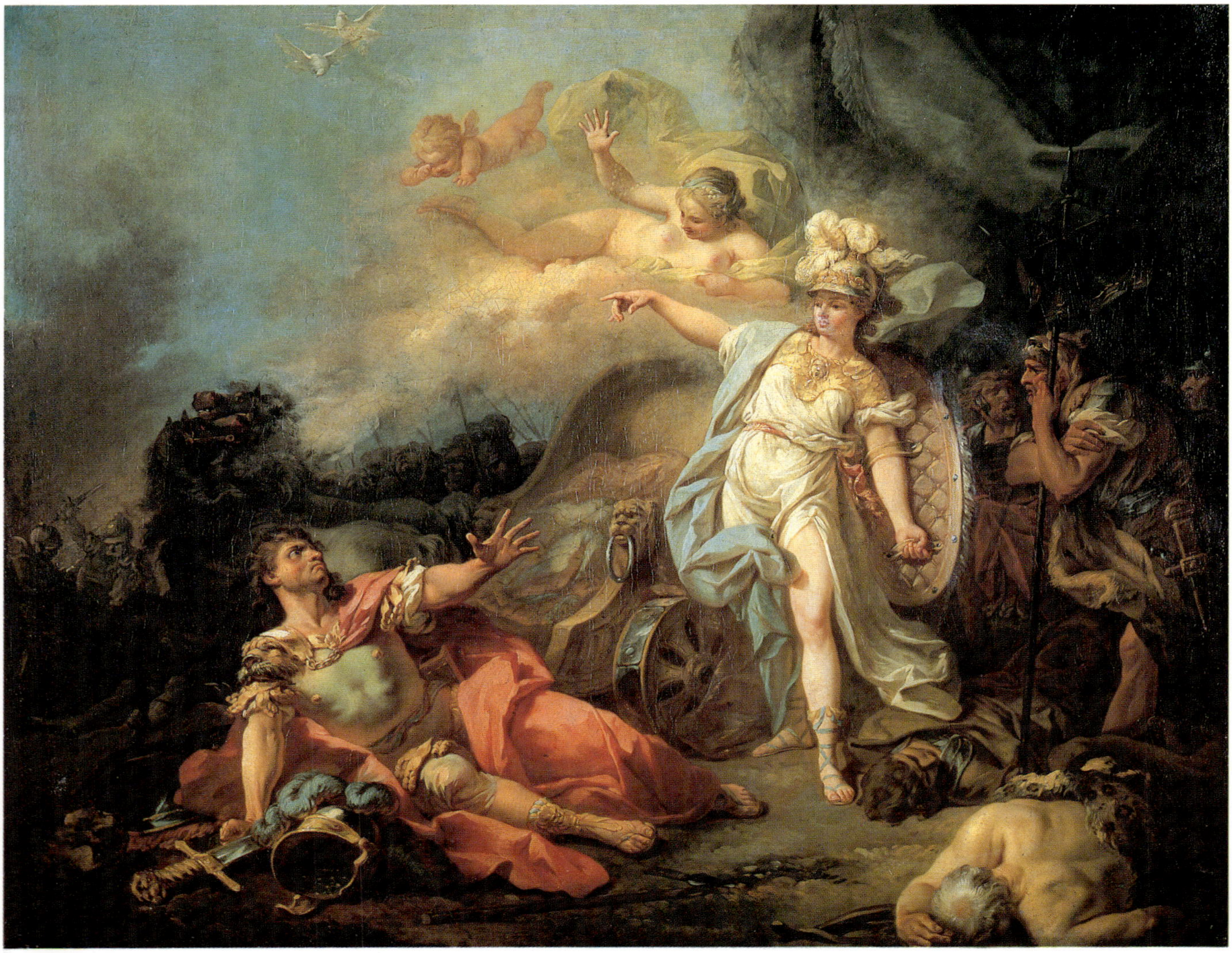

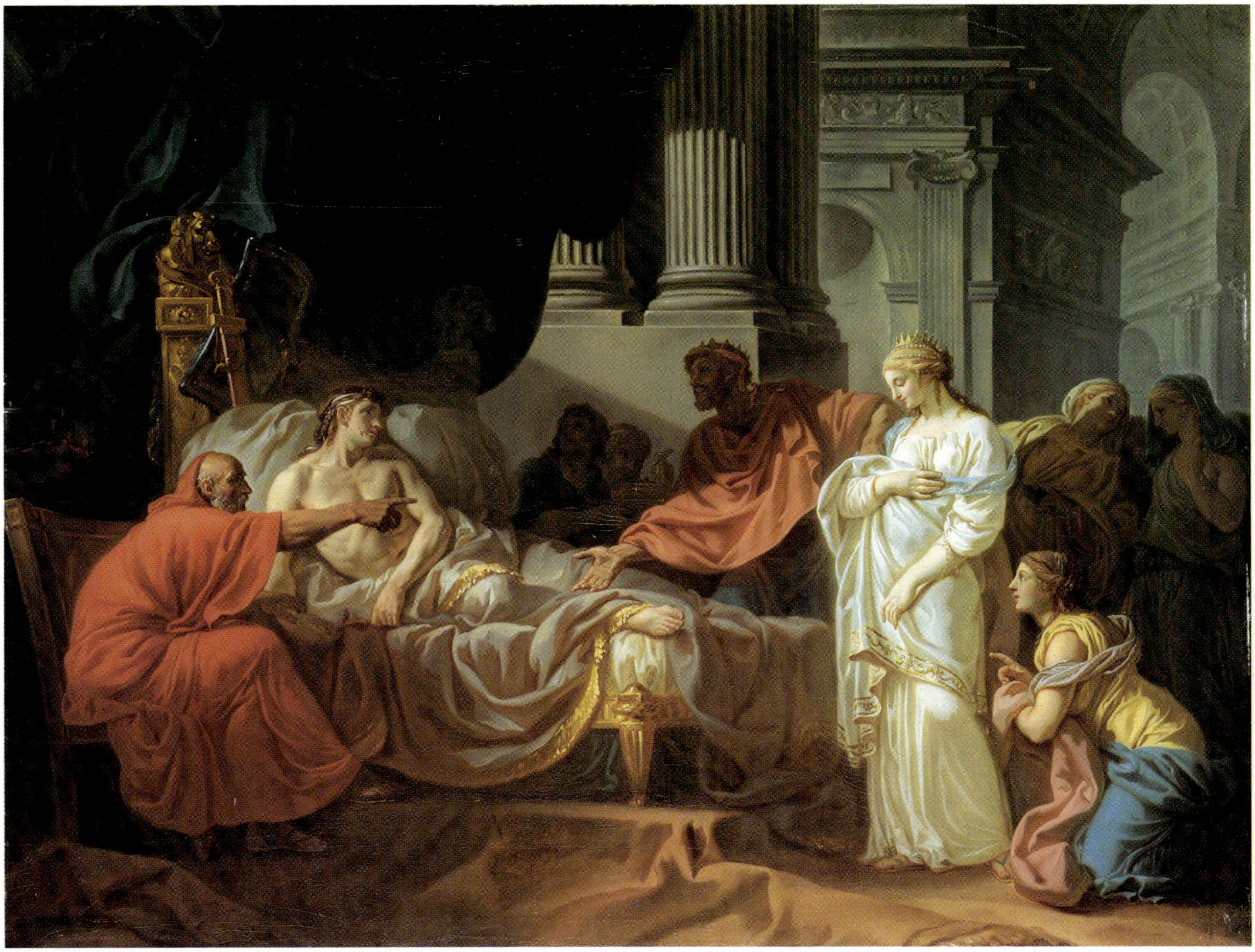

ANTIOCHUS AND STRATONICE, 1774
Oil on canvas, $46\frac{1}{4}$″ × 63″ (122.5 × 160 cm)
École Nationale Supérieure des Beaux-Arts
Paris

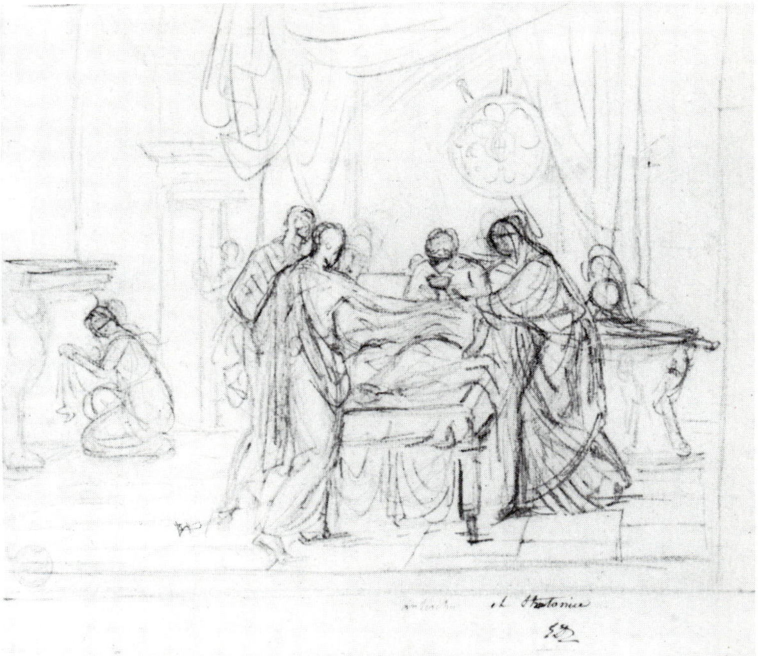

*Antiochus and Stratonice, n.d.*
*Black chalk, $9\frac{7}{16}$″ × $11\frac{1}{2}$″ (24.6 × 29.2 cm)*
*The Metropolitan Museum of Art*
*New York. Rogers Fund*

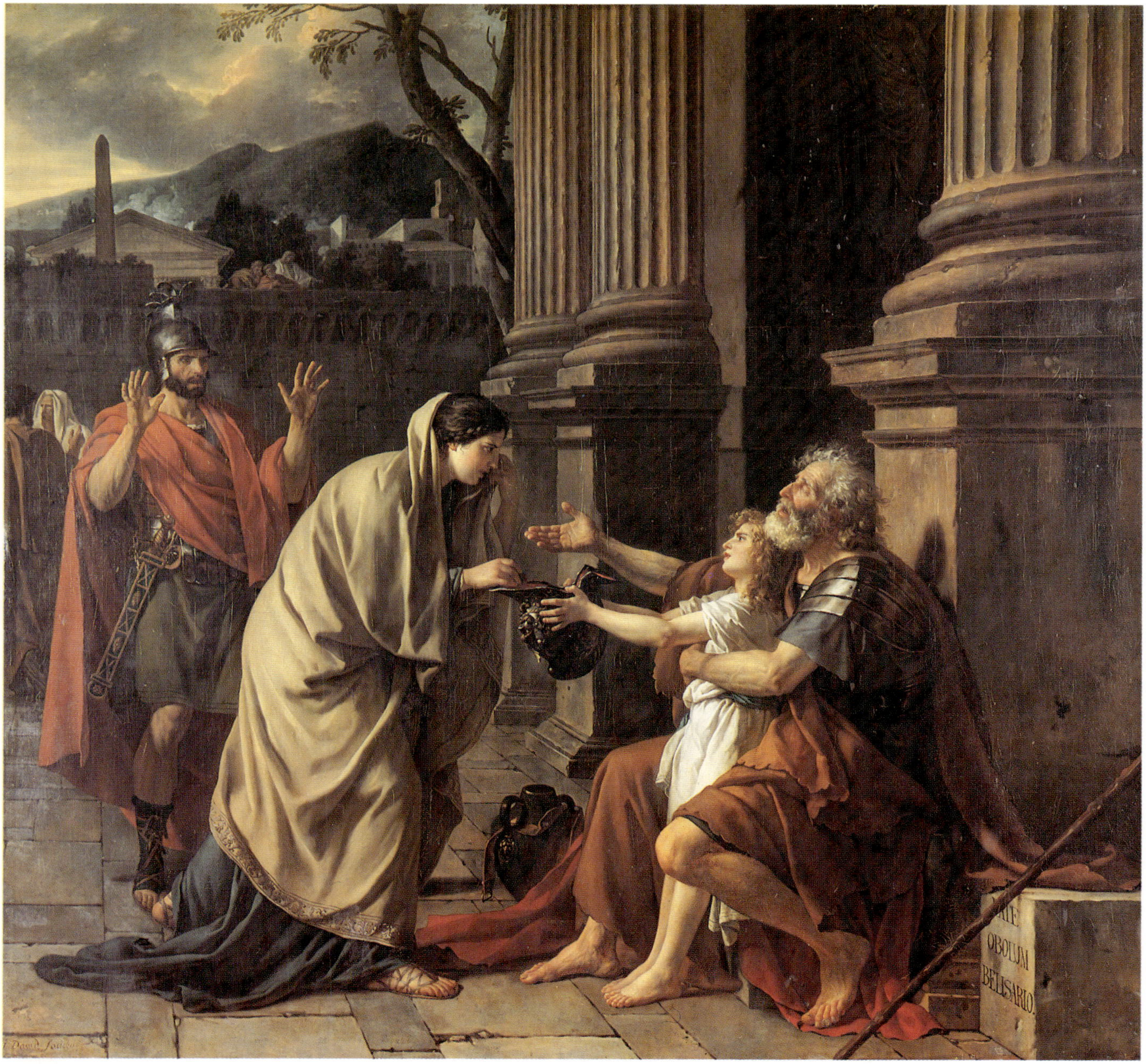


Belisarius Receiving Alms, 1781
Oil on canvas, 9′5 7/16″ × 10′2 7/8″ (288 × 312 cm)
Musée des Beaux-Arts, Lille, France

art, both decorative and libertine, the most representative of which was the work of Boucher, about whom the philosopher Denis Diderot was to write, "This man has everything, except truth."[1]

Major art at the end of the eighteenth century was defined as a presentation of heroic actions, the exemplary effect of which must impress the viewer with the hero's virtue. Truth becomes visual: One learns about truth by seeing it and one expresses truth by resembling it. Everything is in the realm of pure appearance. One absorbs the meaning of reality through the picture. One becomes a painter — that is to say a creator of pictures — by copying model pictures rather than by turning reality into a picture. To copy is to take part in the virtue of an existing work and the process of copying, like an efficient grace, may give the artist the ability eventually to rival his masters.

The growing desire for renewal and morality was a response to a need to break away from pictures of pictures and rediscover nature. At the same time fiction was first challenged in Laurence Sterne's "Tristram Shandy" (1759-1765); Jean-Jacques Rousseau established the voice of the first person singular in his "Confessions"; and the Encyclopedists replaced God by a book that answered all questions. Things artificial and transcendental were to be dismantled like an old and useless theater set. Jean-Baptiste Greuze could have been the great painter of this turning point, but he lost himself in mawkish sentimentality.[2] Jean-Baptiste Deshaye died too young.[3] This role was finally taken by Joseph-Marie Vien (1716-1809), who restored the "major arts" through the observation of nature. He was David's teacher, first in Paris and later in Rome, where he was appointed director of the Académie de France the same year David became a student there.[4]

David made many copies from the antique. He looked to the arts of antiquity to find an ancient moral energy, but he also observed the postures and bodies of his contemporaries. He carefully studied the light in the works of Caravaggio, the definition of space in the works of Raphael, and the expressive tension in that of Nicolas Poussin. He was partial to intelligence, precision, and line over color. He wanted to triumph through rigor rather than through the emulation of charm as in the work of his teacher Vien or his rival Jean-François-Pierre Peyron, who was awarded the Grand Prix in 1773.

When David returned to Paris in the summer of 1780, he had to be accepted by the Académie Royale de Peinture in order to exhibit at the Salon, which was the only place one could show works to the public. With this in mind, he executed a large painting in which he wished to assert himself as a history painter who could renew the genre. He chose to paint a scene constructed around four figures and he set it against a background of paving stones and columns opening in the back onto a landscape in the style of Poussin. A seated old man raises a sightless face; he extends his right arm and clutches against him a young boy who, his arms stretched forward, holds a helmet upside down. A woman bends over and drops something in the helmet. Behind her a soldier gestures in surprise. In the foreground, an inscription on a block of stone states, "Date obolum Belisario."[5] This brief description sets the place and the theme, which was then so significant in painting. The as yet unresolved problem was how to create a harmony between words and pictures. According to artistic rules of the time,

(1) Born in 1713, Diderot was enormously influential in shaping the rationalist thought of the eighteenth century. His life work was the *Encyclopédie*. His *Salons* pioneered modern art criticism. (Note of the translator).

(2) Born in 1725, Greuze was a genre and portrait painter, best known for his moralizing pictures. He died in 1805. (Note of the translator).

(3) Born in 1730, Deshayes was Boucher's son-in-law. His pictures on mythological themes were similar to Boucher's, but his large paintings of the martyrdom of Saint Andrew expressed a dramatic action and realism which created a stir at the 1761 Salon. He died in 1765. (Note of the translator).

(4) An academy founded in 1666 and the residence of the winners of the Prix de Rome. Under the old regime it was seated at the Palazzo Mancini. Since 1803 it has been seated at the Villa Medici. (Note of the translator).

(5) Give alms to Belisarius.

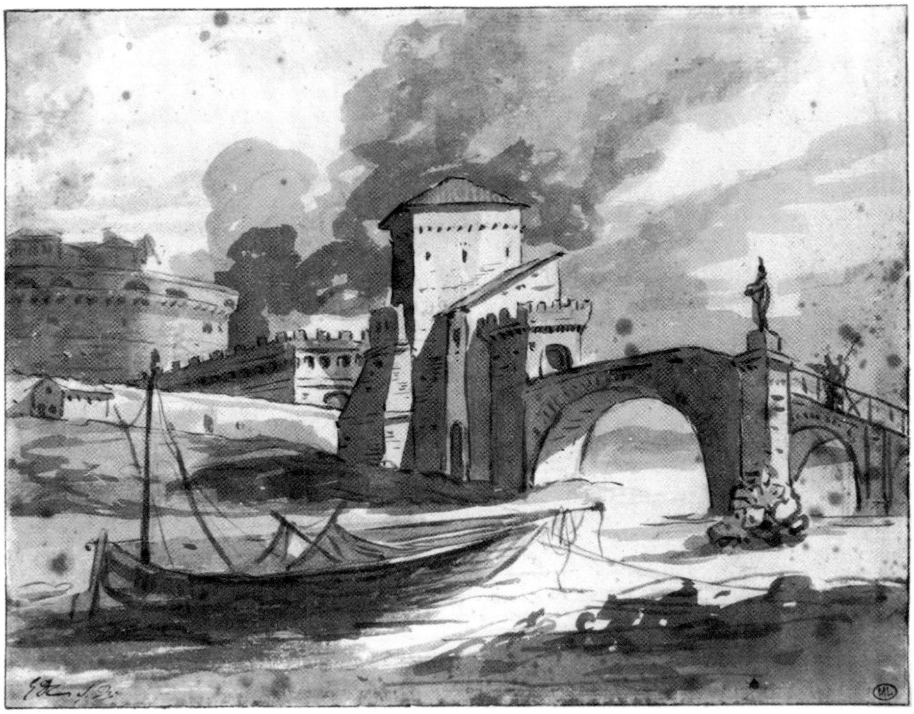

*Roman Landscape, n.d.*
*Black crayon*
*and India ink wash*
*6⅜" × 8⅜"*
*(16.7 × 22.1 cm)*
*Musée du Louvre*
*Cabinet des Dessins, Paris*

David must choose a theme which the viewer could identify easily, and the recognition of this theme was to create an effect of intelligence and generosity through the visual impression. The construction and design were to express David's ideas, and they were, therefore, more important than color, which carried the emotions. The painterly effect was more conceptual than visual. One spoke then of "coloring" rather than color, and this coloring needed to be justified by its use on a very specific object, whether clothing, architecture, or a landscape. Much later David was to change his mind, saying to Etienne-Jean Delécluze, "Coloring is the most material in art; it is that which first seizes the senses." [1] In the 1780s, however, David claimed not to be interested in "the material in art," although the *Portrait of Count Potocki* shows that he happened to take pleasure in it.

The posture of each of the four figures expresses something which can be immediately understood: The old man and the boy are beggars; the woman gives them alms; the soldier is surprised to recognize the old man. The viewer in turn may be surprised to find his counterpart in the soldier, who is looking on from the other side and who blocks the space with his two raised hands, thus focusing the viewer's attention on the scene between them and away from the background. That background is only painting, while the figures stand for the meaning, which is the reason for the painting.

The art critics of the time — Diderot first comes to mind — were more interested in meaning than painting. They felt that the strength of meaning carried the rest. Here the meaning stems from the fact that the viewer recognizes Belisarius, the great Byzantine general. The victim of an ungrateful Justinian, he had been blinded and deprived of all his possessions. As he was reduced to begging, Belisarius was a symbol of the injustice of rulers and the moral strength of their victims. The soldier

(1) E.-J. Delécluze became David's pupil in 1796. In 1855, he published *Louis David, son école et son temps. Souvenirs,* which was reissued in 1983. (Note of the translator).

recognizes him, as does the viewer who has been informed by the title of the painting, *As a Woman Gives Him Alms Belisarius Is Recognized by a Soldier Who Has Served under Him* (see page 12).

David submitted this painting to the Académie on August 24, 1781. He was unanimously accepted and met with triumph at the Salon. This was the first French neoclassical work. In a pastiche of the playwright Jean Racine, Diderot exclaimed, "I see him every day, and every day I think I am seeing him for the first time." Switching to criticism, he added:

> This young man shows a grand manner in his work; he has spirit; his heads are expressive without affectation; his attitudes are natural and noble; he can draw, he knows how to throw a drapery and make beautiful folds; his colors are beautiful without being brilliant. I wish there were less stiffness in the flesh; in some places the muscles are not flexible enough. It would be better also if thought could tone down the architecture. If I were to mention the soldier's admiration, the woman giving alms, or these arms crossing, I would spoil my pleasure and sadden the artist. I cannot help but ask him, however: Don't you think Belisarius is humiliated enough as a beggar? Must he also ask for alms? Forget this arm raised around this child, or raise it to the sky, which he will reproach for its harshness.[1]

This rather long quote is typical of an art critic who gives pride of place to the moral commentary, so much so that he criticizes attitudes and not the painting. David shared the spirit of his time, and one can assume that he intentionally made Belisarius hold out his hand; the expression on the face matches the movement of the arm. The hero lives his humiliation heroically. There is also a small engraving dated 1784, curiously signed L. David for the painter and J. David for the engraver, the

(1) *Salon* of 1781, in Denis Diderot, *Salons*. Ed. by Jean Seznec and Jean Adhémar. Oxford : Clarendon Press, 1957-1967, p. 377.

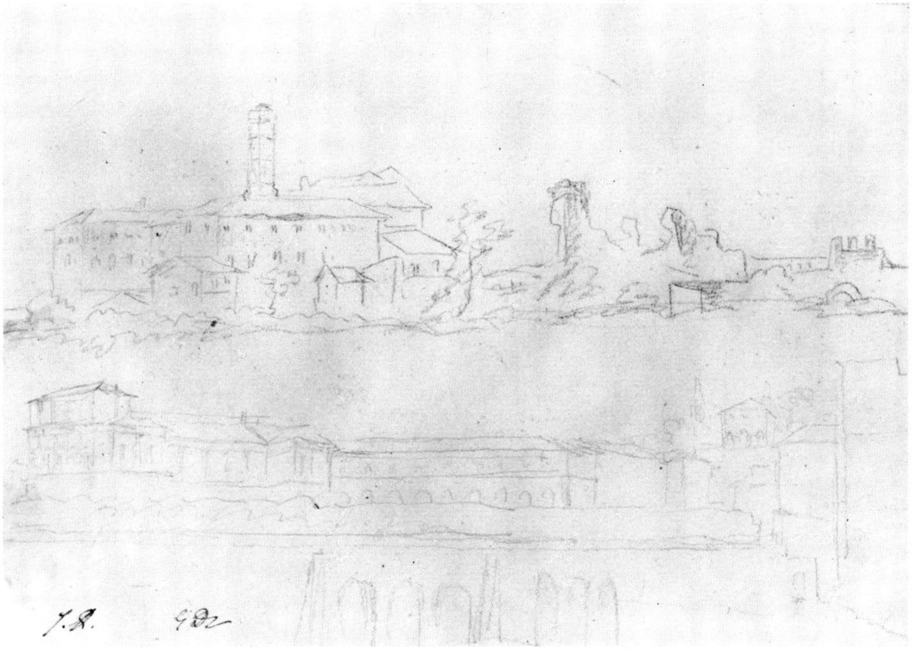

*Roman Landscape, n.d.*
*Roman Album p. 11*
*Black crayon on*
*white antique laid paper*
*5⅜" x 7¼"*
*(13.7 x 19.7 cm)*
*The Fogg Art Museum*
*Harvard University*
*Cambridge, Massachusetts*
*Bequest of*
*Grenville L. Winthrop*

J as a mirror image of the scroll of the L. The engraving focuses on the figures and emphasizes Belisarius's gesture.

Nevertheless, the success of the painting at the Salon was due to its painterly qualities: the truth in the figures, the clear definition of their attitudes, their expressiveness, and above all, the rigorous simplicity of the whole composition. The public may have reacted to the theme, which had become very fashionable after Jean-François Marmontel published in 1767 his epic novel, "Bélisaire," but the "virtue" perceived in the painting was mostly due to a strong relationship between a composition eschewing superfluous effects and a clarity of meaning devoid of affectation and pathos. Some criticized David for his muted tones, but they could see at the same Salon these tones brilliantly used in the *Portrait of Count Potocki*. Colors had to be unobtrusive in *Belisarius* to avoid distracting the viewer from the painting's simple tension and emotion.

*Belisarius* and *Potocki* seem to contradict each other as paintings and to indicate two different roads in David's development: the very reasonable path of the past and the freer one of the present. Soon these two paths were to cross. David combined past and present in his history pictures by mixing copies from the antique with drawings after live models. He admitted to the fact that he needed the latter to record a posture or a drape. Philippe-Auguste Hennequin mentioned *Belisarius* in his memoirs, "for which I sat for the young boy holding a helmet." Unlike academic painters who limited themselves to the surface, David needed to capture that which lay beneath it.

The body is the matter and shape beneath the surface. Stones seem to be the matter and shape of time: They are prominent in history pictures, in which they outline the central scene in walls, slabs, columns, arches, and caryatids. They disappear in works depicting the present, in which they are replaced by color rubbings that are pure painterly texture and create a strong effect of space.

On August 22, 1783, Vien presented David's *Andromache Mourning Hector* to the Académie Royale de Peinture. The painting was accepted by a unanimous vote. It was very favorably received when it was exhibited at the Salon (see page 17). The scene is outlined and set forward by a stone pavement and a wall, which is as high as that in *Potocki*, but smooth and half covered with a drape. The dead man's torso is naked. His ribs stick out. An open wound can be seen under his right collarbone. The light leads the viewer to the face of Andromache, who is as ecstatic with pain as Bernini's Theresa is ecstatic with pleasure. Her open right hand lies on the dead man's side, and she pays no attention to her son Astyanax, whose left hand rests on her throat. So many arms and hands linked to one another to form a spiral, so many creases and folds.... The drama is overshadowed by the pleasure of following the downstrokes and upstrokes of light that give the painting a glorious body.

David had established himself with only two history pictures. He was already regarded as a master, and students crowded his studio. His favorite among them was Jean-Germain Drouais (1763-1788), with whom he could talk and in whom he placed high hopes. Little is known about David's teaching. He did not write much, and when he did, he used the declamatory style of the time:

> To achieve their goal, masterpieces must charm but must also penetrate the soul and make on the mind a deep impression that is similar to reality.... Therefore the artist must have studied all the motives of mankind and he must know nature thoroughly. In short, he must be a philosopher. Socrates was a skillful sculptor; Jean-Jacques [Rousseau] was a good musician; the immortal Poussin created the most sublime philosophical lessons on canvas; they all testify to the fact that in art the genius should have no guide other than the flames of reason.

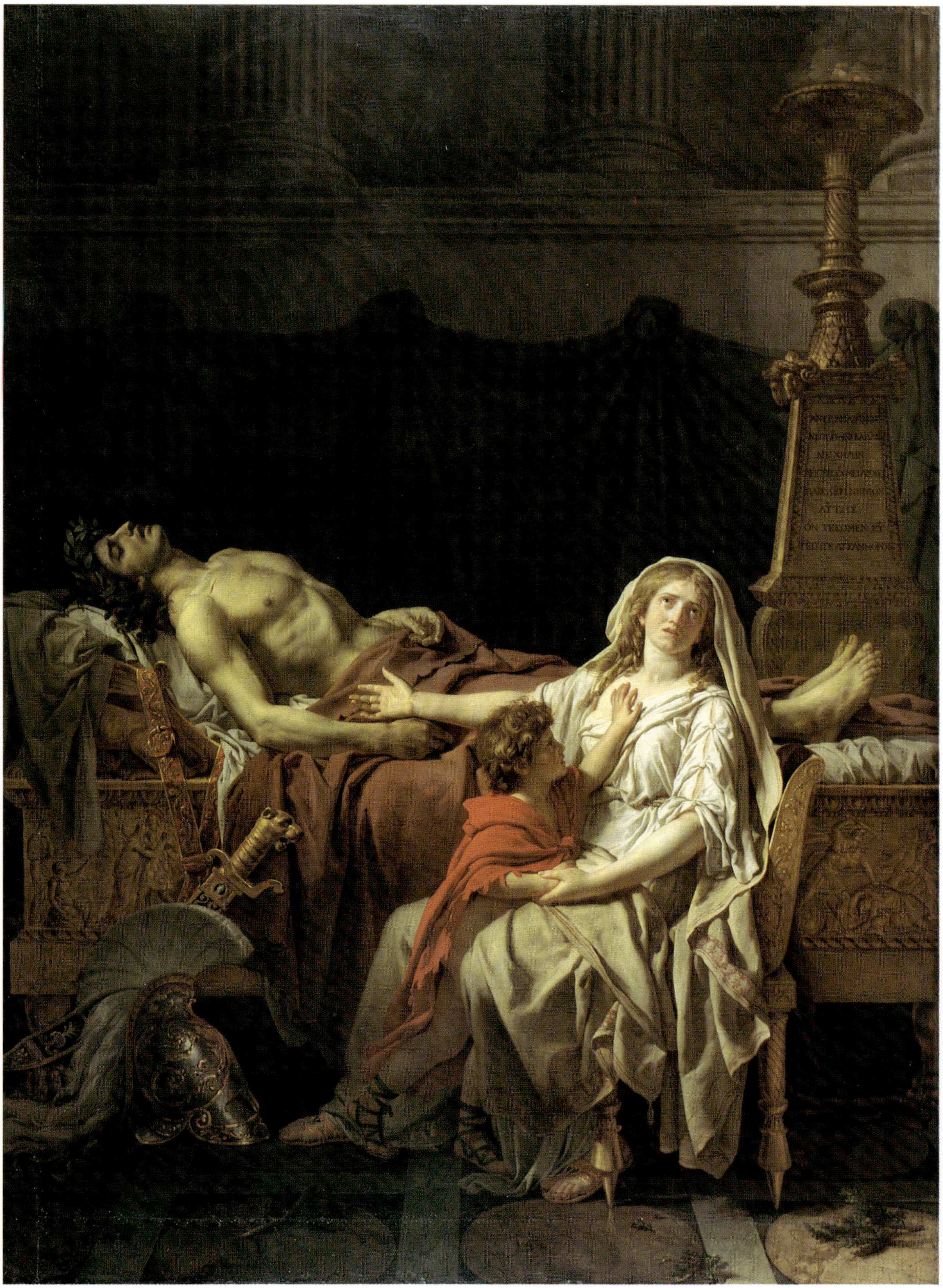

Andromache Mourning Hector, 1783. Oil on canvas, $9'10\frac{1}{4}'' \times 6'7\frac{15}{16}''$ (275 × 203 cm)
École Nationale Supérieure des Beaux-Arts, Paris

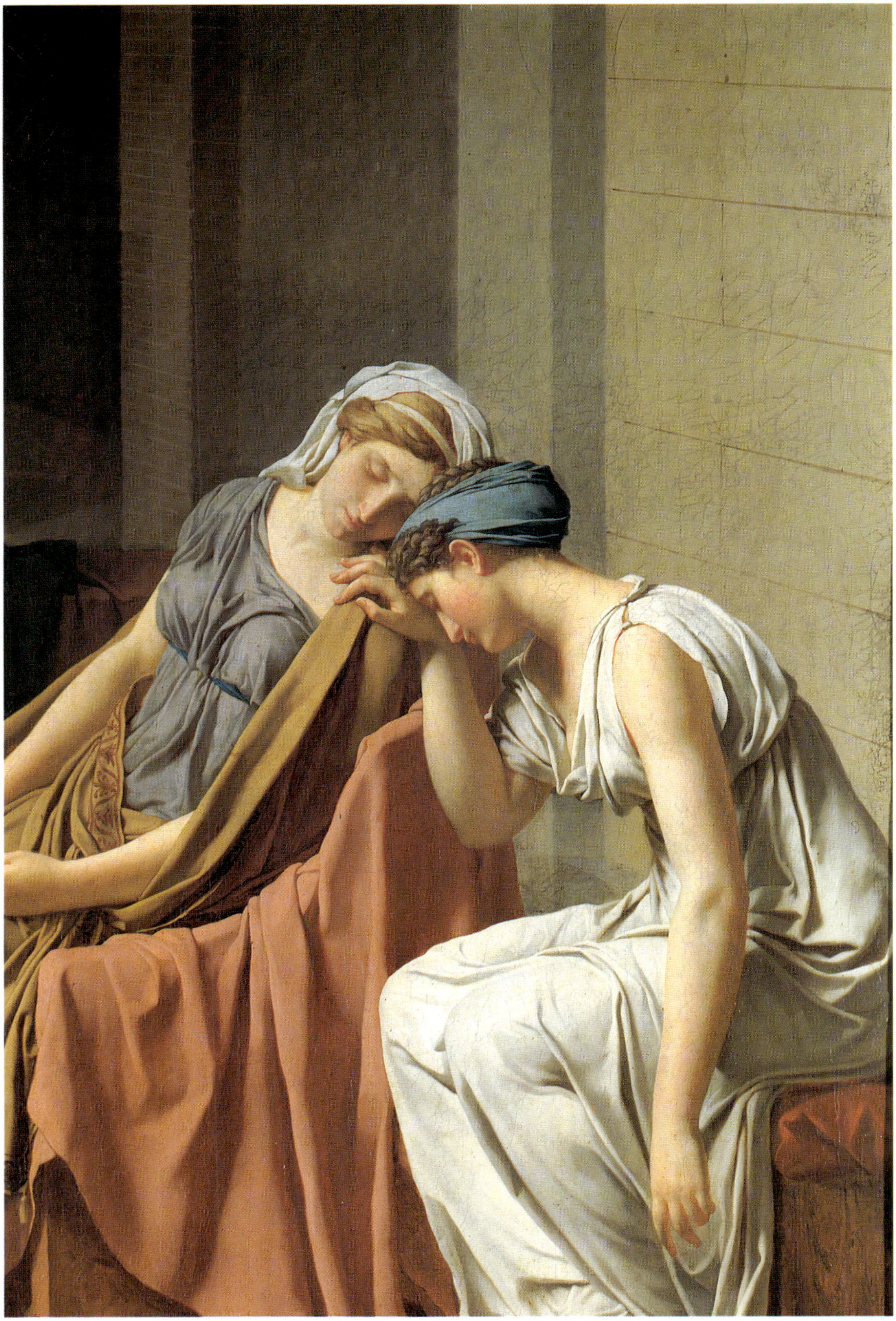

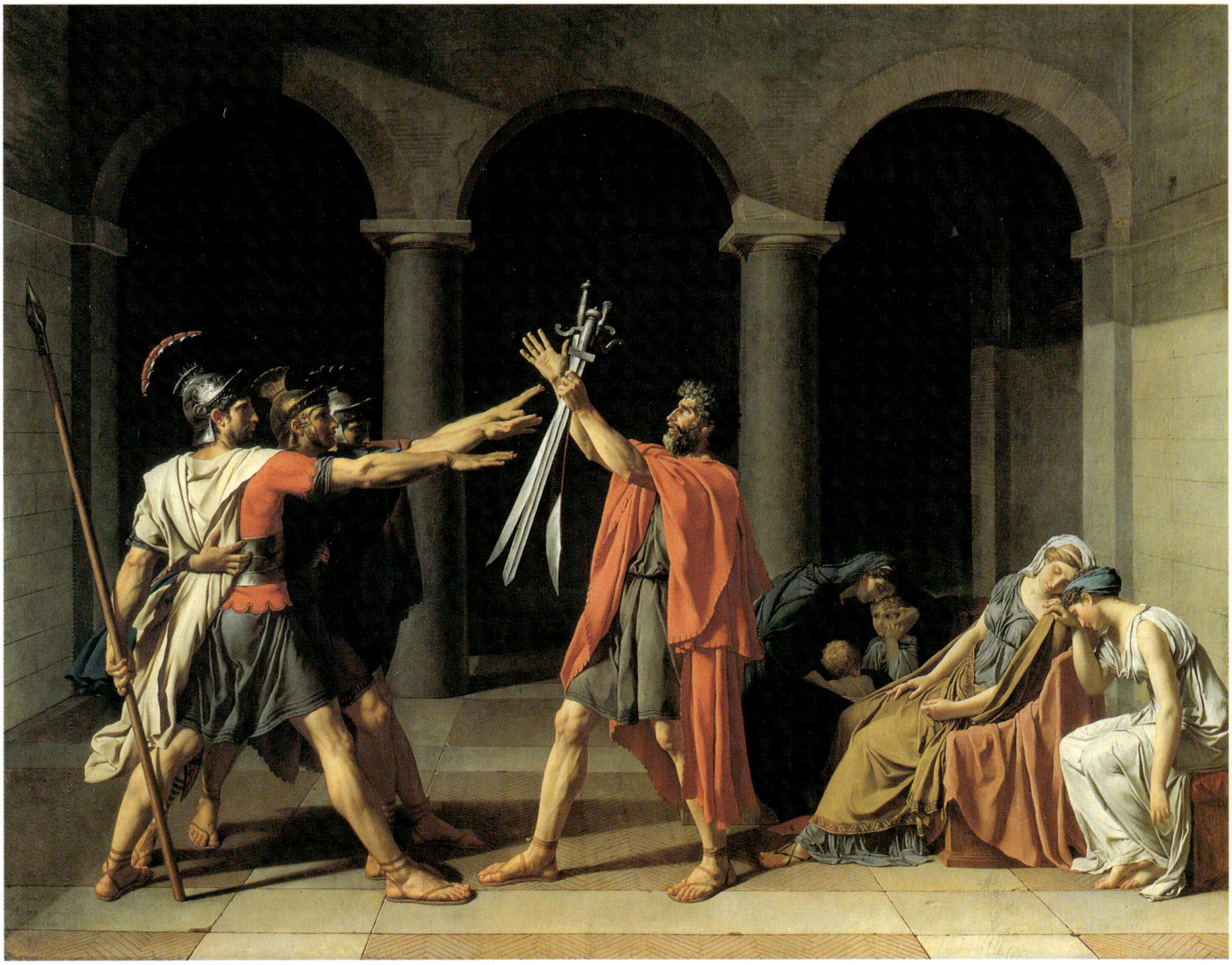

THE OATH OF THE HORATII, 1784
Oil on canvas, 10′9$\frac{15}{16}$″ × 13′11$\frac{3}{8}$″ (330 × 425 cm)
Musée du Louvre, Paris

THE OATH OF THE HORATII.
Detail

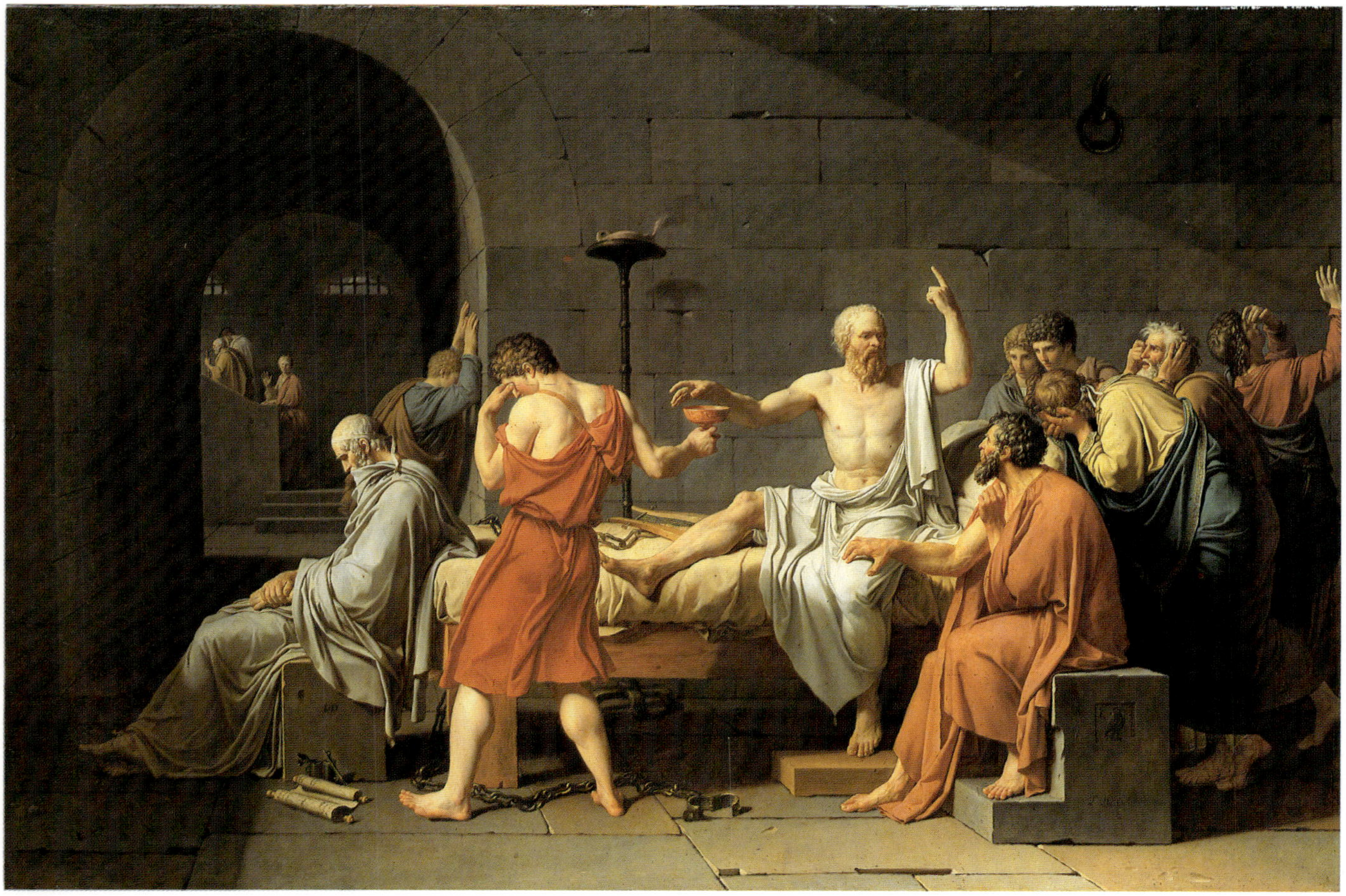

THE DEATH OF SOCRATES, 1787
Oil on canvas, 51″ × 77¼″ (129.5 × 196.2 cm)
The Metropolitan Museum of Art
New York. Wolfe Fund
Catharine Lorillard Wolfe Collection

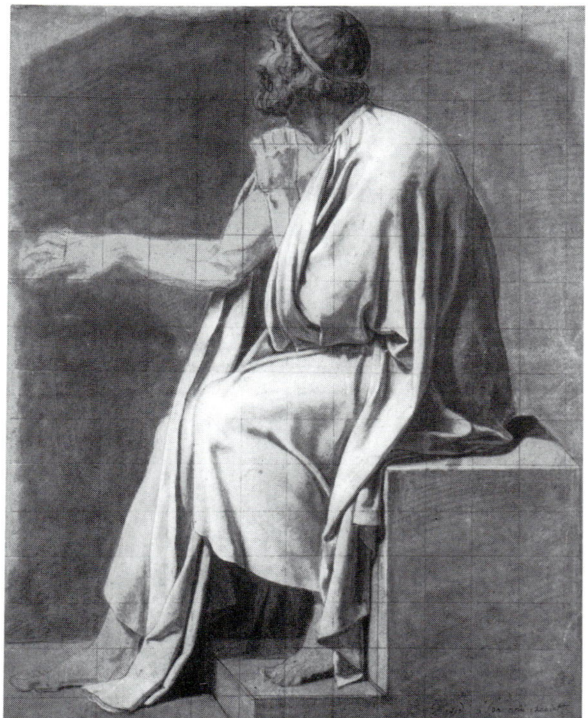

*Study for the Figure of Crito*
*in "The Death of Socrates," ca 1787*
*Black chalk, gray wash, heightened with*
*white chalk on brownish paper, squared off*
*in black chalk, 31¹⁄₁₆″ × 16⁵⁄₁₆″ (78.8 × 41.3 cm)*
*The Metropolitan Museum of Art*
*New York. Rogers Fund*

His students produced thoughtful paintings, in which today's viewer sees mainly the theatrical effect. Their themes prevent us from from perceiving anything else, although a century of modernism ought to have taught us to look through the theme in order to see the painting itself. Painting and theme may not be separated: The theme is there to give intelligence to painting and turn it into thought, and no modern painter has understood this necessary encounter better than René Magritte.

In five history paintings executed before the Revolution, David tied ever more tightly that which today we would prefer to separate, now that we believe that painting is not contingent on the source of its inspiration or its content. His pictures contain both accessory ornaments and vital organs. The ornaments depict history, which is indicated through the helmets, togae, and cross-belts, and these are meant to be signs rather than things. The problem lies in the fact that things always appear as things because they cannot be to painting what Latin or Greek is to our language and culture. Moreover, the picture does not depict a period but an exemplary situation, the case of which can only be found in the past, more specifically in antiquity. The situation is the vital element of the picture: To see that situation the viewer must be able to recognize it, and this is only possible if the painting contains recognizable signs.

The signs have aged because, since David's time, antiquity has ceased to be a readily available source of myth and imagery, the elements and characters of which would form a natural part of our vocabulary. History has since become a flow instead of a warehouse of heroic characters and deeds. What was then regarded as history painting is seen now as its opposite, as morality made visible. It is also a painting, however, and this becomes obvious when one stops looking at reproductions and returns to the actual pictures.

What does one see? The space of a canvas, and within this space a theme for reflection, which is exactly what the painter intended one to see. The picture establishes an ambiguity, that leads the viewer to information, pleasure, thought, or even all of the above at the same time, and the viewer cannot master this overlap. The likeness may open the space of the canvas toward the spiritual instead of limiting it to the representation of things, and this likeness becomes the picture's virtue and the shape of its beauty.

In 1785 David started work on his most famous history picture. He recalled, writing in the third person singular:

> In 1784 he realized that he needed to see Italy again, and he was persuaded to go by his friendship with Drouais, his student, who had been awarded the Grand Prix that year. For these reasons he decided to travel with him and in 1785 he executed *The Oath of the Horatii*, which was decisive in establishing his reputation in both Italy and France. While he received much acclaim in France, he was showered with praise in Italy. For three weeks, he had a constant stream of visitors at his lodgings, and to avoid any mishap coaches arrived on one side of the street while others left on the other. Forgive me these minor details, they are only meant to depict the effect this painting created in Rome.

The old Pompeo Batoni, a famous Roman painter, who was to die soon and leave his brushes and palette to David, told him, "Tu ed io, soli, siam pittori: per rimanente si puo gettarlo al fiume."[(1)]

*The Oath of the Horatii* (see page 19) caused a sensation at the 1785 Salon. It is one of David's paintings most dulled by reproductions in school textbooks and dictionaries. It regains its energy when seen

(1) You and I alone are painters: The rest can be thrown into the river.

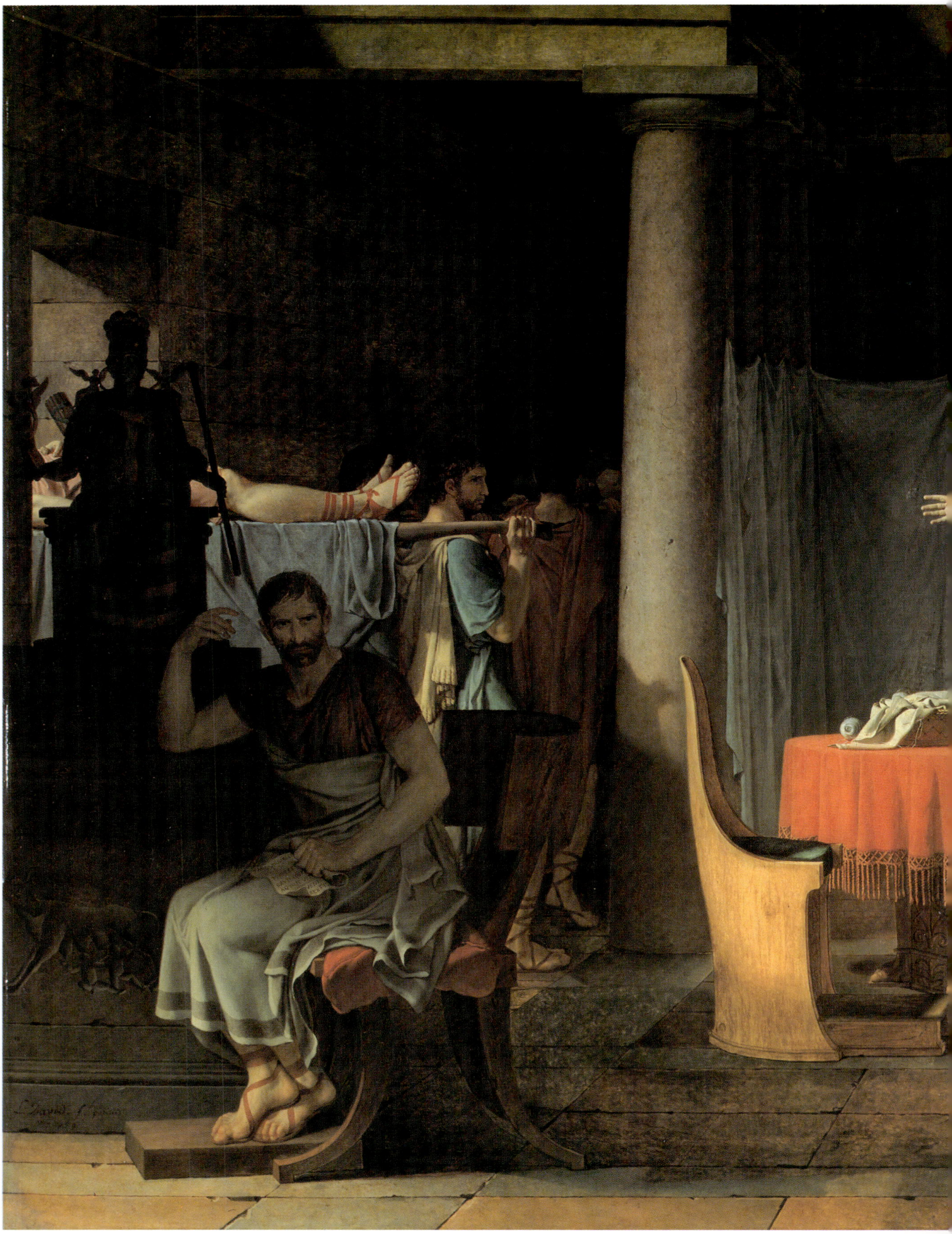

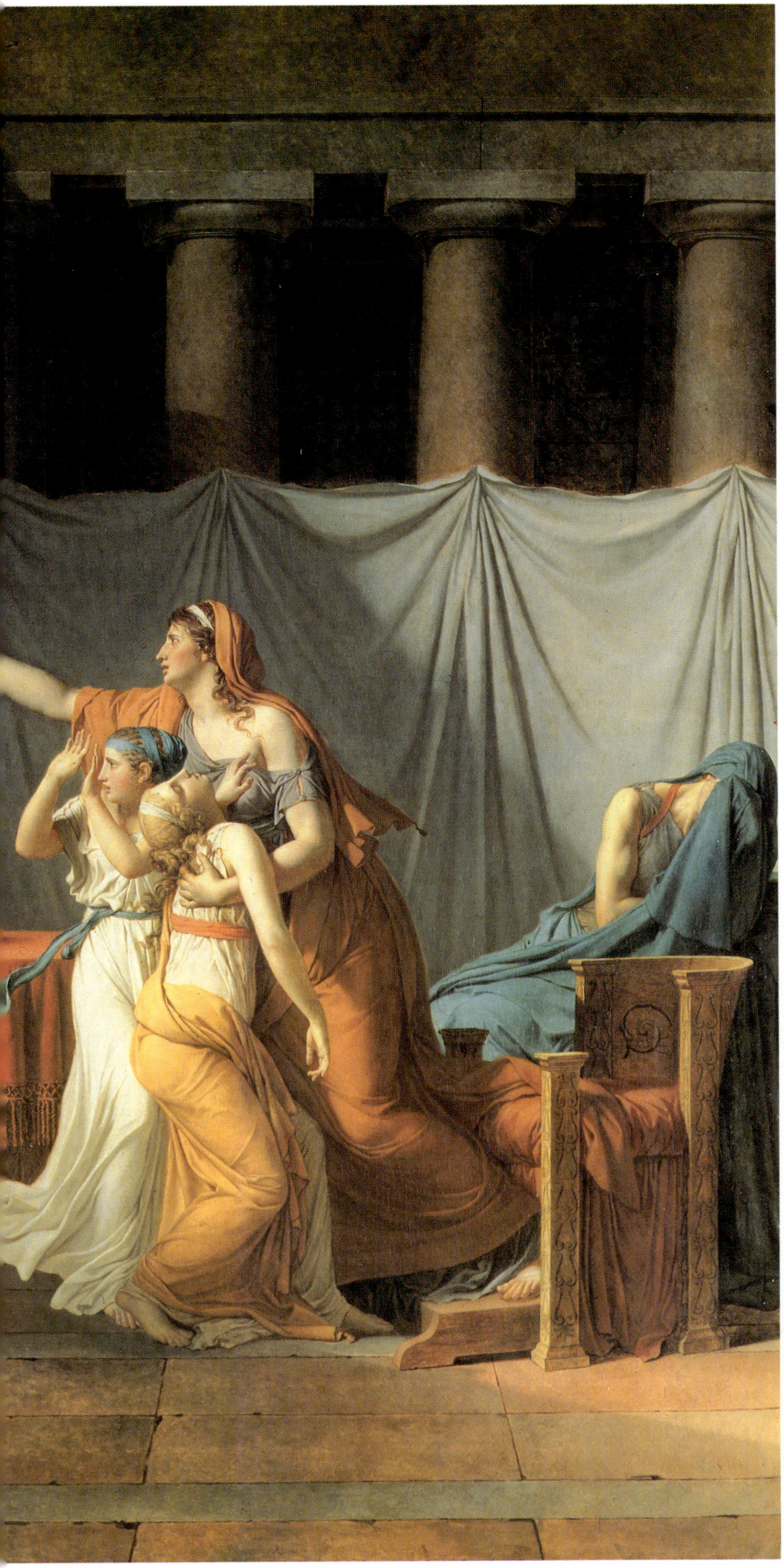

Lictors Bringing Brutus
the Bodies of His Sons, 1789
Oil on canvas
10′7³⁄₁₆″ × 13′10³⁄₁₆″ (323 × 422 cm)
Musée du Louvre, Paris

at the Louvre: Its rigorous composition triumphs over cliché. Reason, which David claimed to be the flames of art, shines out in a severe picture, the construction of which is both effective and dynamic. Everything is said in the double movement by which the Horatii brothers take the oath and are given their sword, and a mystery can be felt in the shadow of the arches and the grief of the women. The contradiction between shade and light, violence and pity, straight and curved lines creates a pensive movement in the space of the canvas, and it draws from the harsh contrasts a harmony that is fascinating to see.

David claimed the significance of reason more forcefully in this painting than in his four other history pictures. It is the reason championed by the Enlightenment, which was soon to govern France. This reason is already perceived as a secular virtue, because the oath of the Horatii, taken from their father, is only directed at the fatherland. There was nothing transcendental other than patriotism. One may wonder about the significance of the Horatii's will to sacrifice themselves to an idea which has become the Absolute. The Revolution of 1789 was made in the name of reason, which it turned into a supreme value. Only the government needed to be changed for the nature of this Absolute to be changed also, and this led to a furious and very French application of reason — a terrorism contradicting the very purpose of the Revolution.

David's last two history pictures were *The Death of Socrates* (see page 20) and *Brutus Returning Home after Having Sentenced His Sons for Plotting a Tarquinian Restoration and Conspiring against Roman Freedom; the Lictors Bring Their Bodies to Be Buried* (see pages 22-23).[1] When Sir Joshua Reynolds returned to London, he commented on *The Death of Socrates*, which he had seen at the Salon of 1787, calling it the greatest work of art since the Sistine Chapel and Raphael's Stanze in the Vatican. The painting had been commissioned by the younger of the two Trudaine brothers, Charles-Michel.[2] Another friend of David and habitué of the Trudaine salon, the poet André Chénier, may have suggested the gesture of Socrates as he stretches his hand toward the cup of poison, without holding it yet because he is entirely occupied with his last words.[3] *Brutus* was seen as a republican manifesto since Brutus had his sons executed for allegedly plotting with "tyrants." The authorities would have forbidden its exhibition at the 1789 Salon if the events of July 14 had not occurred before. Delécluze noted,

> While this painting confirmed rather than increased David's already widespread reputation, its influence was immediately felt on taste, fashion, and even morals. After it was exhibited, fashion returned to hair without powder, and women adopted loose hair styles, soon to be followed by men. Curves in Regency furniture and decoration were replaced by severely square shapes favored in Ancient times. Architecture was also influenced by the taste for antiquity, as can be seen in the Paris tollhouses built by [Claude-Nicolas] Ledoux.[4] Finally, corsets were banished, as were high-heeled shoes, and women got into the habit of replacing so-called court dresses by light and simple clothes, which were more elegant than sumptuous.[5]

(1) A small oil sketch is at the National Museum in Stockholm.

(2) Charles-Michel Trudaine de la Sablière and Charles-Louis Trudaine de Montigny were the sons and grandsons of high-ranking state officials and members of the Academy of Sciences. Their father had been a close associate of Turgot. Their salon attracted the members of the liberal aristocracy as well as the young intelligentsia in favor of political reforms. They remained on very friendly terms with David until 1792. The two brothers and the wife of Charles-Louis were guillotined in July 1794. (Note of the translator).

(3) A great lyrical and satirical poet born in 1764, André Chénier was executed in 1794 for writing pamphlets denouncing the excesses of the Reign of Terror. (Note of the translator).

(4) Born in 1736, Ledoux became the most daring exponent of neoclassicism in France. Although he never went to Italy, he was profoundly influenced by Italian architecture, and Piranesi in particular. In 1772 he completed the Pavillon de Louveciennes, a landmark in the history of French architecture. His Paris tollhouses were built in 1785-1789. His career came to an end during the Revolution. He published his designs in 1804 and died in 1806. (Note of the translator).

(5) E.-J. Delécluze, *op. cit.*, p. 123.

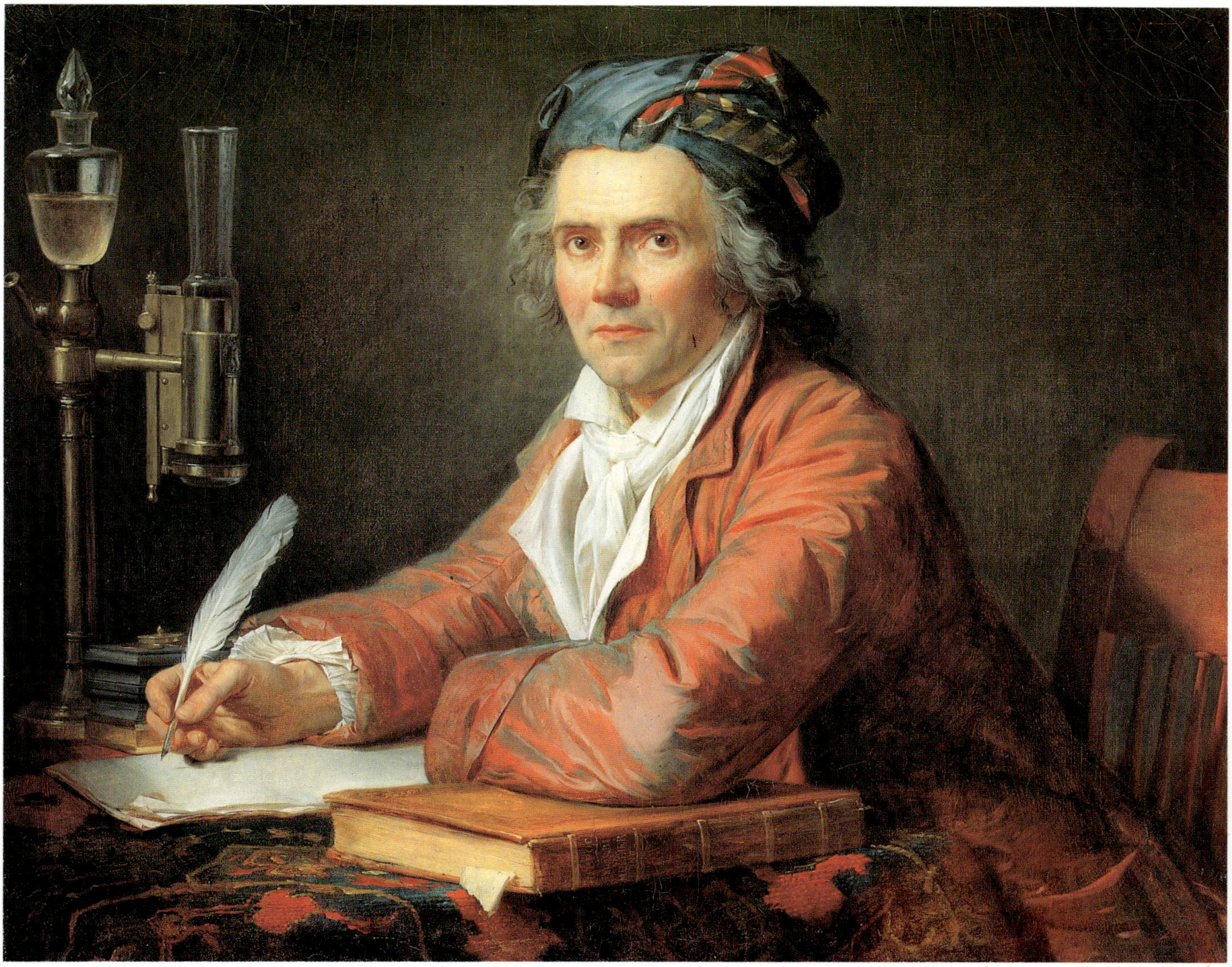

Alphonse Leroy, 1783
Oil on canvas, 28⅜″ × 35⅞″ (72 × 91 cm)
Musée Fabre, Montpellier, France

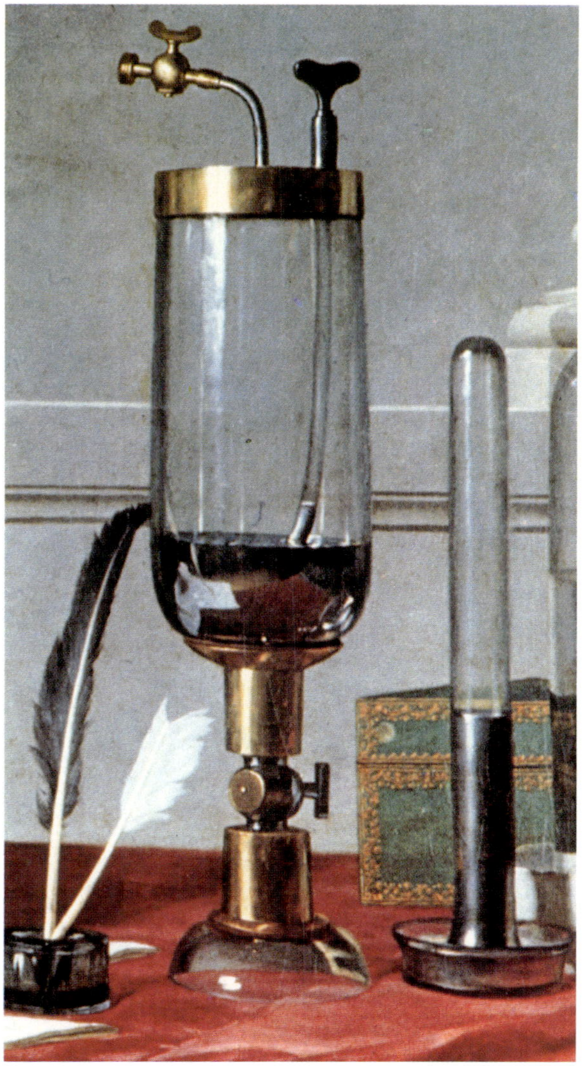

ANTOINE-LAURENT LAVOISIER AND HIS WIFE. Detail

The group of women in the *Horatii* and *Brutus* has a moral significance, which was noted at the time. It also brings a new element created by curves, shapes, and light. The postures, which are supposed to be caused by grief, show a strange abandon, which imparts a flexibility, a despondency, and a freedom from constraints more intense than the situation would require. This is particularly noticeable in *Brutus*: The young girl in the foreground — collapsing against her mother, her head thrown backward, and covered with light and drapery — expresses an emotional softness which could convey pleasure as well as grief. This is the first example of an erotic pathos based on mythology, which was to characterize the most disturbing works of David's young students, works that are also strange in their unrealistic postures and light: *Endymion Sleeping* by Anne-Louis Girodet-Trioson, *Psyche and Cupid* and *Ossian Evoking the Ghosts* by François Gérard, *Sappho at Leucadia* by Antoine-Jean Gros, *The Death of Hyacinth* by Broc, and later *Ossian's Dream* by Jean-Dominique Ingres. All these paintings are overdone, even in their polish, and they are swept by a wind of death.

In *Brutus* neoclassical art comes to a paroxysm and pushes to the limits: In an extraordinary effort it succeeds in remaining true to itself while reaching for the future. It already contains the Romantic movement as well as its opposite, the Realist movement. The group of women also constitutes a magnificent play of lines and colors. One must overlook the theatrical gesture of the mother and simply follow her arm, and the manner in which it outlines an area of the canvas, as if it were gathering an extraordinary bouquet of dresses and coats.

Between *Socrates* and *Brutus*, in 1788, David painted a picture that showed the same freedom, the same energy in colors as *Portrait of Count Potocki*. This was *Antoine-Laurent Lavoisier and His Wife* (see page 27).[1] The background is a realistic rendition of a wall decorated with pilasters; in the left corner, a portfolio of drawings is lying on an armchair; but the eye focuses immediately on the two faces at the center of the picture. The viewer's attention switches between the expression on the faces and the blocks of colors in the painting: the white dress, the black suit, the red rug on the table.

(1) Born in 1743 and a founder of modern chemistry, Lavoisier was the first to use effective quantitative methods in the study of reactions. He created a modern classification of substances, proposed the oxygen theory of combustion, and described oxygen's role in respiration. He was also a very rich farmer-general, a financier, and a social reformist. His wife is said to have been one of David's pupils. He was guillotined in 1794 during the Reign of Terror. (Note of the translator).

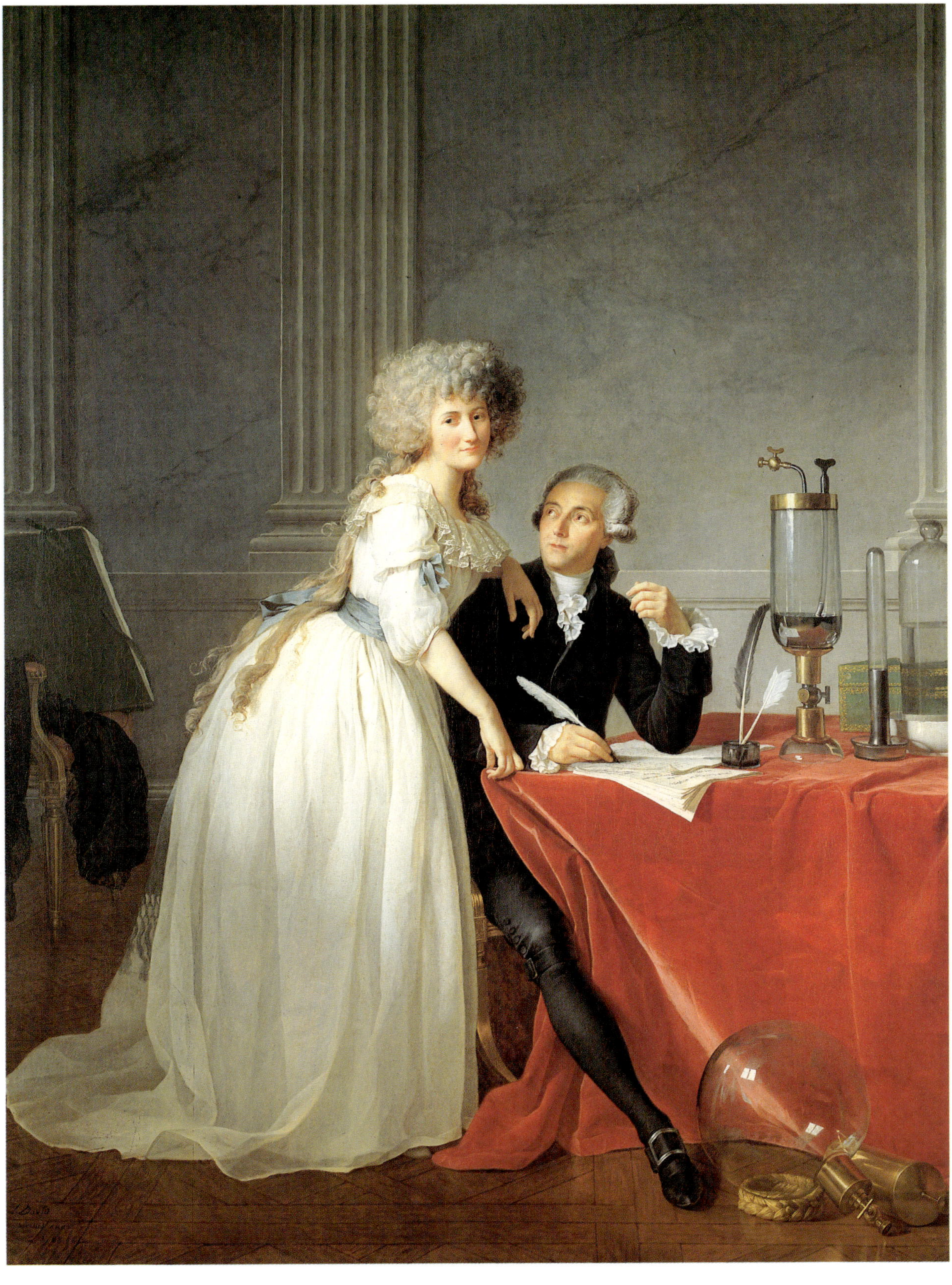

Antoine-Laurent Lavoisier and His Wife (Marie-Anne Pierrette Paulze), 1788
Oil on canvas, 102¼″ × 76⅝″ (259.7 × 194.6 cm)
The Metropolitan Museum of Art, New York. Gift of Mr. and Mrs. Charles Wrightsman

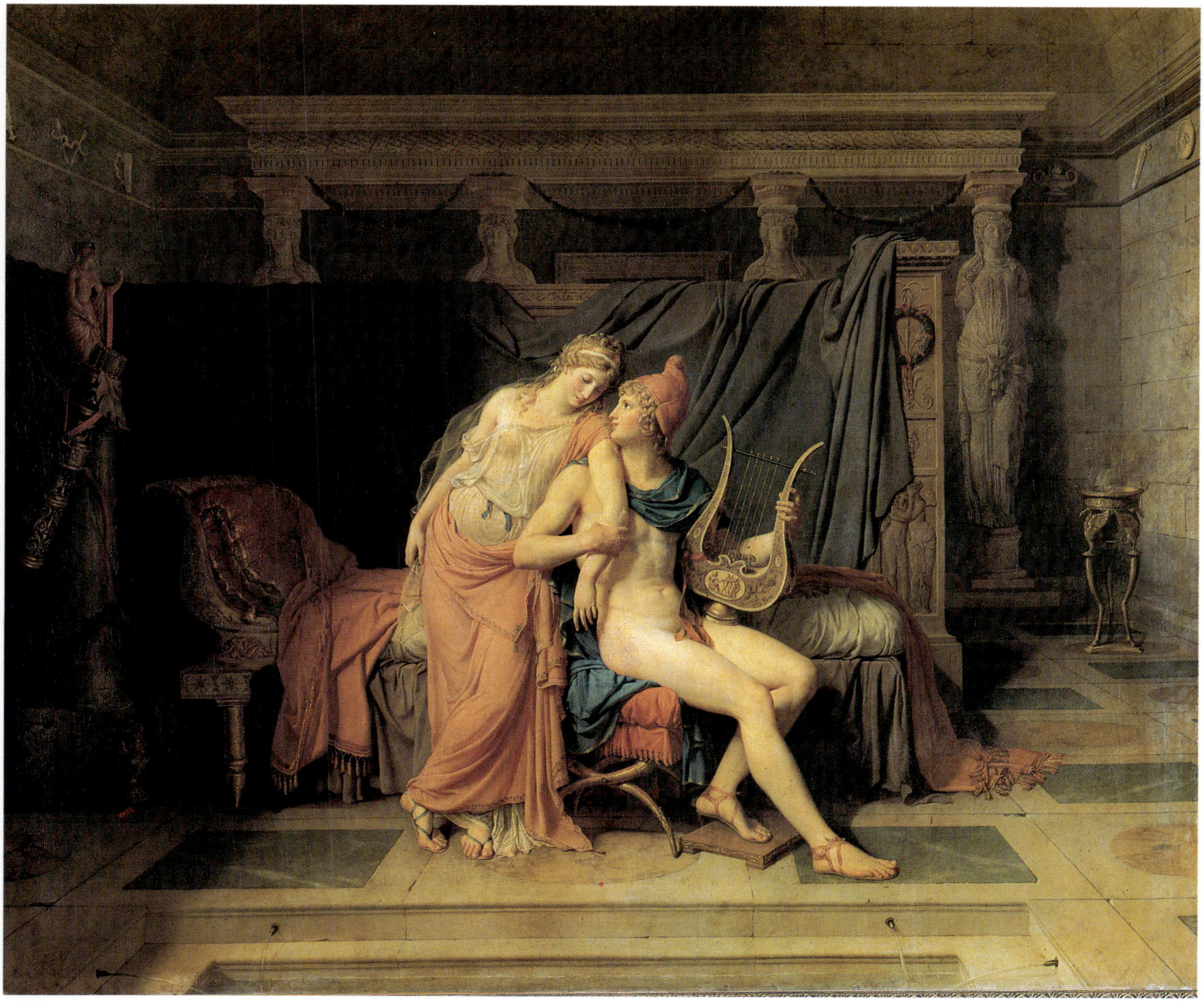

Paris and Helen, 1788
Oil on canvas, 57½″ × 71¼″ (146 × 181 cm)
Musée du Louvre, Paris

Light seems to shine out of the white and reflect on the red and black. At first glance the unexpected oblique line created by Lavoisier's right leg appears to threaten the perfect harmony in the composition, but in fact it reinforces this harmony, as do the various glass objects. These are featured to evoke the chemist's work, but also to show David's mastery at rendering transparent glass, whether thin and almost invisible as in the balloon-flask, or thick and almost cloudy as in the test tube and bottle. This painting illustrates the difference between classical and modern concepts of color. Classical color is only an accessory: The more airy and lighter the color, the more it becomes part of the shape that justifies its use. David never used color for its own sake, except in the backgrounds of his later paintings. There is always something underneath the color that is the reason for its covering the canvas. In modern painting color has become independent of the bodies and objects it covers and it invests them with its own power of expression and emotion instead of drawing this expressiveness and emotion from that which it covers. This independence may be the origin of abstract art, although the geometric shapes in some abstract works have regained the role of the underlying shape justifying the use of the color covering it.

In 1788 David painted another picture that anticipates a style which he was to use mostly at the end of his life. The painting was commissioned by the king's brother, Count d'Artois, later to be Charles X, who suggested the theme: *Paris and Helen* (see page 28). The background fills a large part of the space of the canvas; it is done in the style of David's other history pictures, with an ashlar wall, paving stones, and a portico with caryatids. The area where the story is being told on the canvas is outlined by a red hanging behind a bed covered with a disarray of red, white, and gray fabrics. Helen is standing, leaning her left breast against Paris's right shoulder. He is seated, his profile raised toward his lover. Her face is bent over his but she is looking away. The two bodies form a triangle, in which critics have seen the shape of an A. Helen is wearing a transparent tunic. Paris is naked, but a cumbersome lyre is standing on his left thigh, the ribbon of which hides his virility. The scene differs from the rococo paintings of the time inasmuch as it is dedicated to beauty rather than to sensuality, and beauty succeeds in outshining the mythological pomp.

It could be said that, when David painted *Paris and Helen*, he was abiding too much by the theory of Johann Joachim Winckelmann, "Beauty is like the clearest water drawn from a pure spring: The healthier it is, the less taste it has." Winckelmann (1717-1768) was the most significant theorist to champion the return to antiquity that engendered European neoclassical art, and in 1764 he published his most influential work, "History of Art in Antiquity." David must have been indirectly inspired by him when he stayed in Rome, as he was by Anton Raphael Mengs, a Roman by adoption, who was then regarded as one of the greatest artists of all time. In 1762 Mengs published a book on thought and taste in painting, "Pensées sur la Pensée et le Goût dans la Peinture."

In 1788 David was bereft by the death from smallpox of his student Drouais. The significance of this event may not have been assessed adequately in most biographies of David. Drouais had astonished the Académie Royale de Peinture with his *Christ and the Canaanite*, for which he was awarded the Grand Prix in 1784. C.P. Landon wrote about this painting, "Never has a student submitted a work to this competition that was so strong in its composition and execution.... It aroused everybody's enthusiasm." David had followed Drouais to Rome to paint his *Horatii*. He admitted in a letter, "I decided to join him because of my devotion to art and to him. I could not do without him. I was learning from the teaching I was giving him, and his questions will be lessons for the rest of my life. I lost my emulation."

*Brutus* met with a triumphant success at the Salon of 1789. It was a painting about the past that had a contemporary meaning. The times were receptive to the past because History was becoming an immediate reality. The painting itself does not express this momentum between reality and history. On the contrary, one is struck by a void at its center, which is wedged between the three parts of the scene: the women on the right, Brutus in the shadow, and the funeral procession far on the left. In the central empty space, a sewing basket is left as a symbol of the lost texture of daily life. There cannot be a better representation of History than this juxtaposition of daily objects and the exaggerated gestures caused by an event. Here David goes beyond the theatrical to find an extraordinary simplicity.

Events were moving fast: The States-General[1] convened on May 5, 1789; on June 17 the Third Estate — the Commons — joined by some of the clergy and nobles, proclaimed itself the National Assembly; it took an oath on an indoor tennis court on June 20;[2] on July 9 the National Assembly proclaimed itself a Constituent Assembly; the Bastille was stormed on July 14. Current events were becoming history. David joined the Club of the Friends of the Constitution, which was named the Club of the Jacobins after the monastery where it met.[3] The role of the Academy was challenged as early as September 1789. In December about twenty members of the Academy, led by David, demanded that Vien — who had been director since May — revise its bylaws and review its teaching of art and the giving of awards. In the summer of 1790 the protesters suggested in a memorandum that the Academy be abolished and replaced by a "free and universal" Commune of Fine Arts.

David owed his political following to the success of his paintings. The ideas expressed in his pictures were already revolutionary in spirit. He did not need to advance his career, since he was already successful, and critics often forget this in their effort to belittle him. David's studio was already the most sought after in Paris throughout Europe. He was teaching the best artists of the generation that followed his: François Gérard, Anne-Louis Girodet-Trioson, and Antoine-Jean Gros. He was aware of his role as a ferryman to the future. He may have been accused of wishing for the abolition of the Academy as revenge for having failed several times to win the Prix de Rome, but he would have wrought greater revenge by gaining control over the Academy, which he could have done. In point of fact, he himself had suffered from the deadening effect of academic teaching, and he felt that a radical break was necessary if the Revolution was to be extended to the arts also. This was achieved when, on August 8, 1793, the National Convention abolished all academies.[4] The portrait painter Elizabeth Vigée-Lebrun, who had fled abroad as early as 1789 and who was David's natural enemy, acknowledged that he loved art so much that no amount of hatred could prevent him from doing justice to someone's talent. David was entirely devoted to the arts: He arranged for several masterpieces to be put into safe keeping, he protected artists, and he secured commissions for them. Because he survived the coup d'état of 9 Thermidor,[5] however, it has since been generally held that he was immoderate and violent during the Revolution and was finally saved by his cowardice.

Like Louis-Antoine de Saint-Just,[6] David felt that "The world had been empty since the Romans." He believed that the Revolution would bring back civic virtue. Both his realism and his reason committed him to those ideals. The paradox is not that bourgeois rationality could lead to a reign of terror, rather that the bourgeoisie could find in this reign of terror the reason to oppose any new revolution. The bourgeois repression of the Paris Commune in 1870 produced ten times more victims in Paris than

(1) French national assembly in which the clergy, nobles, and commons were represented as separate bodies. (Note of the translator).
(2) The National Assembly took an oath not to separate until a constitution had been drawn up. (Note of the translator).
(3) Jacobins was the Parisian name of the Dominicans. (Note of the translator).
(4) Aside from the Académie Royale de Peinture et de Sculpture, there was the Académie Royale d'Architecture, founded in 1671 in Paris by Jean-Baptiste Colbert, who was then controller general of finances under Louis XIV. It also ran a school. (Note of the translator).
(5) A new republican calendar had been established on November 24, 1793, the eleventh month of which was named Thermidor (July 20-August 18). On July 27, 1794, a coup d'état led to Robespierre's execution and a period of political reaction. (Note of the translator).
(6) Born in 1767, Saint-Just was a member of the Committee of Public Safety. He was executed with Robespierre, whose close associate he had been.

had the Reign of Terror, but the Commune is regarded as responsible for the bloodshed. The bourgeoisie succeeded in benefiting from a revolution but it also sacrificed that revolution in the name of that benefit. It put an end to the revolution by killing the revolutionaries and making them responsible for their own deaths. The point here is not to try to justify the Reign of Terror by claiming that it had relatively few victims, but to compare it to repression. During the Reign of Terror, people of substance were executed daily in a sacrificial ritual that made such an impression that one talks of "rivers of blood" — a lasting image believed to be an accurate description. In the repression that occurred later, masses of people were killed, and their murder was forgotten as a matter of course. The penalty for repression is never paid, although on one occasion "war criminals" have been put on trial. There was an atonement for the Reign of Terror, however, as all its participants were sacrificed one after the other and finally Maximilien Robespierre himself, "The Incorruptible," was guillotined.[1]

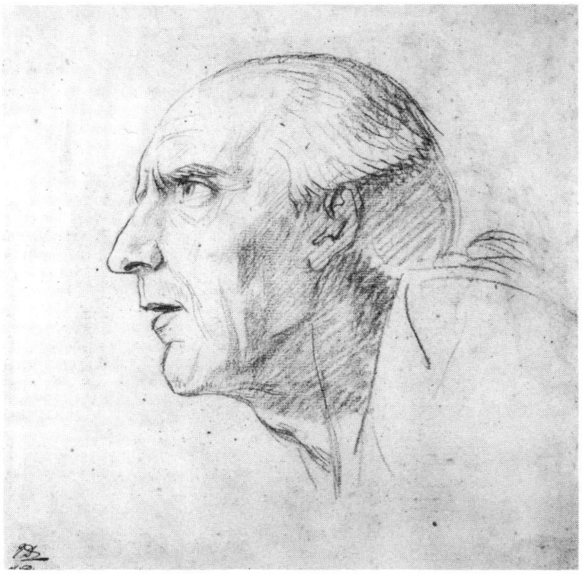

*Profile Portrait of an Old Man*
*(Prieur de la Marne?), n.d.*
*Black chalk on ivory laid paper, 9″ x 9⅛″*
*(22.7 x 23.1 cm)*
*The Art Institute of Chicago*
*Helen Regenstein Collection*

"I was devoid of all ambition. I was seeking only the glory achieved through the Fine Arts. I accepted official appointments only in order to serve the Fine Arts and secure their prosperity." This statement clarifies David's position; the power in which he was interested was the "glory" of the artist. As a revolutionary, he saw nothing unusual in being commissioned to represent a Revolution. Moreover, he had been the first to paint it. Thus he became the pageant-master of great revolutionary celebrations: the first Freedom Day for the rehabilitation of the Swiss Guard of Châteauvieux, on April 15, 1792; Fraternity Day on August 10, 1793; the Day of the Supreme Being[2] on June 8, 1794, for which he choreographed the processions and designed costumes, ornaments, and allegories. The young Delécluze saw David for the first time on the Day of the Supreme Being. He watched him "wave a hat with big three-colored plumes to maintain the distance between the marching groups of civil servants."[3] He found David's revolutionary persona distasteful, but he was dazzled by the artist's glory.

The Cordeliers[4] wrote a petition for the dethronement of the king, which David signed on July 17, 1791, at the Champ-de-Mars. On August 17, 1792, he was elected to the National Convention in Paris. On October 2, he was appointed a member of the Committee on Public Education. On

(1) A lawyer born in 1758, Robespierre was elected to the Sates-General and the National Convention. He became leader of the Jacobins in their struggle with the Girondists. In 1793 he dominated the Committee of Public Safety through the Reign of Terror. He eliminated both the extreme left and the moderates in the Convention, until he was overthrown by an alliance of the right wing and the Plain. (Note of the translator).

(2) Robespierre instituted a new civic religion based on J.-J. Rousseau's deistic theories. (Note of the translator).

(3) E.-J. Delécluze, *op. cit.*, p. 8.

(4) This revolutionary club on the left bank in Paris was created by Georges Danton, Jean-Paul Marat, and Camille Desmoulins. It was so named after its meeting place, the Convent of the Cordeliers—the French name for the Franciscan monks. It was instrumental in the fall of the Girondists in 1793 and drifted to the extreme left under J.R. Hébert. (Note of the translator).

October 18, he joined the Commission on the Arts. On January 17, 1793, he voted for the king's execution. He was the president of the Jacobins between June 17 and July 14, 1793. On July 25 he was elected secretary to the Convention. On September 14, he became a member of the Committee of General Security. He was the president of the Convention between January 5 and January 20, 1794. On 9 Thermidor (July 27), when Robespierre was overthrown, David's life was probably saved by the fact that he was ill and did not attend the Convention. He was arrested on August 2 and jailed until December 28, 1794. He was imprisoned again on May 29, 1795, and freed in August of the same year.

Aside from his different appointments, David was also working at the temporary Commission for the Arts and the Commission of the Museum, and — most important of all — he was painting. On October 28, 1790, Edmond-Louis-Alexis Dubois-Crancé had the Jacobins commission David for a picture commemorating the Oath of the Tennis Court.[1] The painting was supposed to be "thirty feet high and twenty feet wide" (9.15 meters by 6.10 meters). The Jacobins were to present it to the National Assembly as a decoration for the House. It was to be financed by a subscription for an engraving after the painting; the Jacobins were counting on three thousand subscribers, each paying twenty-four pounds, or a total subscription of seventy-two thousand pounds. Honoré de Mirabeau[2] brought this proposal to

(1) Dubois-Crancé is mainly known for the law of February 21, 1793, on the reform of the army. The corps of volunteer and professional soldiers were to be grouped together; some officers and the non-commissioned officers were to be elected; only a third of the commissions were related to years of service. This radical law was instrumental in turning the French revolutionary army into an effective military force. (Note of the translator).

(2) Born in 1749, Mirabeau first led a life of excess and was repeatedly imprisoned. In 1789 he was elected to the Third Estate in spite of his aristocratic origin. His fiery eloquence and intelligence gave him a prominent role in the Constituent Assembly. He tried to create a constitutional monarchy that would permit him to become prime minister. He died in 1791, just before his dealings with the king were discovered. (Note of the translator).

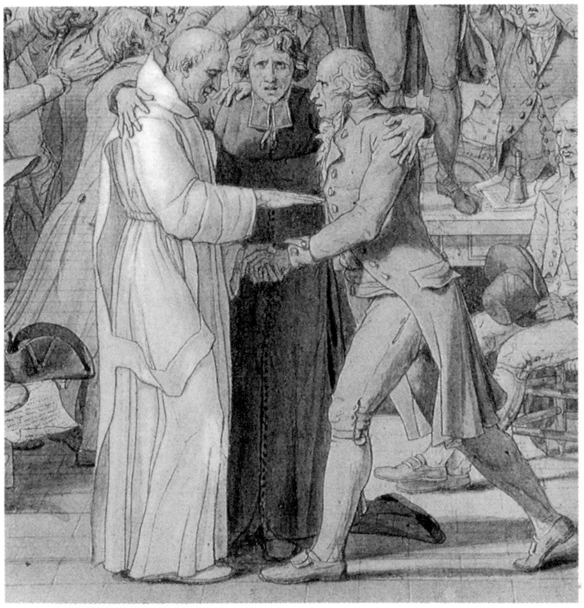

*The Oath of the Tennis Court*
*Detail. Symbol of the Fraternization of Churches: Dom Gerle (the Carthusian monk), Abbé Grégoire, and Pastor Rabaut Saint-Etienne*

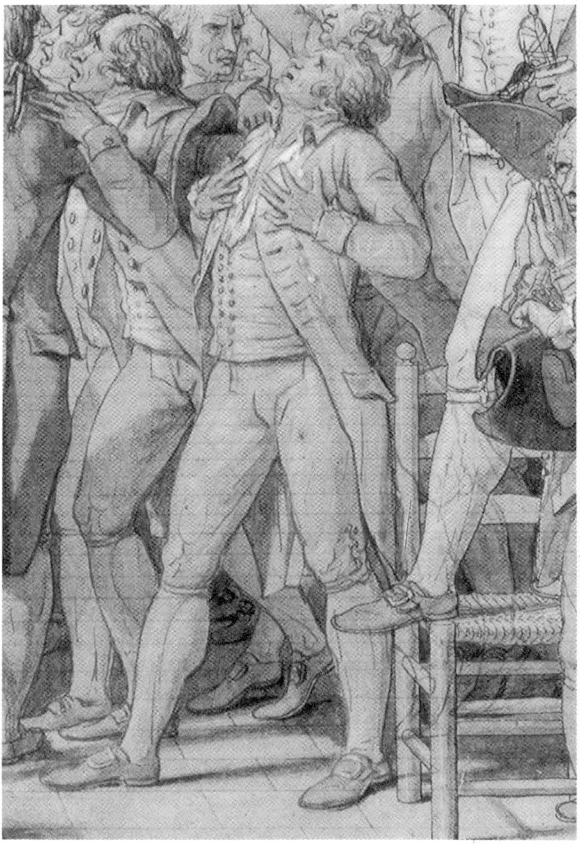

*The Oath of the Tennis Court*
*Detail. Robespierre*
*David depicts him with an expression of enthusiasm and emotion*

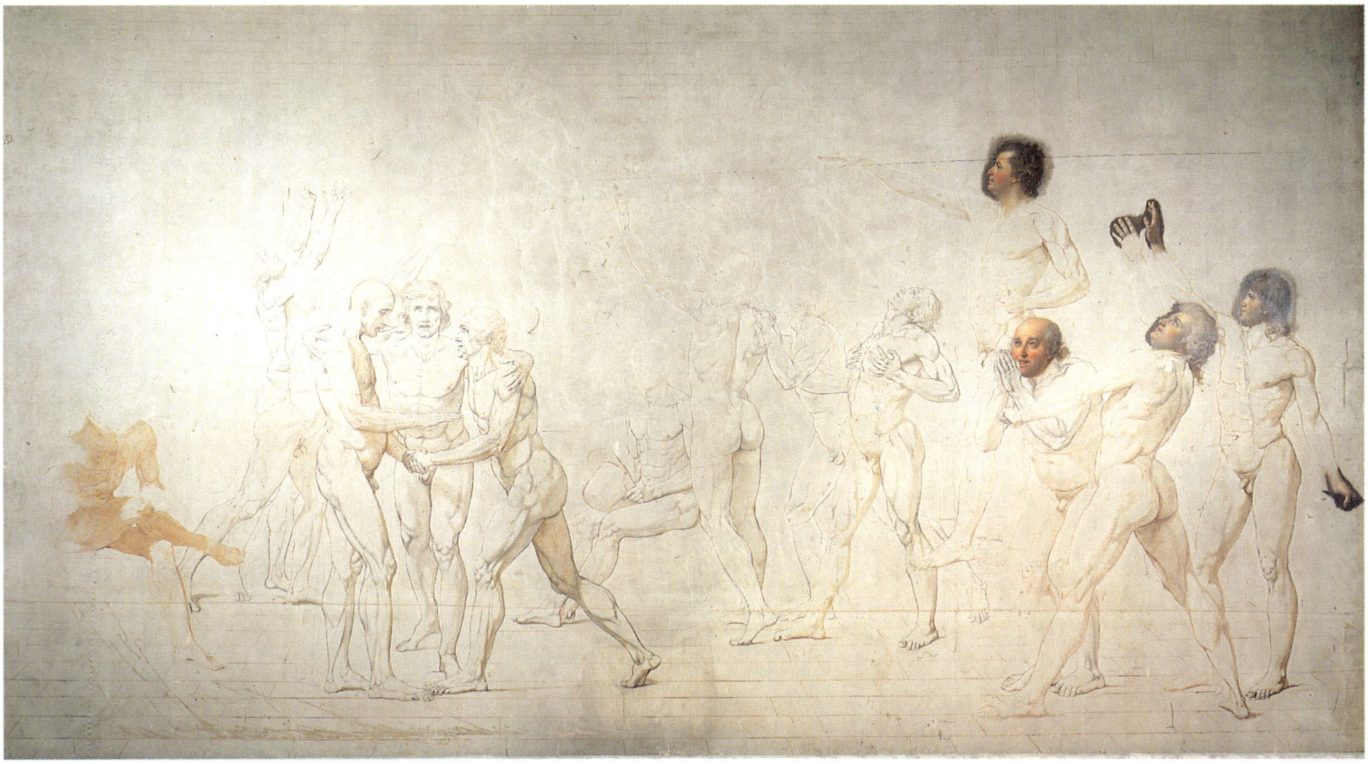

THE OATH OF THE TENNIS COURT, 20 JUNE 1789, 1791-1792
Sketch, white and black pencil, brown wash and oil on canvas
13′1½″ × 21′7⅞″ (400 × 660 cm)
Musée National du Château de Versailles et des Trianons

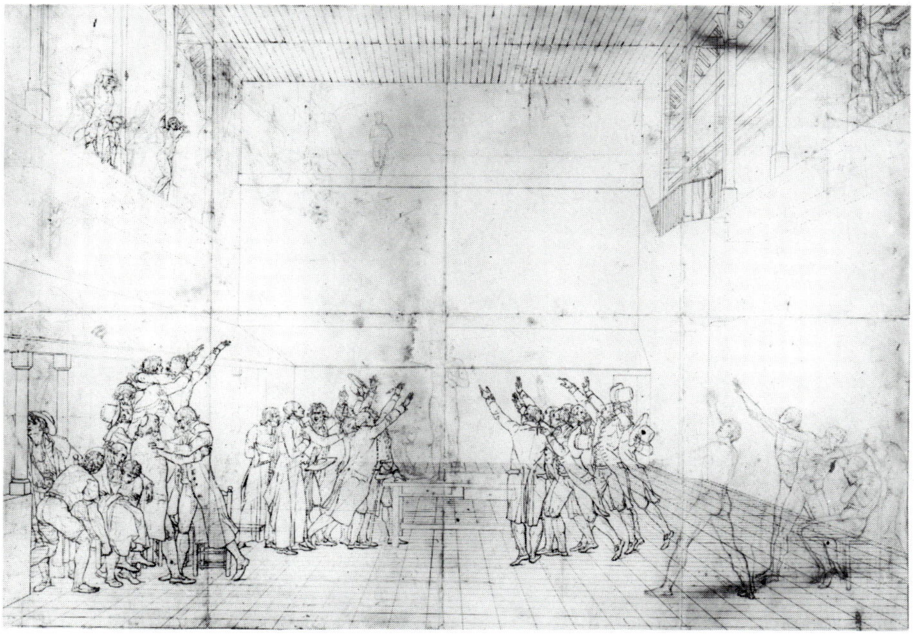

*Study for "The Oath of the Tennis Court"*
*ca 1790*
*Pen and brown and black inks over black chalk and graphite on white laid paper*
*26″ × 38⅞″ (66.2 × 99 cm)*
*The Fogg Art Museum*
*Harvard University*
*Cambridge, Massachusetts*
*Bequest of*
*Grenville L. Winthrop*

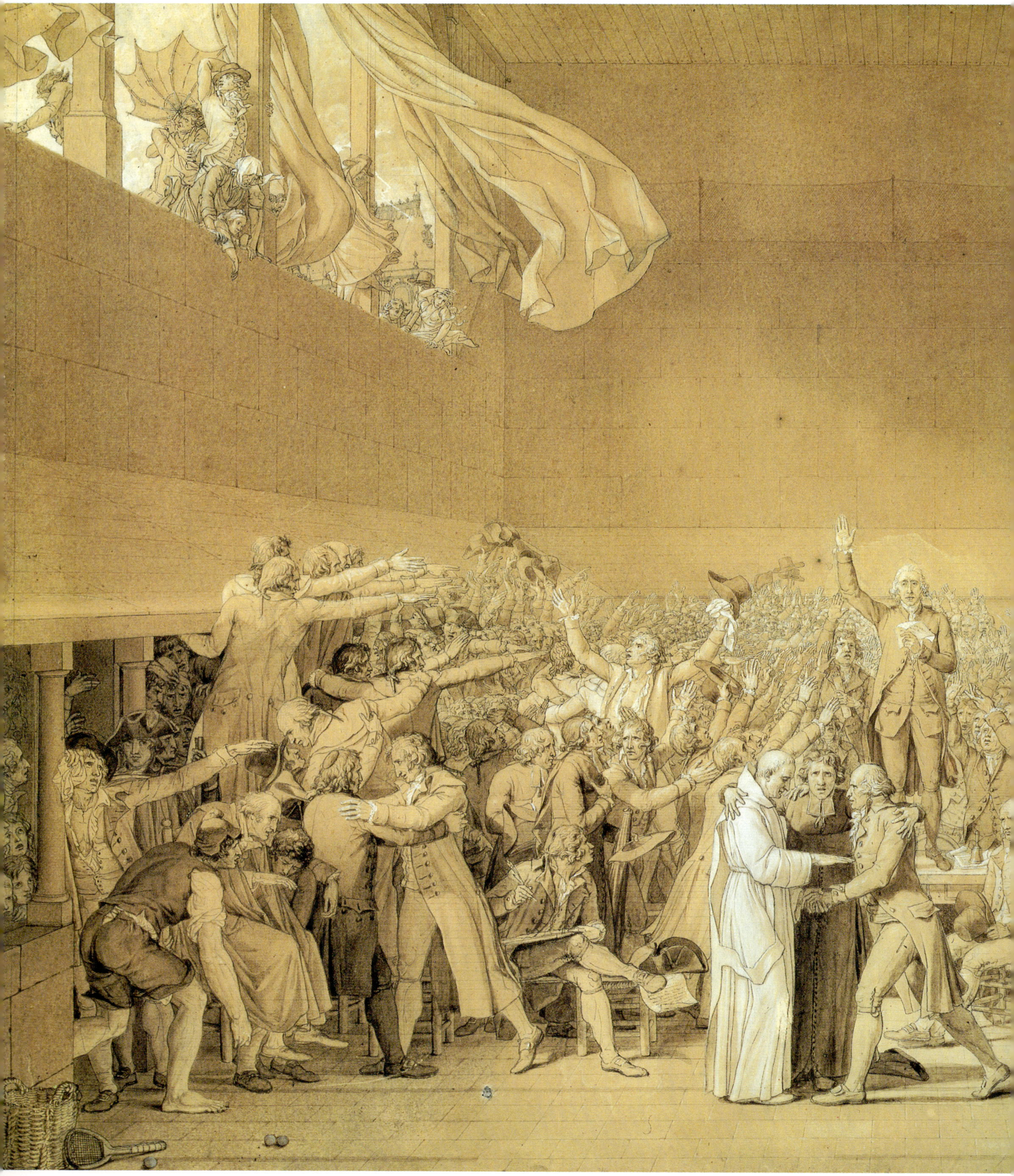

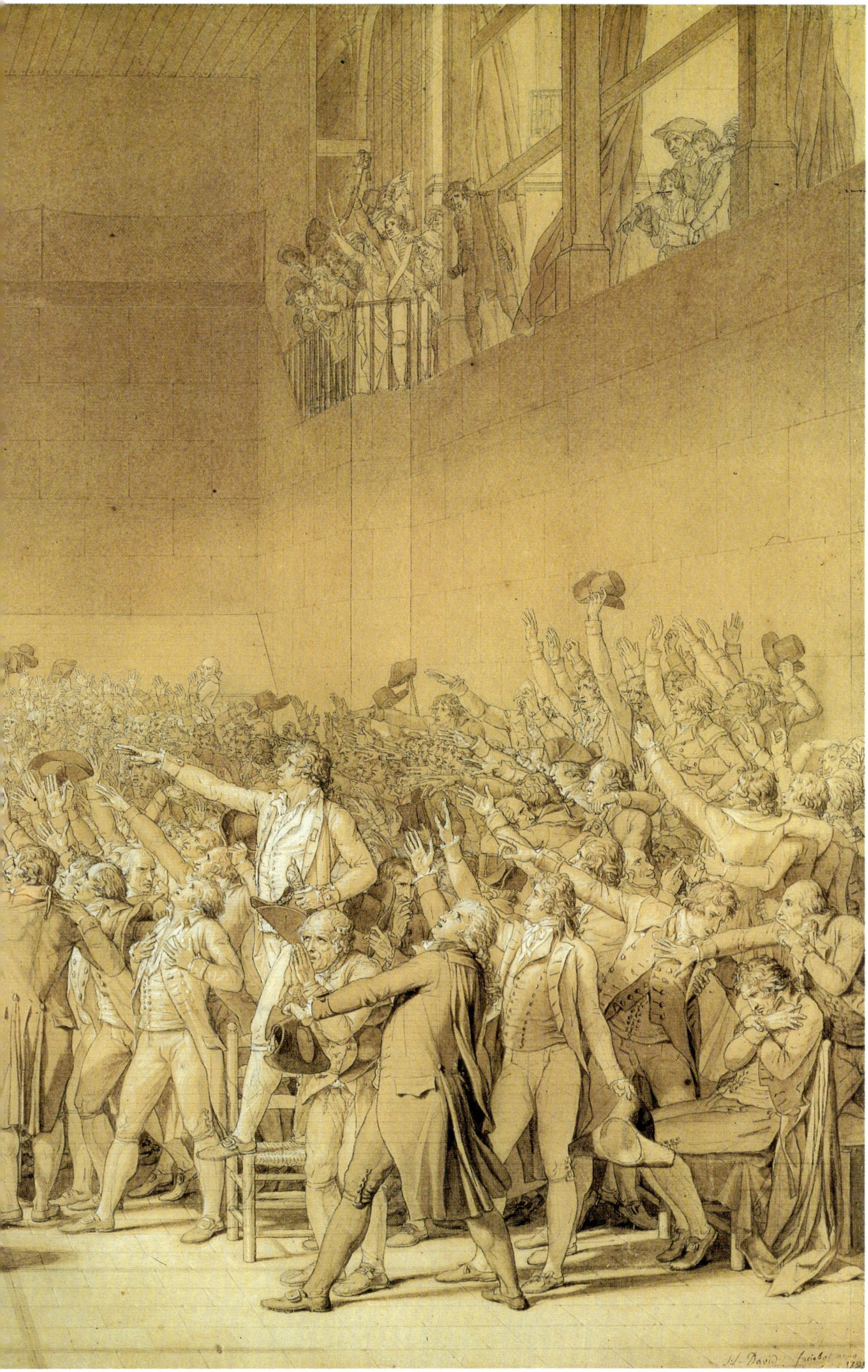

THE OATH OF THE TENNIS COURT AT VERSAILLES ON 20 JUNE 1789, 1791
Pen and ink drawing with brown wash and white highlights on paper
25$\frac{15}{16}$″ × 39$\frac{11}{16}$″
(66 × 101 cm)
Musée National du Château de Versailles et des Trianons

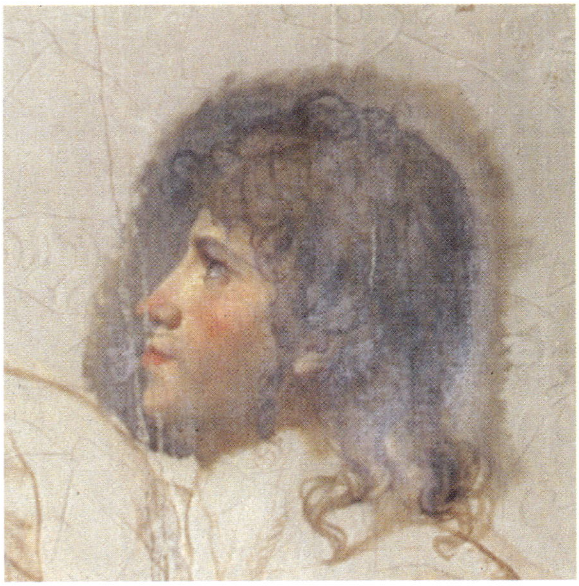

Barnave

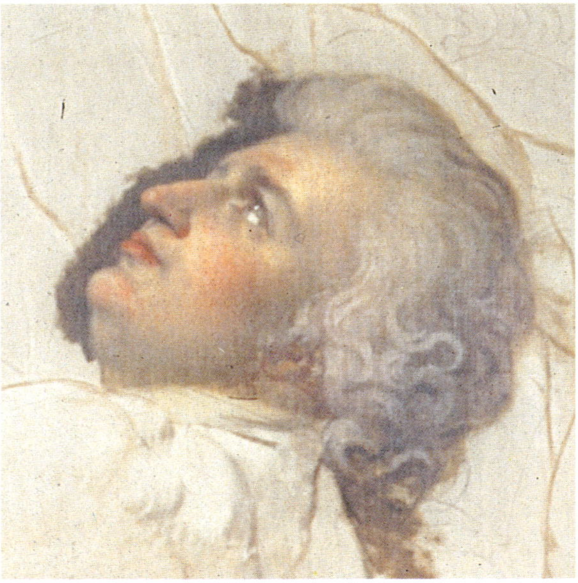

Mirabeau

Details from page 33

Gérard

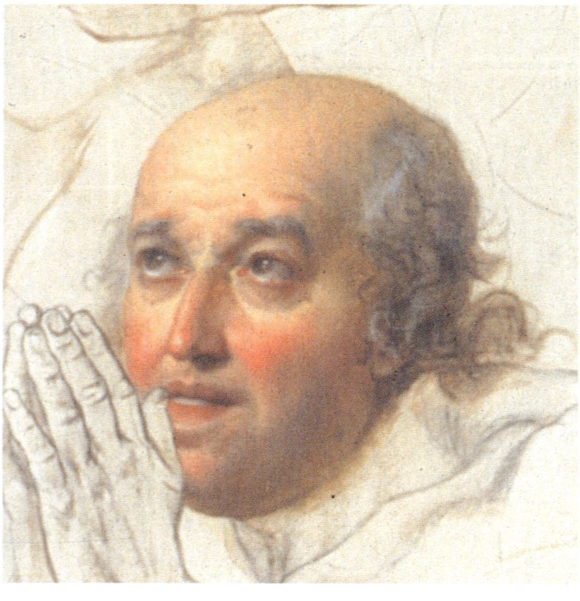

Dubois-Crancé

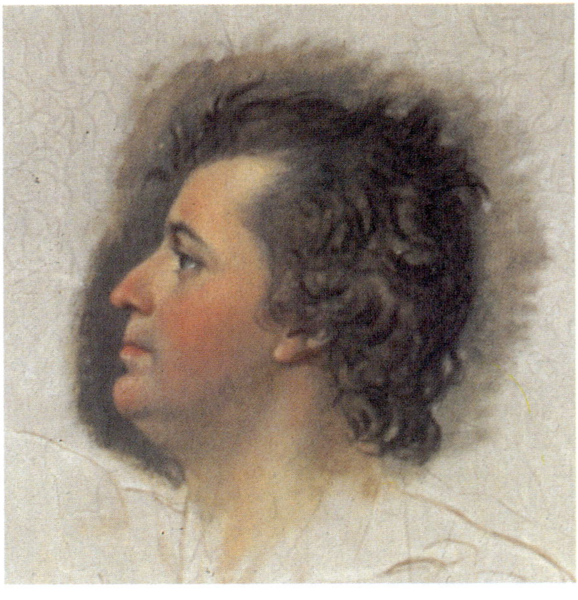

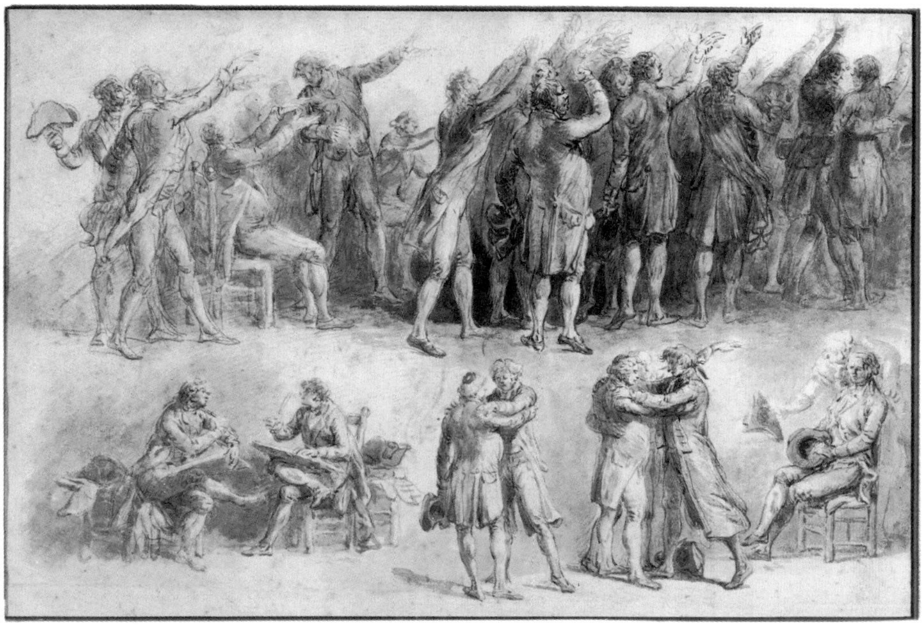

*Study for "The Oath of the Tennis Court" recto, n.d.*
*Brush and black and brown ink with gray wash over traces of graphite on ivory paper*
*11$\frac{7}{16}$" × 17"*
*(29 × 43.3 cm)*
*The Art Institute, Chicago*
*The Helen Regenstein Collection*

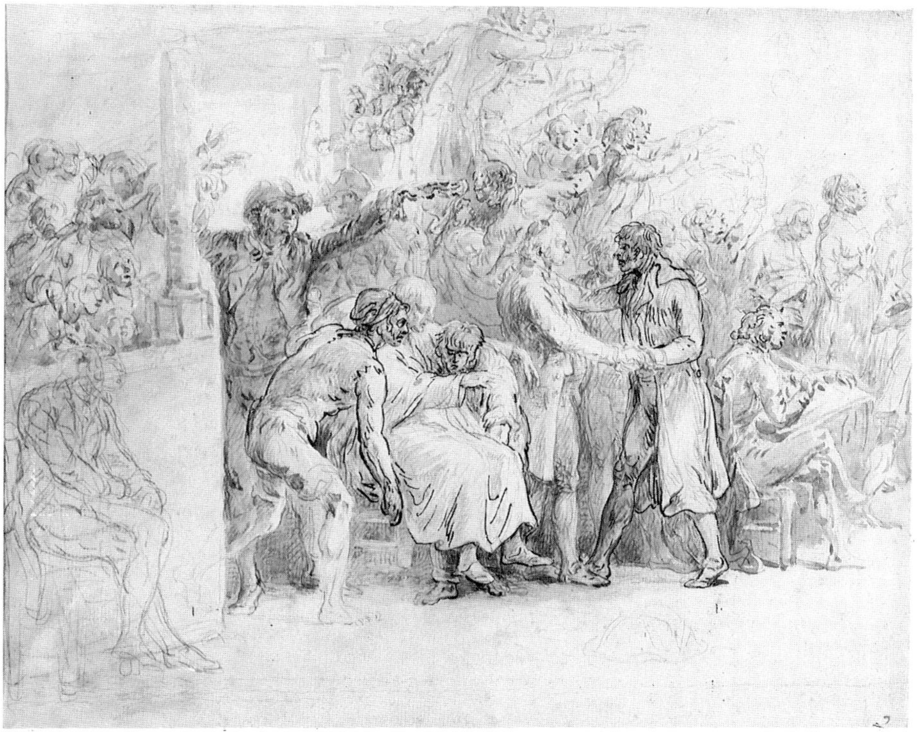

*Study for "The Oath of the Tennis Court", verso, n.d.*
*Group with Maupetit de la Mayenne Carried by His Two Sons*
*Brush and black and brown ink with gray wash over traces of graphite on ivory paper*
*11$\frac{7}{16}$" × 17"*
*(29 × 43.3 cm)*
*The Art Institute, Chicago*
*The Helen Regenstein Collection*

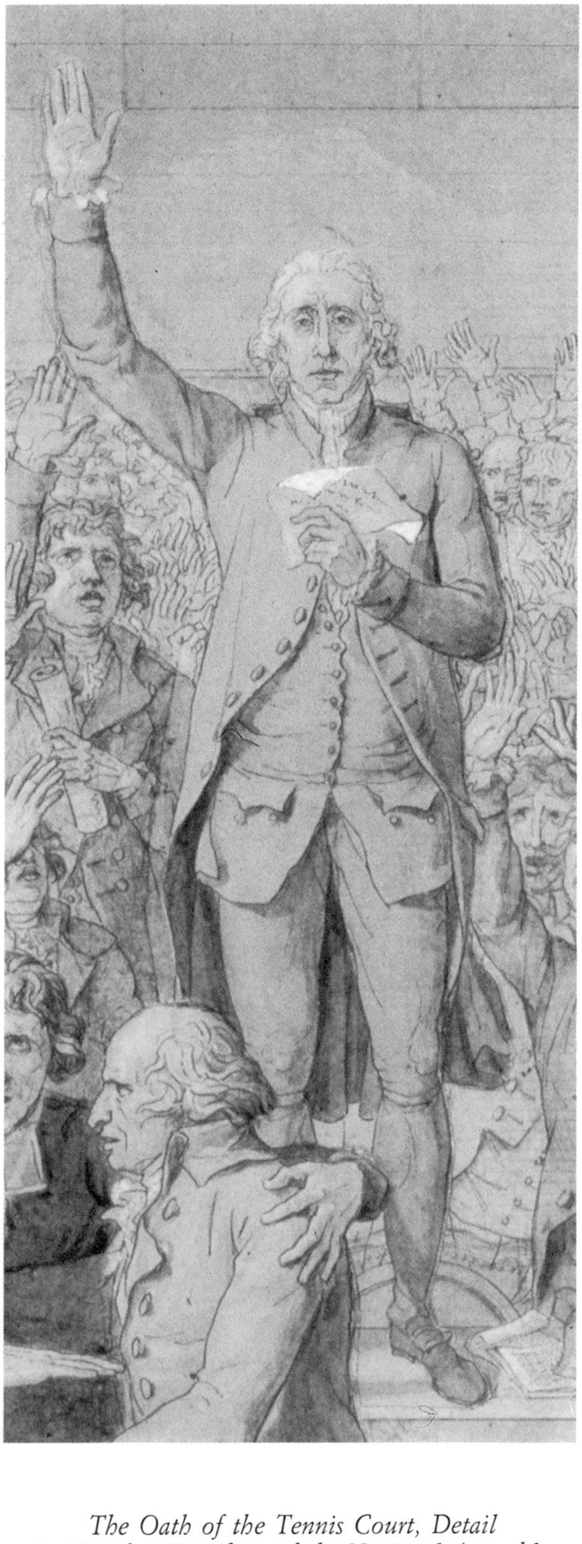

*The Oath of the Tennis Court, Detail*
*Bailly, then President of the National Assembly reads the text of the Oath of the Tennis Court*

the Assembly and Joseph Barnave accepted it in its name.[1]

David set himself to work and composed a large sepia drawing on paper that was to be the model for both the painting and the engraving (see pages 34-35). Around the end of May he exhibited the drawing in his studio and in September at the Salon of 1791. It was hung next to the *Horatii*, creating an arresting juxtaposition between past and present oaths. The subscription was a failure but the exhibition attracted large crowds. On September 28, 1791, two days before the dissolution of the Constituent Assembly, Bertrand Barère had a motion carried that the commission for the painting be paid by the Treasury.[2] David had already made his studio in the deconsecrated Church of the Feuillants, near the Tuileries, and he had made a sketch of the painting. He put an advertisement in the "Moniteur" asking members of the National Assembly to come and sit in his studio or send him their portrait.

It seemed that historical themes could now be found in the present time and the revolutionary enthusiasm created examples of virtue. While painting had easily found a support in past history, the immediate present could be a burden. David was still unaware of this when he exclaimed in the wooden, declamatory tongue of the time: "O beloved fatherland! No more shall we need to seek in the history of ancient people the themes to exercise our brushes. Themes were lacking, artists were forced to repeat themselves. Now there are more themes than there are artists. No, there is no people whose history offers anything as great, as sublime as this Oath of the Tennis Court which I must paint."

(1) A lawyer born in 1761, Barnave was elected to the Third Estate of Dauphiné. In October 1790 he was elected president of the National Assembly. In 1791 he brought the royal family back to Paris after its arrest at Varennes. He became a champion of the monarchy and was imprisoned on August 15, 1792. He was executed on November 29, 1793. (Note of the translator).

(2) A lawyer born in 1755, Barère was a representative of the Third Estate of Brionne, Normandy. Later he was elected to the Convention. He made his reputation during the king's trial. He was elected to the Committee of Public Safety on April 7, 1793, and again on July 10. He was reluctant to rally Robespierre's adversaries and was imprisoned after Thermidor. He supported the coup d'état of 18 Brumaire (November 9-10, 1799). (Note of the translator).

He started on the huge canvas. One can see naked figures with historic faces. On the left, three men embrace: Abbé Grégoire,[1] Pastor Rabaut,[2] and Dom Gerle.[3] On the right, Barnave, Mirabeau, "Old Man" Gérard,[4] and Dubois-Crancé. Robespierre stands between the two groups, among headless figures. The figures are all drawn in white pencil over the gray primer. Four faces are painted in: Barnave, Mirabeau, Gérard, and Dubois-Crancé. So are three hands: Barnave's two hands, and the raised hand of Mirabeau. The canvas was left unfinished, and the version we know is smaller than it was originally. After David died it was cut to 21 feet 7 7/8 inches by 13 feet 1 1/2 inches (6.6 meters by 4 meters) in order to be sold more easily (see page 33).

It is easy to understand why David never finished the painting. The heroes of the Oath of the Tennis Court were quickly becoming politically suspect because politics changed faster than the painter could work. As it stands unfinished, the painting creates a three-dimensional effect owing to the combination of the finished parts, which give an idea of the painting that could have been; the parts sketched in, which are indicative of the manner in which David worked; and the unpainted areas, which reveal the surface. Thus, the whole process of painting is shown in its successive stages, with an unwitting strength.

It may be assumed that David put aside *The Oath* as of March 1792. He was very busy with the reorganization of the arts, the revolutionary celebrations, and the design of ceremonial clothes for civil servants and elected officials. The drawing of 1791 gives an idea of the whole composition. The truly interesting aspect of the drawing lies with the arresting contrast between its two different approaches to space — empty on top and overcrowded at the bottom. In the foreground, details abound: gestures, postures, grimaces, connections between figures, attitudes, which impart an astonishing liveliness, whatever the point from which the scene is observed. When the whole picture is considered, this profusion converges in one movement because all the elements hold together so well and the sharpness of each detail leads from one to another. Consequently, the viewer cannot look at the documentary aspect of the work without being also carried by the painterly form. Here art does more than illustrate history. It captures history's meaning through an image that is itself an act of rebellion: The picture is neither a description nor an explanation because it reconciles the artist's inner vision with an exterior view and combines two different approaches to the space of the drawing.

History painting often results in imagery. It may also create miraculously an image so strong as to become blurred and reveal a face that is both impersonal and deeply moving. This encounter takes time off its hinges, when a wind blows that used to be called Fate. History paintings resemble French classical tragedies, but, while the theater's rule of unity of time, place, and action applies naturally to history painting, the latter is deprived of action and depicts everything within one scene. Therefore, the artist must include painterly suggestions and readable indications of the painting's context. David's education made him believe in a hierarchy between genres, and he probably did not realize that his portraits of *Potocki* and *Lavoisier* express so much character that they create the effect he was seeking in his heroic compositions. In 1793 he painted his masterpiece, *Marat Murdered* (see page 45), which is at the crossing between the two genres, between history and portrait painting.

(1) Born in 1750, Henri Grégoire was sent to the States-General as a member of the clergy of Nancy, Lorraine. A bishop and a defender of the rights of Jews and Blacks, he took an oath to the civil authority on September 27, 1790. He was elected to the Convention and worked on the Committee for National Public Education. (Note of the translator).

(2) Jean-Paul Rabaut Saint-Etienne, born in 1743 in Nîmes, Languedoc, was a Calvinist minister and a Girondist. He was executed in 1793. (Note of the translator).

(3) The Carthusian monk, Dom Gerle, was a surrogate representative of Riom, Auvergne, who sat at the Assembly after December 1789 but did not attend the meeting of June 20. In April 1790, he tried and failed to maintain the Catholic religion as a State religion. (Note of the translator).

(4) A representative of the seneschalsy of Rennes, in Brittany, Gérard became instantly famous because he kept his Breton peasant dress. (Note of the translator).

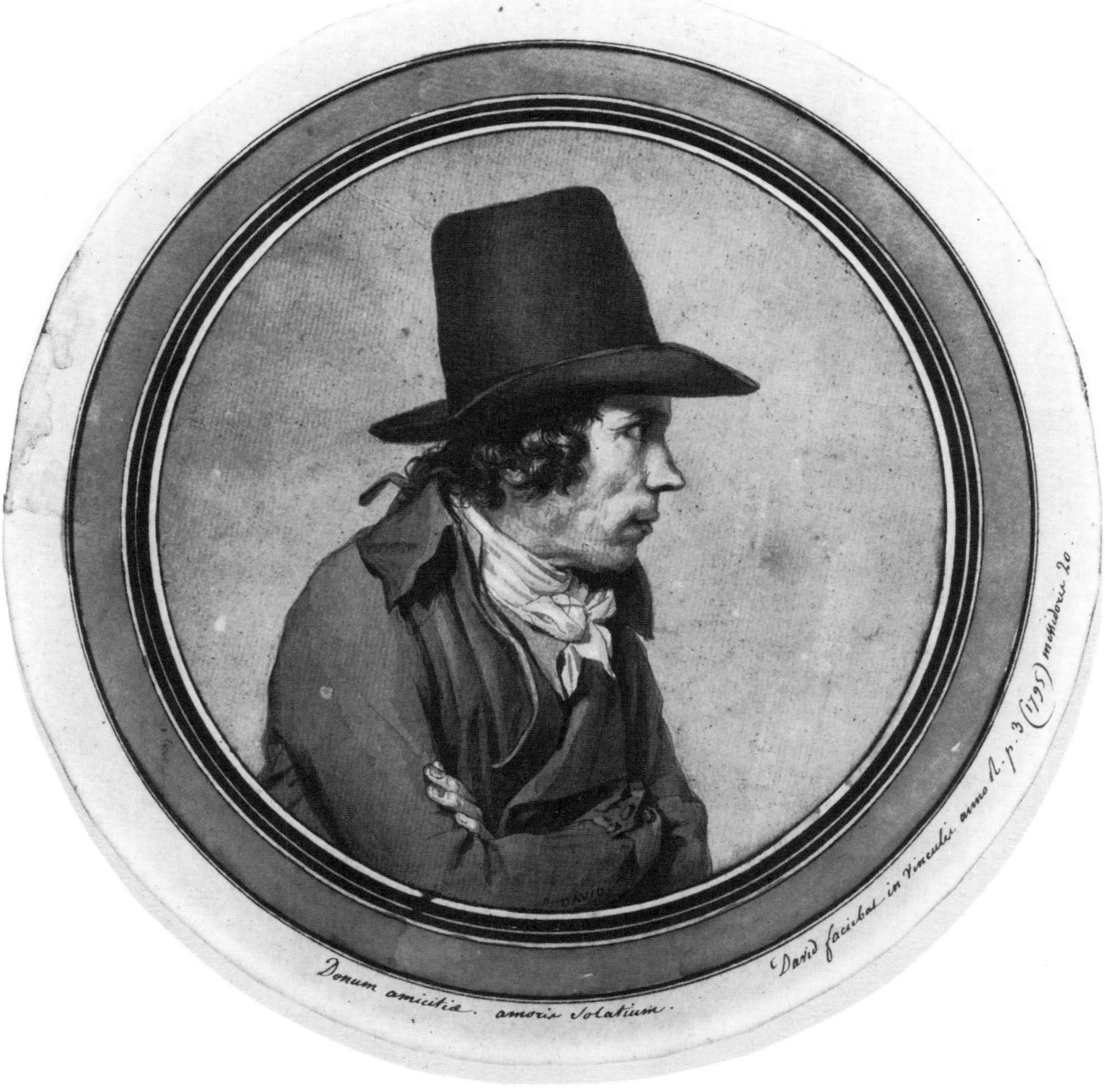

*Portrait of Jeanbon Saint-André, 1795*
*Brush and black ink with gray wash, heightened with white gouache on ivory laid paper, diameter 7⅛" (18.2 cm)*
*The Art Institute of Chicago. The Helen Regenstein Collection*

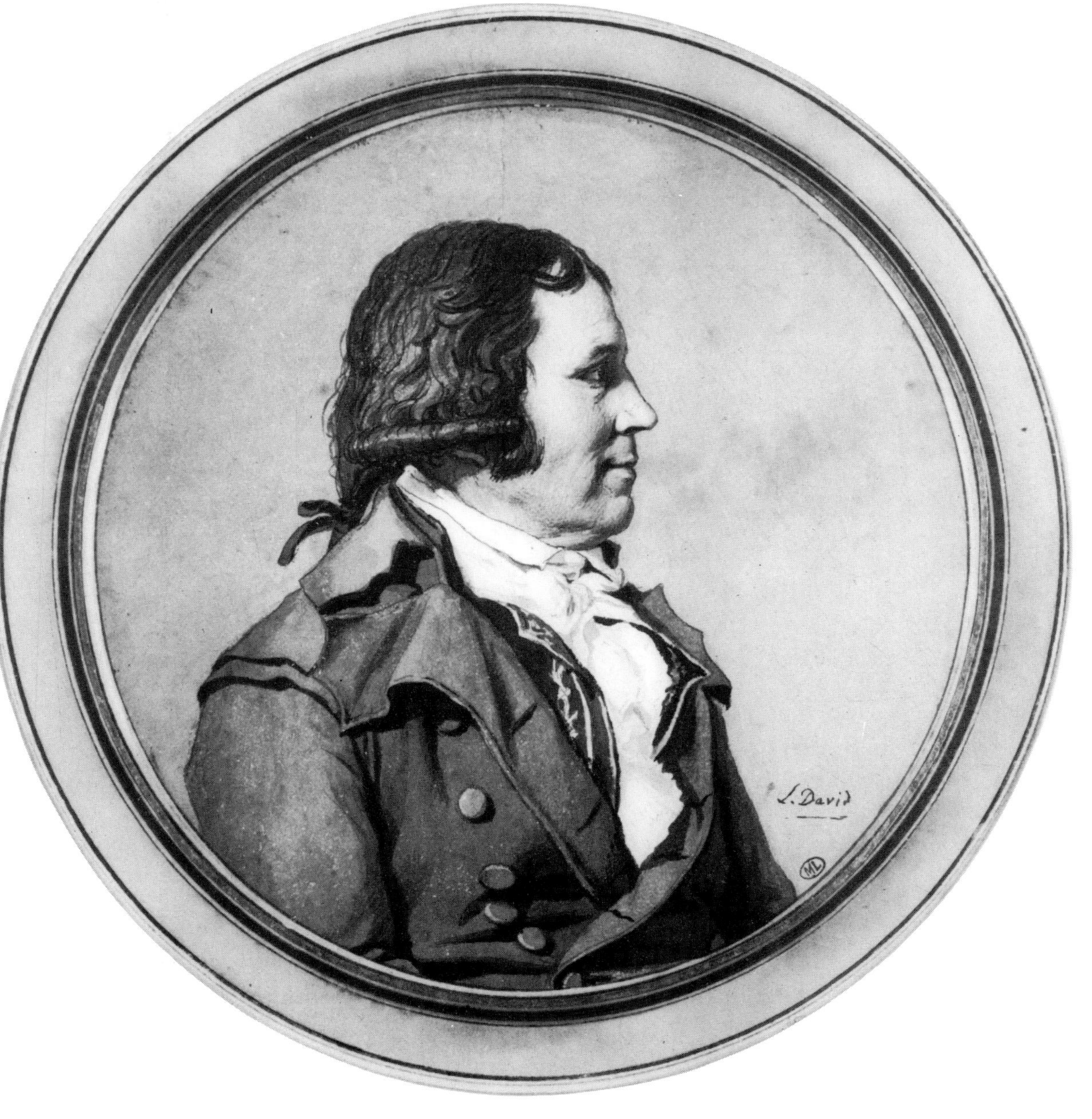

*Portrait of Dubois-Crancé, n.d.*
*Drawing*
*Musée du Louvre*
*Paris*

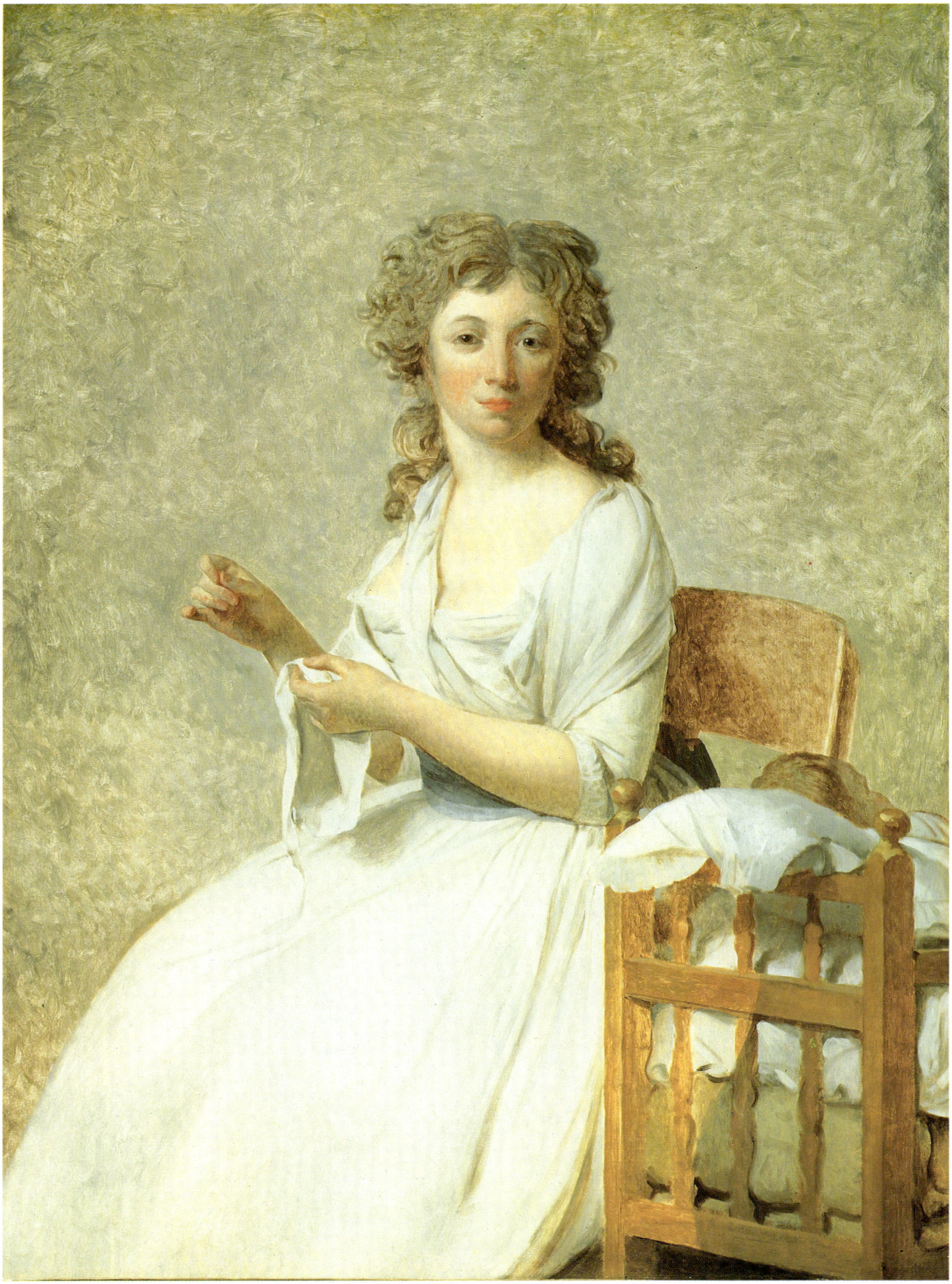

Madame Pastoret and Her Son, 1791-1792. Oil on canvas, 51⅛″ × 38¼″ (129.9 × 97.1 cm)
The Art Institute of Chicago. Clyde M. Carr Fund

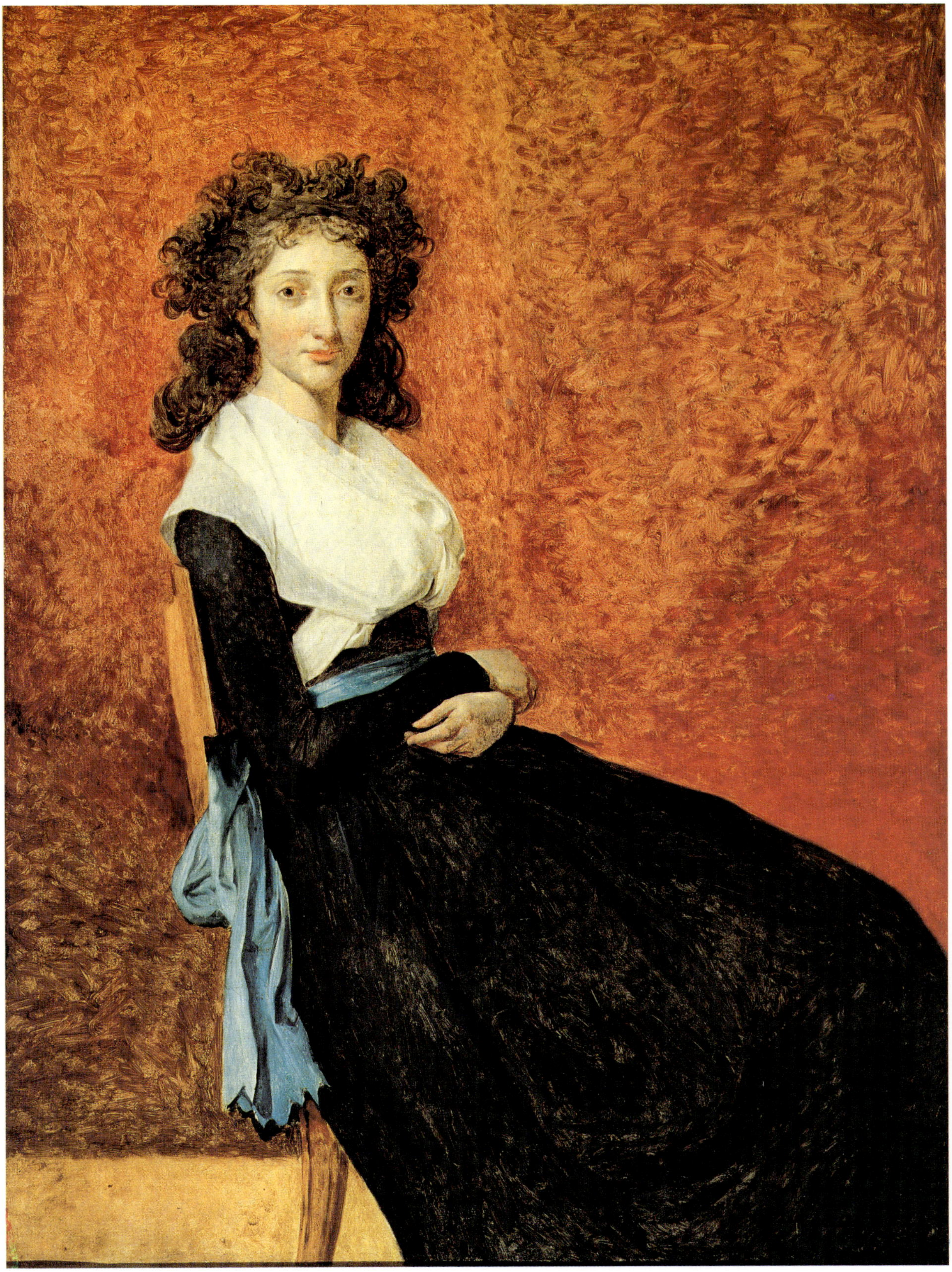

PORTRAIT OF MADAME TRUDAINE, 1791-1792. Oil on canvas, $51\frac{3}{16}'' \times 38\frac{1}{2}''$ (130 × 98 cm)
Musée du Louvre, Paris

In 1790-1792 David produced four portraits which were to become famous. This is where he invented his background of pure space, which was as unexpected then as was Turner's Impressionism in his time. There are *Monsieur de Joubert* (the date of which is uncertain),[(1)] *The Marquise d'Orvilliers* (1790),[(2)] *Madame Charles-Louis Trudaine* (1791-1792), and *Madame Pastoret* (1792), the latter two being the most beautiful (see page 42 and 43). One wonders about the meaning of beauty in this case. There is a name under each painting, which provides little explanation since the viewer cannot verify the portrait's resemblance. One could inquire and collect biographical data, but this would have little to do with the painting. There is a face, and the viewer is told that it is a portrait; but the portrait, as such, is of no interest to the present viewer, for otherwise the painting would merely be a historic document. The paradox is that while a portrait is based on resemblance, its beauty owes little to that resemblance. One may wonder about the significance of a face in painting. A particular face remains still in the middle of time, staring at us. History is the past, being always that which passes. Heroic painting consists in marking this passage of time in heroic terms, but heroism stops short in front of *Madame Trudaine*. Her attitude and eyes express an anxiety, a doubtful expectation, that transform this face, the identity of which has become unimportant to us, into the essence of painting. While the portrait becomes more anonymous, it turns into the representation of the condition of women rather than that of an individual.

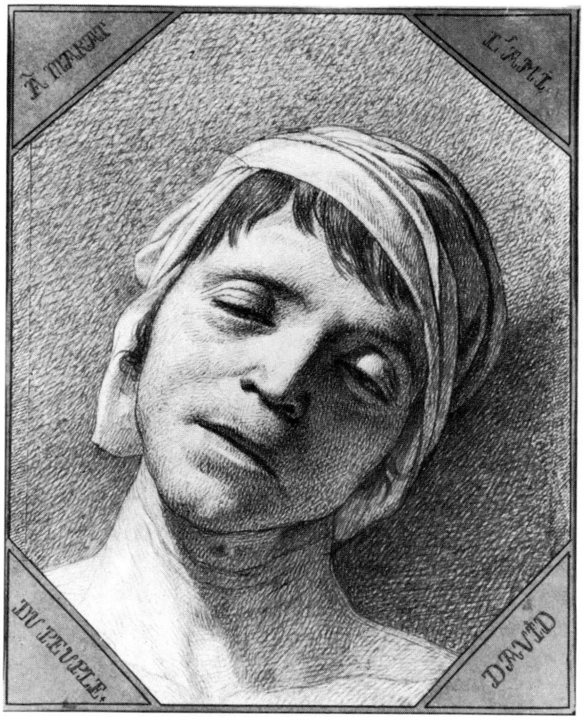


*Head of Marat Murdered, 1793*
*Pen and ink on white paper mounted on brown paper, 10⅝" × 8¼" (27 × 21 cm)*
*Musée National du Château de Versailles et des Trianons*

The very lessons of history become timeless as they become exemplary and they obliterate history itself. To paint after the antique was therefore a false problem, related to signs helping the viewer's recognition rather than to virtue. If an artist wants to depict virtue based on a contemporary event that could be compared to antiquity, and make it exemplary, he must paint that virtue both in its contemporary context and with an element of timelessness. David's *Marat* succeeded in this feat: It is both a portrait and a history painting, both a revolutionary icon and a tragic knot.

David was the president of the Jacobins when Charlotte Corday killed Jean-Paul Marat on the evening of July 13, 1793.[(3)] The day before, he had visited Marat, whom he admired, and the murder caused the setting of the visit to stick in his memory: the tub, the sheet, the green rug, the wooden packing case, the inkwell, and the pen. The tub and the pen are the signs by which the viewer can recognize Marat: He spent long hours in a tub to soothe the itching caused by a skin disease and his pen was

(1) Musée Fabre, Montpellier. Philippe-Laurent de Joubert was a patron of the arts. The painting was left unfinished due to the death of the sitter in 1792. (Note of the translator).
(2) Musée du Louvre, Paris. She was the daughter of a wealthy financier. (Note of the translator).
(3) A physicist, born in 1743, Marat founded the journal *L'Ami du Peuple,* in which he bitterly attacked all who were in power. He was elected to the Convention in 1792 and supported the Jacobins against the Girondists. (Note of the translator).

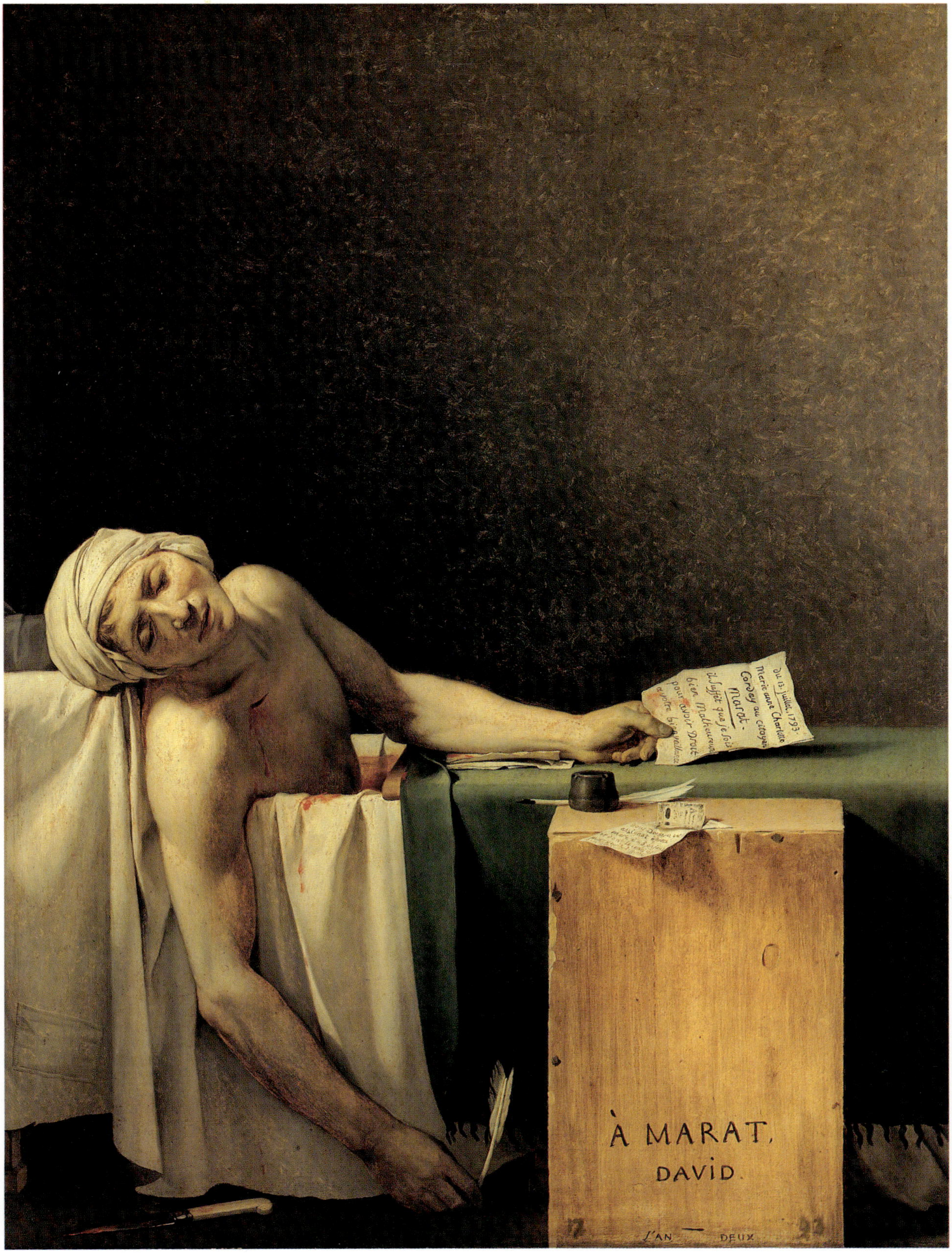


MARAT MURDERED, 1793. Oil on canvas, 65″ × 50⅜″ (165 × 128 cm)
Musées Royaux des Beaux-Arts de Belgique, Brussels

his weapon. The box was his only piece of furniture — a testimony to his austere way of life. Three items are added to the decor; they tell the tragic story and indicate something about Marat's character. On the box, next to the inkwell, there is an assignat [1] with a note by Marat: "This assignat should be given to this mother of five children whose husband died for his country." His left hand holds another note: "July 13, 1793 / from Marie-Anne-Charlotte Corday to citizen Marat. / I am wretched; that alone gives me a right to your kindness." A blood-stained knife lies on the floor. A few words tell us everything that should be known about the dead man's generosity and they add to the visual simplicity of the painting.

Marat was the Revolution's second martyr, after Michel Le Peletier de Saint-Fargeau, who had been murdered in 1793 for having voted for the king's execution. David had painted a portrait of Le Peletier, which may also have been very dramatic, but the painting has since disappeared. [2] After the news of Marat's death reached the Convention, Guiraud, a representative of the section for the Social Contract, concluded his funeral eulogy of Marat with this call:

> The crime! A patricidal hand robbed us of the most courageous defender of the people. He always sacrificed himself for the sake of freedom and this was his crime. Our eyes are still seeking him among us. What a horrible sight, he is lying on his deathbed! David, where are you? You handed down to posterity the picture of Le Peletier dying for the nation. There is another picture you must make. [3]

David replied: "And I shall make it." He also took charge of the funeral ceremony at the Church of the Cordeliers, with Marat's body lying in state, next to his tub and wooden box. The ceremony illustrated a wish to create a revolutionary ritual to consecrate virtue and express it through the sight of a martyr's funeral glory. The organization of official festivities and the design of uniforms had the same purpose.

On November 15, 1793, David presented his painting to the Convention. The dead body calls to mind Christ's Deposition from the Cross. One can see his chest and wound; his right arm is hanging to the ground and his right hand is still holding a pen; the water in the tub is red with blood. His inkwell, another pen, the assignat, and Marat's last letter are displayed on the box, which stands like a stela, bearing an inscription in block letters: "TO MARAT / DAVID." The artist's name is written in smaller letters than that of Marat. The date is on the bottom: "Year two," according to the new calendar. This contrasts with the calendar used by the murderer, whose letter — which Marat holds in his hand — is dated "July 13, 1793."

The curve of the body, the horizontal tub, the vertical box — everything is designed with great simplicity, with an honesty and an economy of means which are the virtue of both the artist and the painting. This honesty also befits the virtue in the man in the painting, whose face expresses a supreme kindness and an exemplary revolutionary spirit carried to the point of sacrifice. The same spirit fills the preliminary drawing, except that the half-closed eyes and dying mouth make the martyr more moving and human (see page 44). In the painting, Marat's face barely reaches the middle of the canvas. The rest is empty — rather it is filled with space that David now uses in his portraits. Here the space is a strange swirling combination of light and shadow which creates an atmosphere of idealism rather than realism.

(1) One of the bills issued as currency by the Revolutionary government of France. (Note of the translator).

(2) Le Peletier's daughter, Madame de Mortefontaine, later renounced her father's beliefs and became a fervent royalist. After David's death, she bought his portrait of her father, as well as the entire edition of prints made after the painting, and the plate. She destroyed everything, except for one damaged print now in the collection of the Bibliothèque Nationale in Paris. (Note of the translator).

(3) E.-J. Delécluze, *op. cit.*, p. 155.

The painting hung in the hall of the Convention until February 1795, after which it was returned to David, as was *Le Peletier*. After David died, the contents of his studio were sold at auction and *Marat* did not find a buyer. The lovers of Romanticism could not understand its pensive emotion devoid of bombast. Charles Baudelaire discovered the painting's power when he wrote in 1846: "The drama is here, vivid in its pitiful horror. This painting is David's masterpiece and one of the great curiosities of modern art because, by a strange feat, it has nothing trivial or vile. What is most surprising in this unusual visual poem is that it was painted very quickly. When one thinks of the beauty of the lines, this quickness is bewildering. This is food for the strong, the triumph of spiritualism. This painting is as cruel as nature but it has the fragrance of ideals. Where is the ugliness that hallowed Death erased so quickly with the tip of his wing? Now Marat can challenge Apollo. He has been kissed by the loving lips of Death and he rests in the peace of his metamorphosis. This work contains something both poignant and tender; a soul is flying in the cold air of this room, on these cold walls, around this cold and funerary tub."[1]

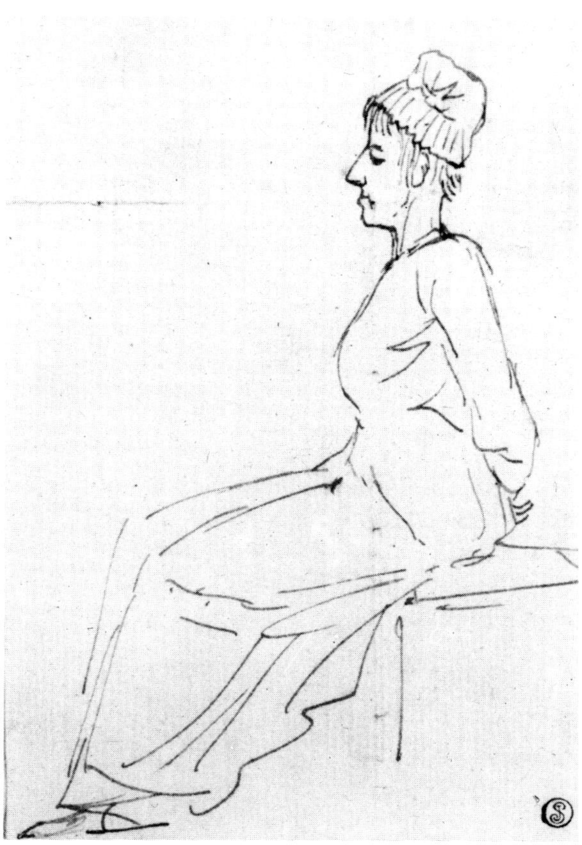

*Marie-Antoinette on the Way*
*to the Scaffold, 1793*
*Pen and ink, 5 13/16" × 3 15/16" (14.7 × 10 cm)*
*Musée du Louvre, Paris*
*E. de Rothschild Collection*

In 1794, David painted his last revolutionary painting, *Joseph Barra*. The theme of this enigmatic work is a very simple event, the circumstances of which David explained clearly: "Young, heroic Barra was only thirteen years old and his mother's sole support. Butchers of mankind surrounded and outnumbered him. He fell alive in their ferocious hands! Virtue shines the most when in danger. When he was called to shout *Long live the King!*, he became indignant and refused to reply with anything but *Long live the Republic!* He was immediately stricken and he fell, holding his three-colored rosette against his heart: He died to live again in the annals of history."

The painting shows only the reclining body of a naked adolescent (see page 48). One can guess that he is holding a piece of paper in his hand as well as a little colored thing. His gender is unclear; there is something feminine in the graceful lines of the body and the face. Where is he lying? One could imagine that he is resting against a fold — a fold of something unfinished, a fold in space, a fold of painting.... This androgynous body is only surrounded with wide strokes — the marks of a brush that can combine light and color and create an extraordinarily airy compost.... Are these brush strokes the "annals of history" David was referring to? They enclose something sexual and disquieting because it is indeterminate. The answer has been for almost two centuries that this is not a body, this is something unfinished about to be dressed.

(1) Charles Baudelaire, "Le Musée classique du Bazar Bonne-Nouvelle," in *Ecrits sur l'art* I, pp. 129-130.

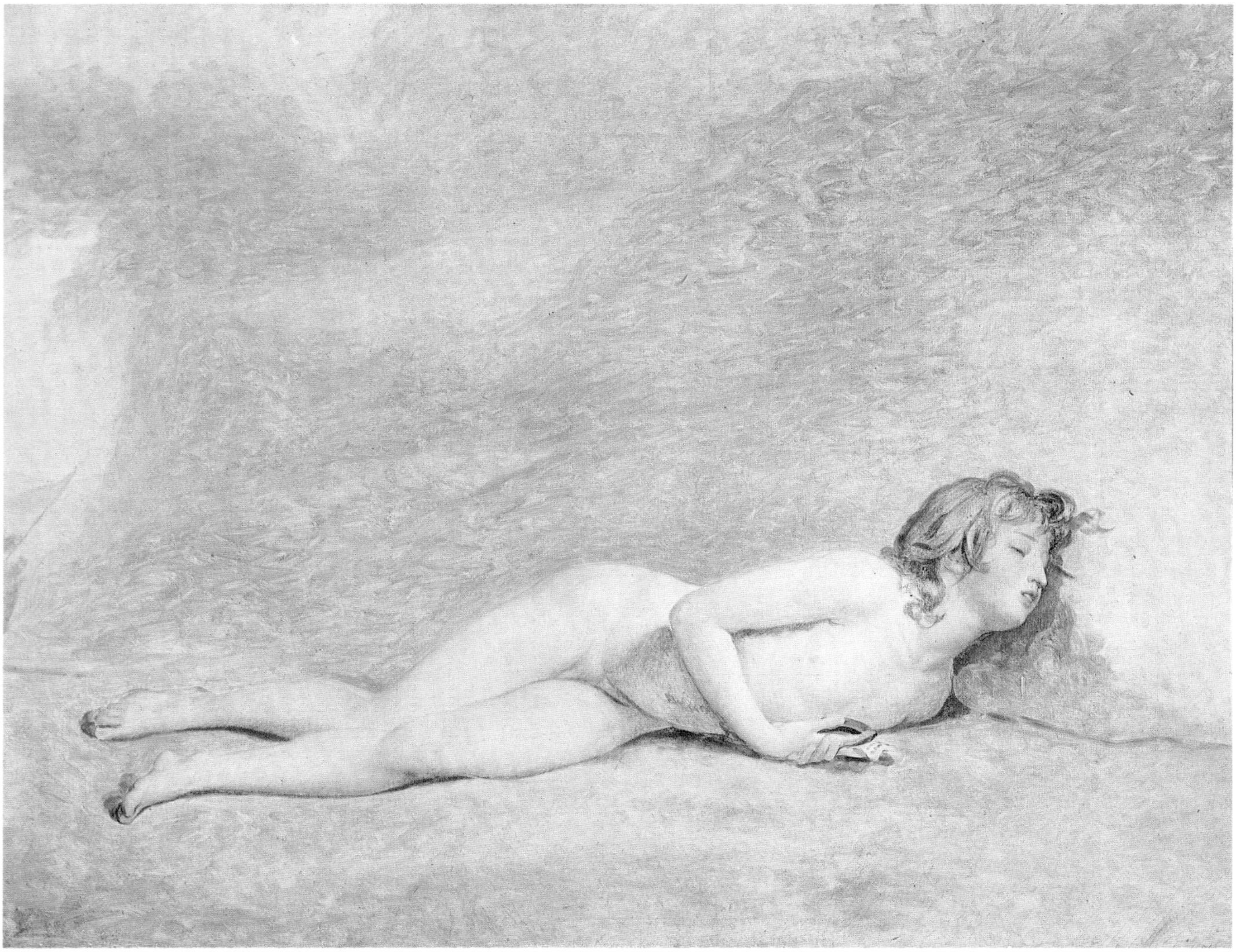

JOSEPH BARRA, 1794
Oil on canvas
46⁷⁄₁₆″ × 61⁷⁄₁₆″ (119 × 156 cm)
Musée Calvet, Avignon, France
Gift of Horace Vernet

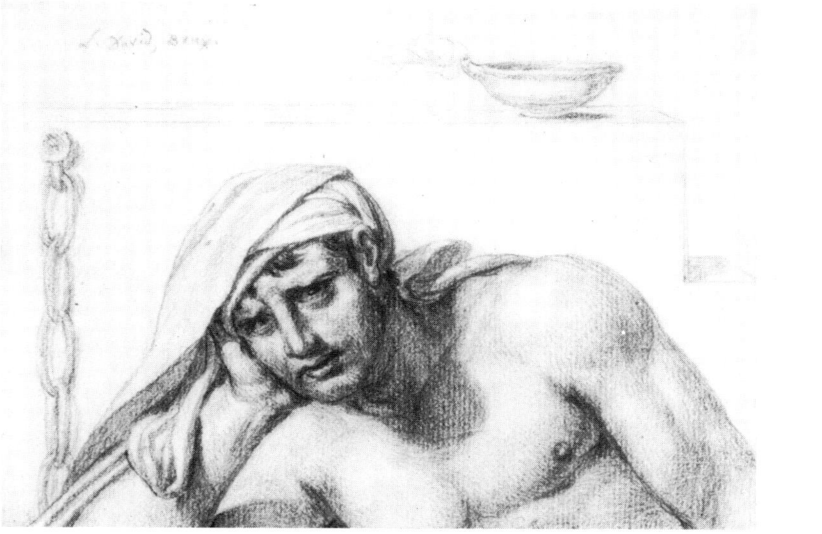

*The Prisoner, n.d.*
*Black chalk*
*5¼″ × 7¾″ (13.4 × 19.7 cm)*
*The Cleveland Museum of Art, Ohio*
*Purchase from the J.H. Wade Fund*

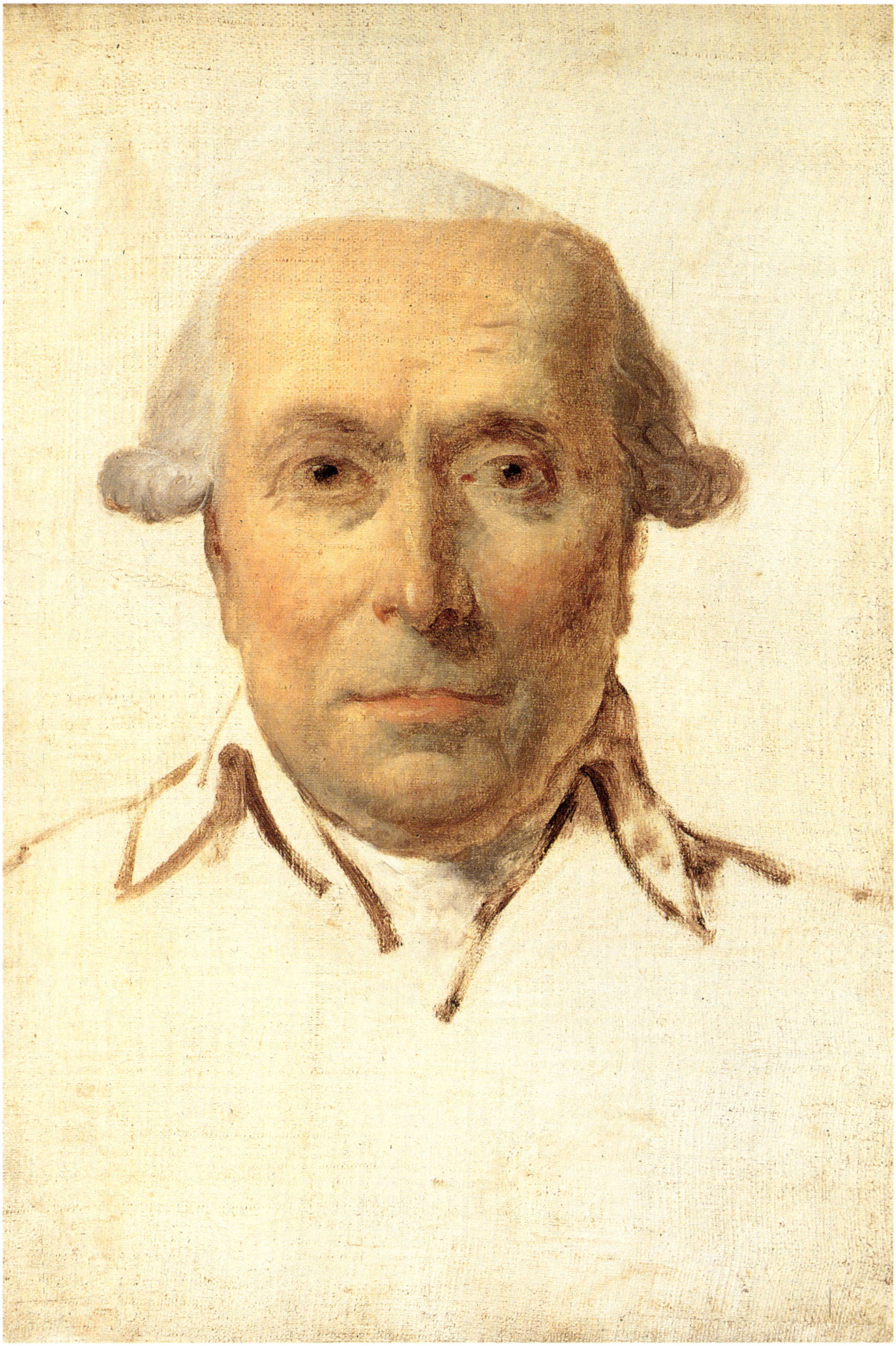

Portrait of the American Rebel Filippo Mazzei
(Also called Portrait of Kervelegan), 1791-1792
Oil on canvas, 19$\frac{5}{16}$″ × 13″ (49 × 33 cm). Musée du Louvre, Paris

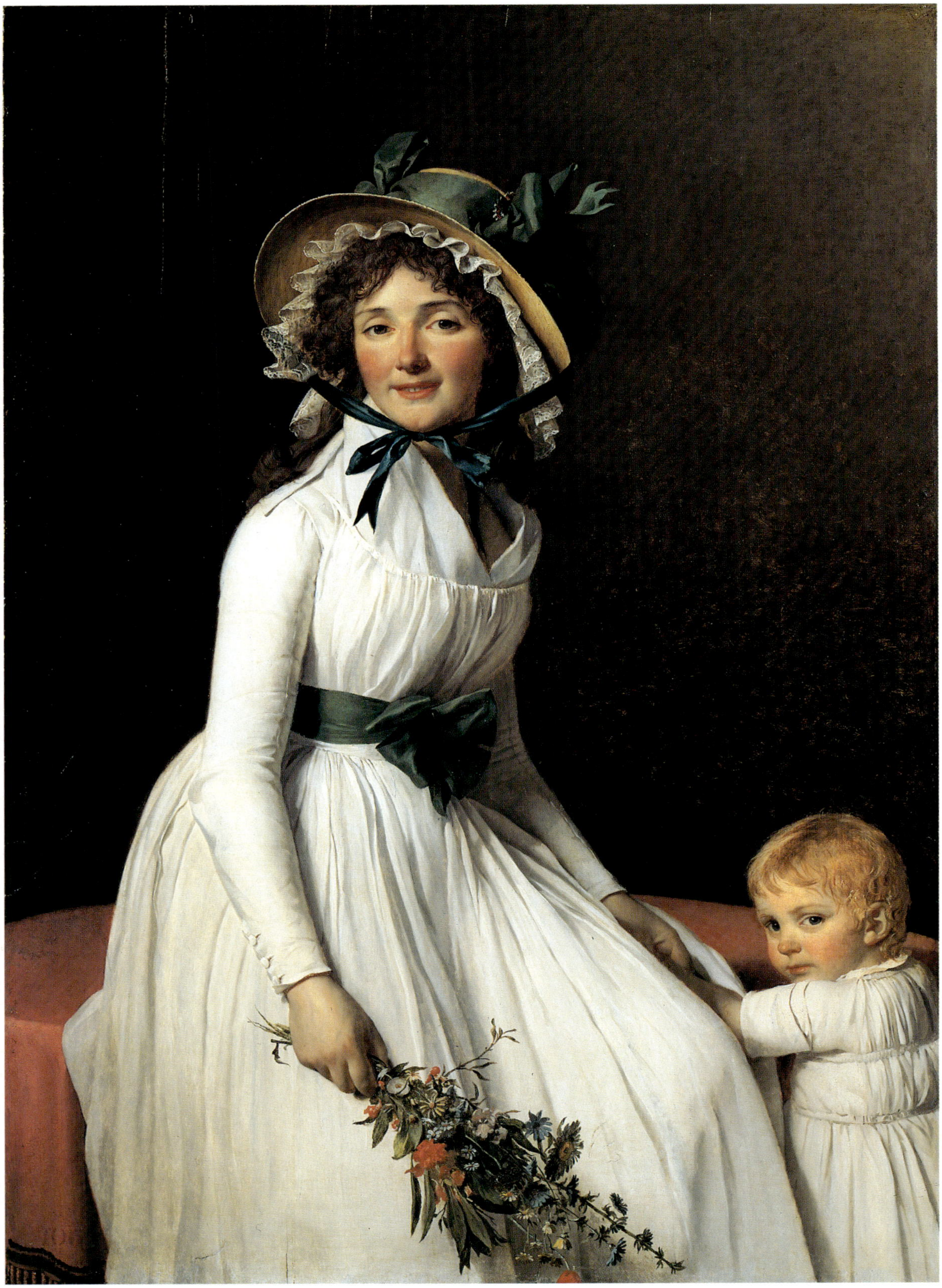

Madame Sériziat, 1795. Oil on panel, 51⁹⁄₁₆″ × 37¾″ (131 × 96 cm)
Musée du Louvre, Paris

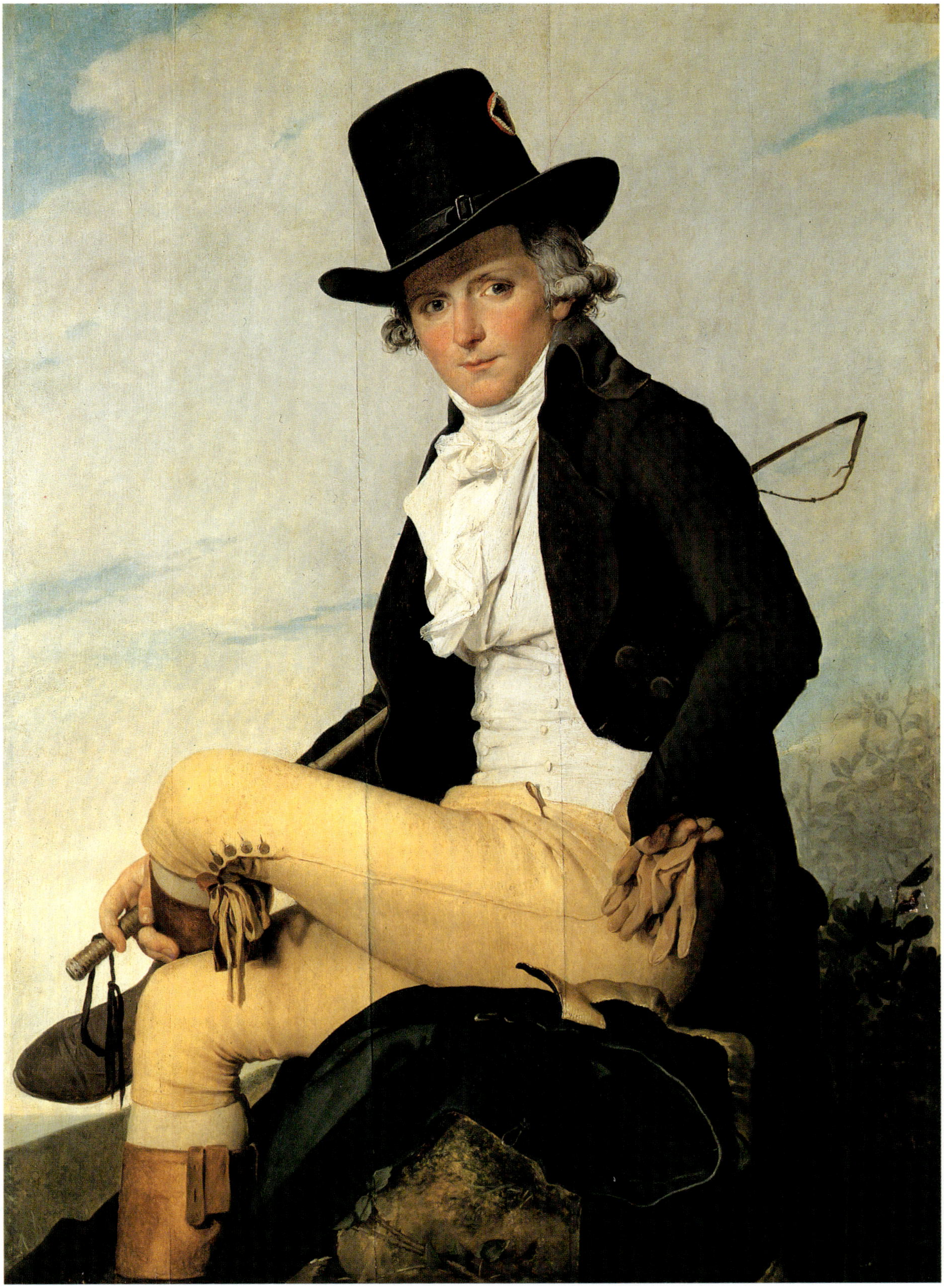

Pierre Sériziat, the Artist's Brother-in-Law, 1795. Oil on panel, 50¾″ × 37⅜″ (129 × 95 cm)
Musée du Louvre, Paris

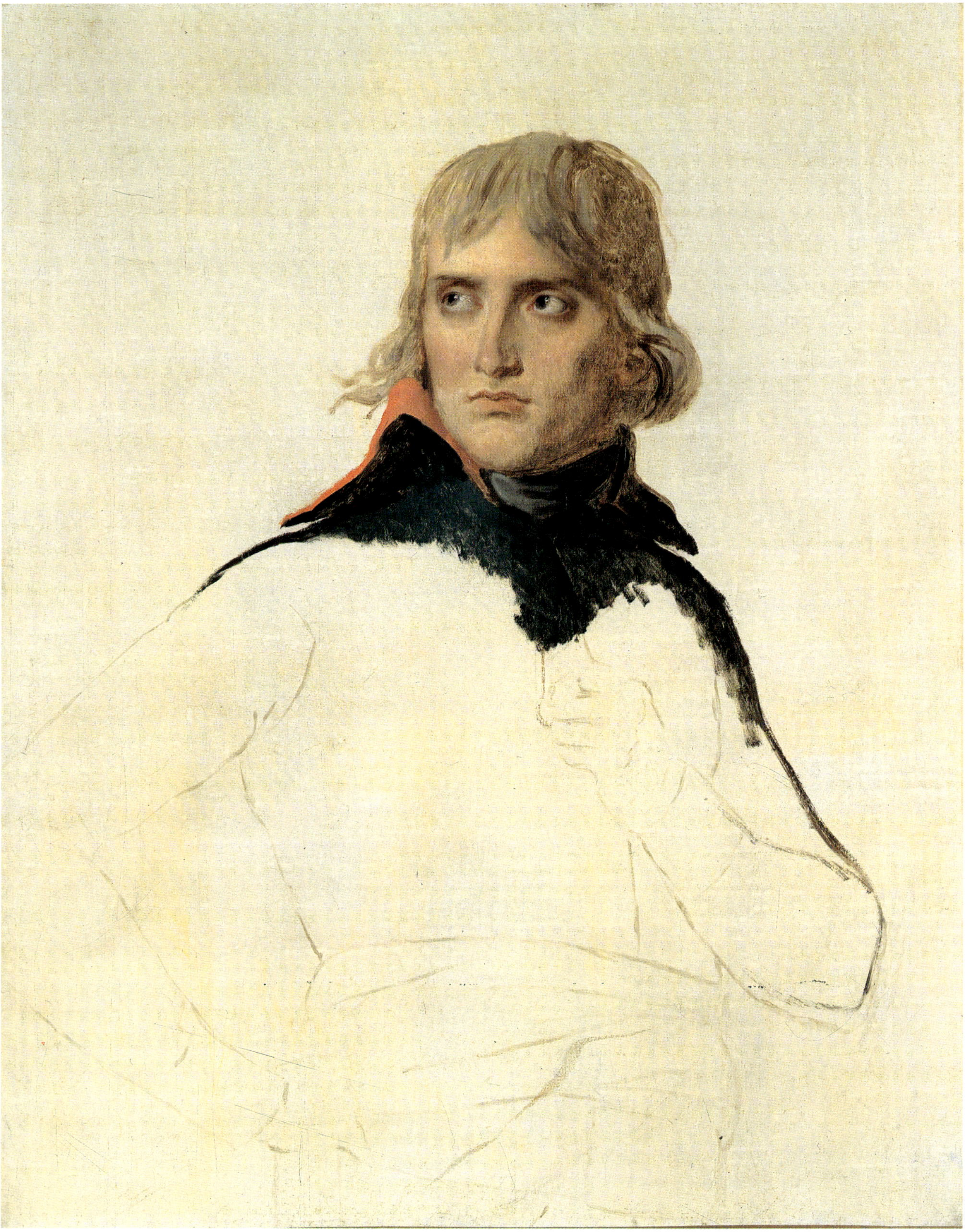

General Bonaparte, 1797. Oil sketch on canvas, 31⅞″ × 25⅝″ (81 × 65 cm)
Musée du Louvre, Paris

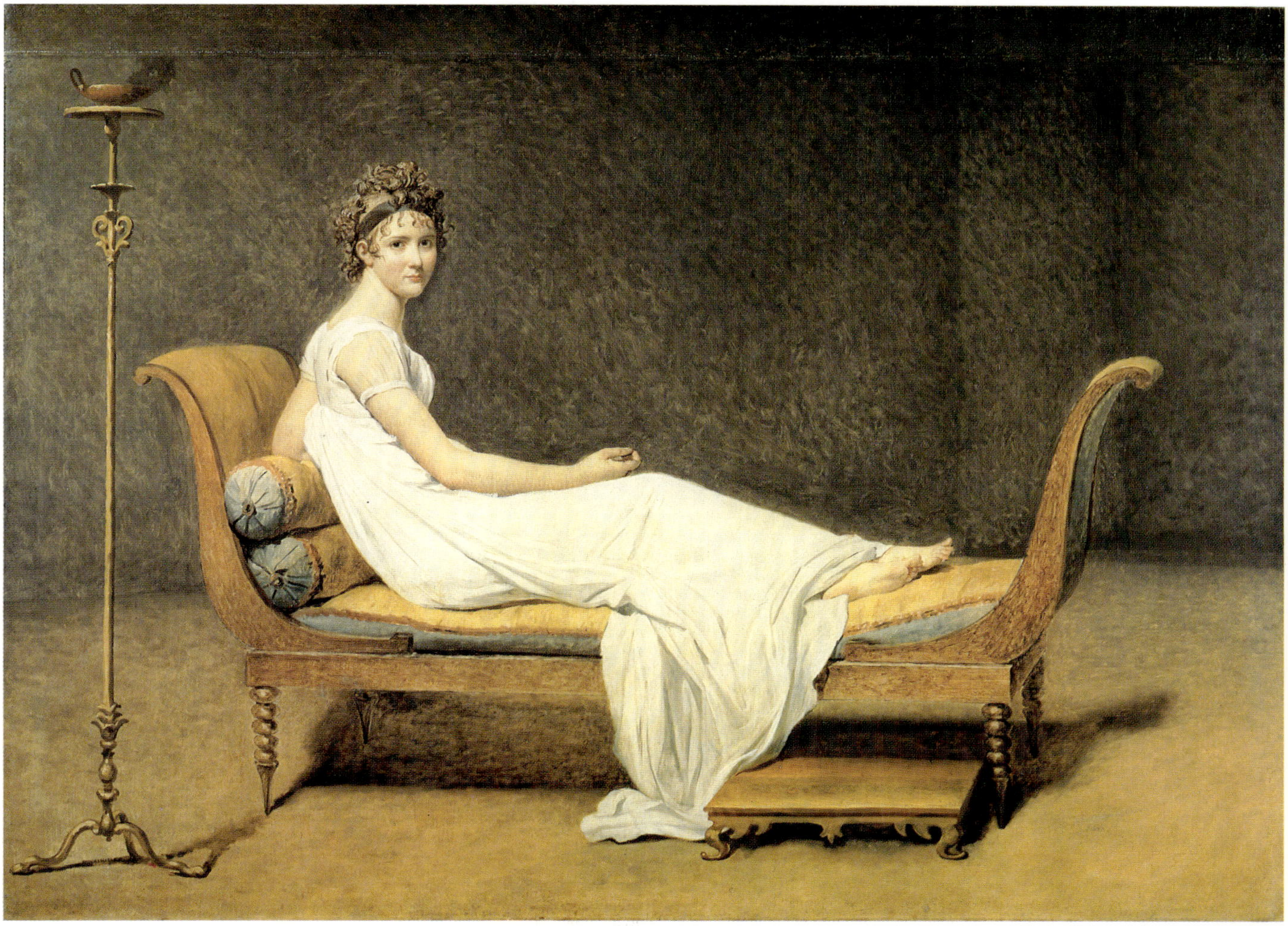

MADAME RÉCAMIER, 1800
Oil on canvas (unfinished), 68½″ × 96$\frac{1}{16}$″ (174 × 244 cm)
Musée du Louvre, Paris

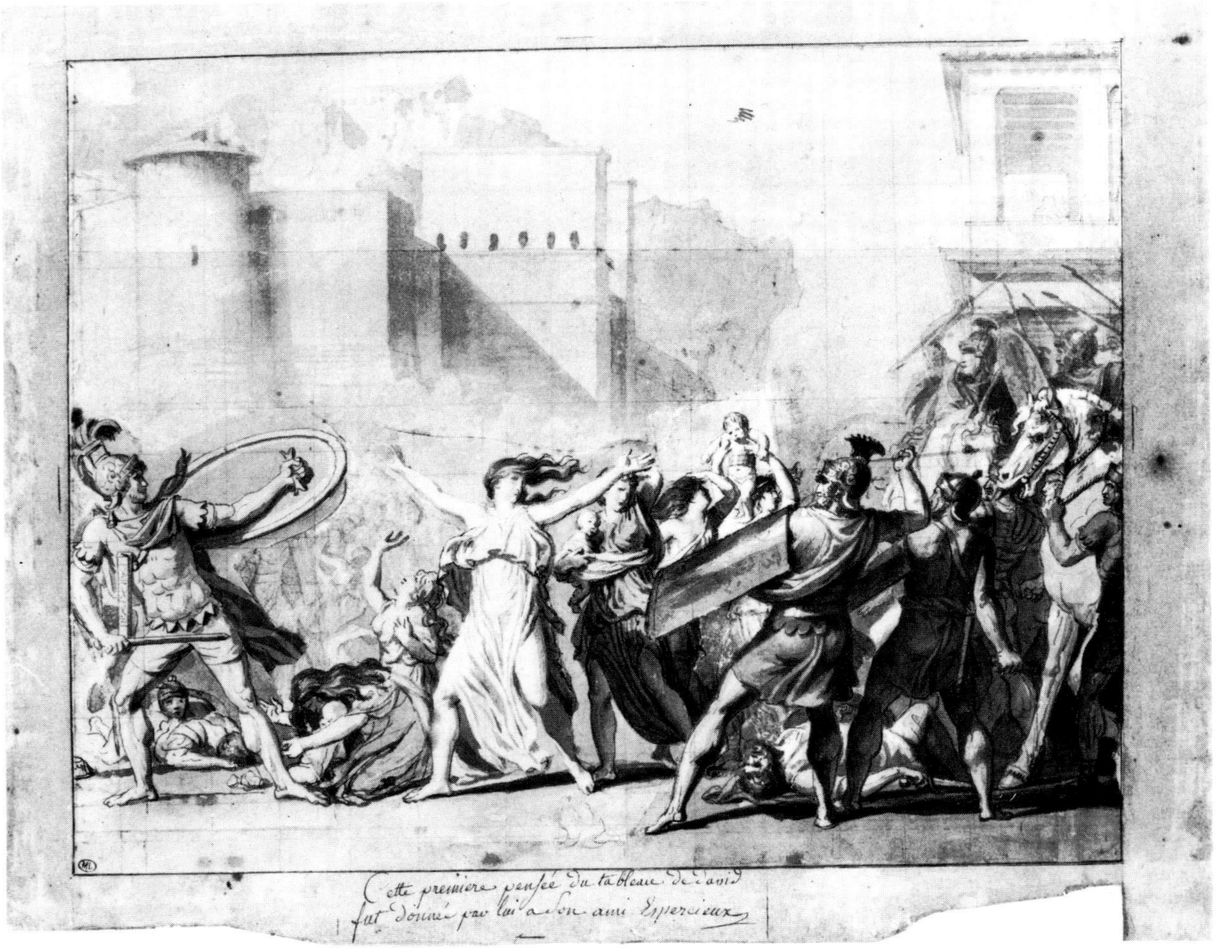


*Study for "The Sabine Women," 1794. Pen and ink over pencil with gray wash and white highlights (made while David was in jail), 10¼" × 13⅜" (26 × 34 cm)*
*Musée du Louvre, Cabinet des Dessins, Paris*

The body has been interpreted as "ephebe from antiquity" stripped of "all effects of costume" and entirely consecrated to glory. The distinction between "finished" and "unfinished" is more interesting. This would be the artist's way to leave his work "in progress" when it seems to have enough meaning. David kept this painting in his studio for thirty years and he never wished to finish it. One wonders whether he was satisfied with it as it was, or whether he just did not want to return to that period. He thought of working again on *The Oath of the Tennis Court*, however. Maybe this figure contained David's secret.

David was arrested on 15 Thermidor (August 2, 1794), after Robespierre, Saint-Just, and about a hundred of their supporters had been executed. He had testified at the Convention on 13 Thermidor and had acquitted himself rather poorly. He reminded the Convention that he had always followed those who had seemed "to love freedom the most." He noted that Robespierre was more interested in David than he, David, was in Robespierre. And he concluded "From now on ..., I shall attach myself to principles rather than to men."[1] David was jailed in what used to be the farmer-general's mansion

(1) E.-J. Delécluze, *ibid.*, p. 171.

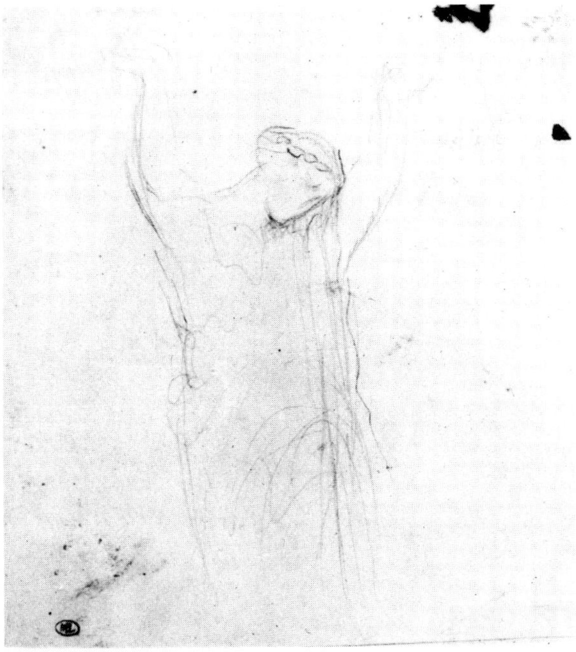

*Study for "The Sabine Women," ca 1799*
*Wash and white highlights*
*18¾" × 25" (47.6 × 63.6 cm)*
*Musée du Louvre, Cabinet des Dessins, Paris*

in the Rue de Grenelle-Saint-Honoré and later transferred to the Luxembourg. There he could paint and draw. He painted a portrait of his jailer(1) and his only landscape, *View of the Luxembourg,*(2) the simplicity of which foreshadows the work of Camille Corot. A *Self-Portrait* stares at the viewer with eyes that are sharp in spite of the questioning anxiety of the face (see title page).

When David was freed in December, he was assigned to forced residence at Saint-Ouen, where he stayed with the Sériziat family, his brother-in-law and sister-in-law. There are two equally famous portraits of his hosts, both painted on panel (see pages 50 and 51). The *Portrait of Madame Sériziat* may have been interrupted when David was arrested a second time and jailed from May 29, 1795, to the end of August of the same year. She is featured with her child, against an abstract background, while *Pierre Sériziat, the Artist's Brother-in-Law* is painted against a background of sky and clouds. These portraits are unique in David's work because of their affectionate vivaciousness and keen enjoyment of life, which are expressed in the harmony of colors rather than in the attitudes. They are a hymn to bourgeois comfort and to the new order of things, which established the rule of

(1) Musée de Rouen.
(2) Musée du Louvre, Paris.

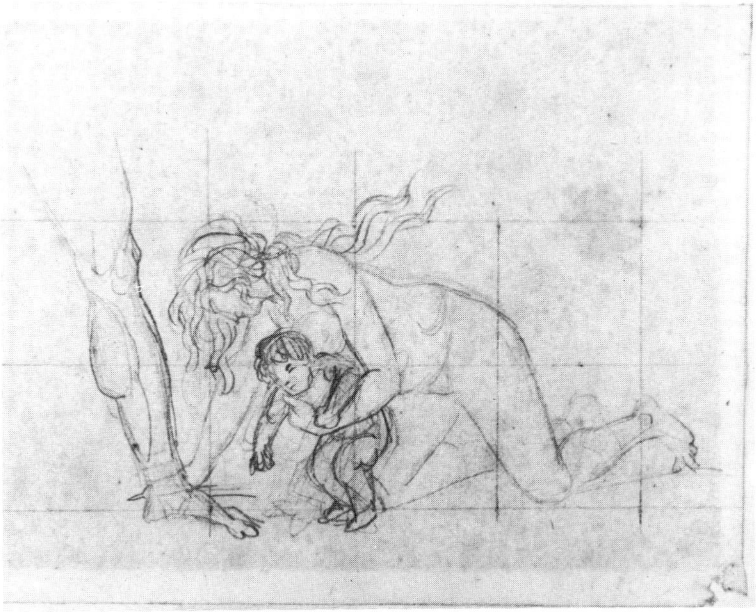

*Mother and Child at the Feet of Tatius. Study for "The Sabine Women," ca 1794-1796*
*Pencil drawing*
*5¼" × 6⅜" (13.5 × 16.3 cm)*
*Smith College Museum of Art*
*Northampton, Massachusetts*

merit. With those two portraits David was claiming that he had not lost his talent. They were very well received at the Salon of 1796.

On October 26, 1795, David received an amnesty and he returned to his studio and his many students. It was then fashionable to make a distinction between his genius and his revolutionary excesses. This has remained the accepted attitude, since artists and writers are regarded as naive and are not supposed to become involved in politics, even when politics are popular. David became silent. Delécluze described him as always carefully dressed and very polite to everybody.[1] He had about sixty students at the time. Tuition was twelve francs a month plus the cost of heating and hiring a model, but half of his students were enrolled free of charge. Delécluze's book, "David, His School and His Time," describes the atmosphere of the studio and recounts some of David's remarks as he was correcting students. To a student who was working while singing some aria by Glück,[2] he said:

> This is the consequence of your love for German music, you prefer harmony to melody. You do the same in painting: You put drawing after color. My friend, this is putting the cart before the horse. It does not matter, however. Do as you feel, copy what you see, study as you wish, because a painter is only regarded as such for the great quality that is his own, whatever that quality may be.[3]

David limited himself to spontaneous remarks. He claimed to know no dogma and no truth, only practice. And Delécluze noted, "He only spoke with great self-effacement of that which

(1) E.-J. Delécluze, *ibid.*, p. 29.
(2) German born composer, whose *Orfeo ed Euridice* (1762) revolutionized opera. He died in 1787. (Note of the translator).
(3) E.-J. Delécluze, *ibid.*, pp. 60-61.

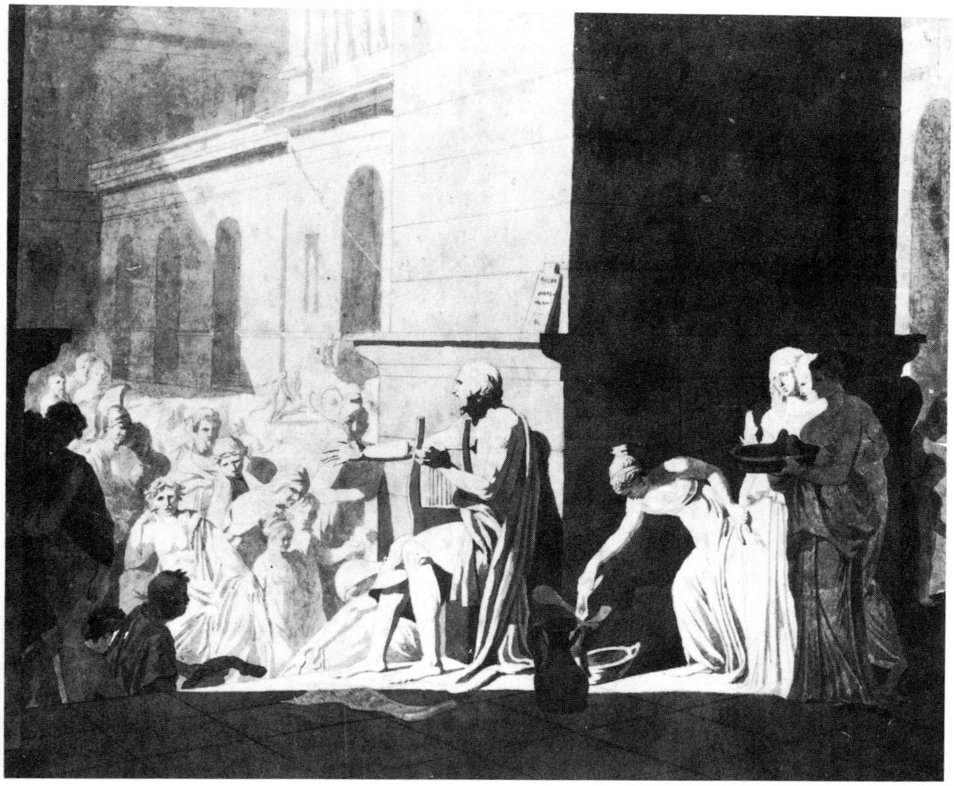

*Homer Reading His Verses to the Greeks, 1794*
*Drawing in black and red crayon and pen with an India ink wash*
*10⅝" × 13⅝"*
*(27 × 34.5 cm)*
*Musée du Louvre*
*Cabinet des Dessins, Paris*

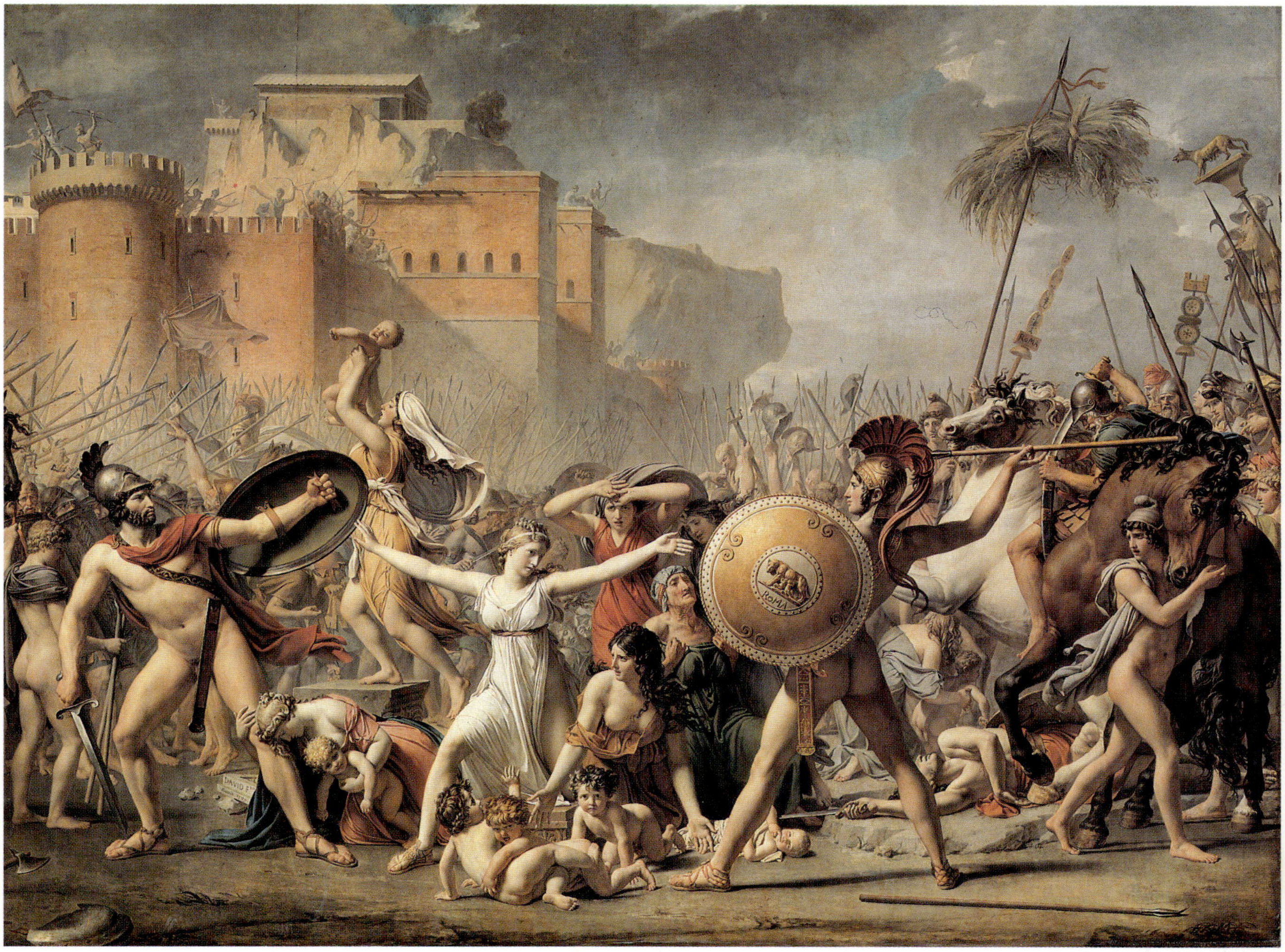

The Sabine Women, 1799
Oil on canvas, 12′7$\frac{3}{16}$″ × 17′1$\frac{1}{2}$″ (385 × 522 cm)
Musée du Louvre, Paris

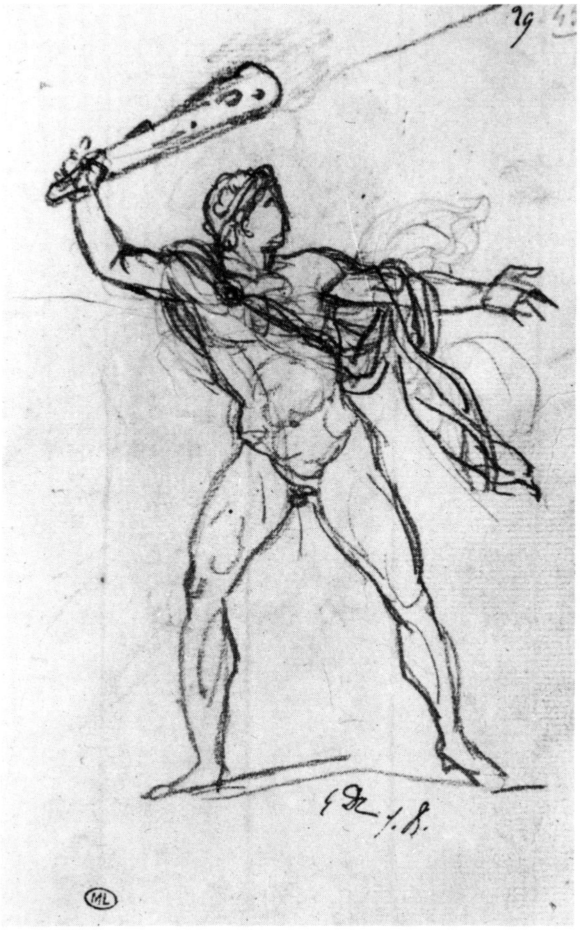

*Study sheet*
*for "Leonidas," n.d.*
*Lead pencil*
*10 9/16" × 13 7/16"*
*(26.8 × 34 cm)*
*Musée du Louvre*
*Cabinet des Dessins*
*Paris*

he knew best, painting. Far from making a display of theories drawn from conversations with knowledgeable people, he preferred not to mention them."

There was a great turmoil of ideas in Paris between Thermidor and the coup d'état of Brumaire.[1] There were many translations; Shakespeare, Ossian,[2] Wolfgang Goethe, Friedrich Schiller, and Vittorio Alfieri were raising a passionate interest. There were many scientific discoveries, by Xavier Bichat in medicine,[3] Pierre-Simon de Laplace in astronomy,[4] Georges Cuvier in

(1) Brumaire was the second month in the republican calendar (October 23 to November 21). On 18 Brumaire (November 9-10, 1799), the French Directory, which had come into existence under the new Constitution of 1795, was overthrown and the Consulate was established with Napoleon as first consul. (Note of the translator).

(2) Legendary Gaelic poet. In the 1760s the Scottish poet James Macpherson represented his own work as Ossian's. (Note of the translator).

(3) The author of an *Anatomie générale*, Bichat contributed also to the development of embryology. (Note of the translator).

(4) With Joseph Lagrange and earlier mathematicians, Laplace established Newton's theory beyond a doubt, and his research results were published in his *Mécanique céleste* (5 vol., 1799-1825). In 1796 his *Exposition du système du monde* gave scientific form to a nebular hypothesis of the origin of the solar system. (Note of the translator).

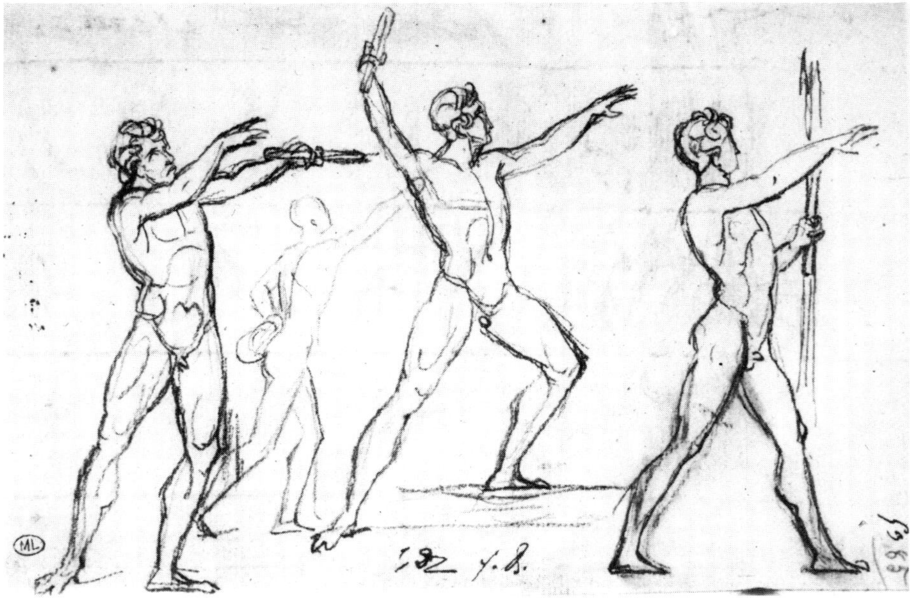

*Nude Studies*
*for "Leonidas," n.d.*
*Lead pencil*
*6 9/16" × 4 7/16"*
*(17.1 × 11.3 cm)*
*Musée du Louvre*
*Cabinet des Dessins*
*Paris*

paleontology and geology.[1] The future became synonymous with progress. There was also a mood for fleeting festivities; it was as if springtime had arrived after a long season of violence and fear. Scientists and artists were the new aristocracy, and David occupied an important place. This was not a Renaissance but a Regeneration.

David was also regenerating since he had found his way: He wanted to progress another step. He worked in secret in a studio he had set in "the attics of the part of the Louvre facing the Pont des Arts." Rumor had it that he was painting a new masterpiece and crowds thronged around the few who had been allowed to see it. David declared to his students: "I set out to do something entirely new.... I want to take art back to the principles laid down by the Greeks."[2] It was a difficult endeavor and the work took him almost four years to complete. Finally, *The Sabine Women* was shown on December 21, 1799, in the rooms of the former Academy of Architecture, at the Louvre, and the exhibition itself was a novelty. David modeled it on shows in England and decided to charge an entrance fee of 1.80 francs. Although he was accused of violating French custom, visitors came in crowds. David replied that his example could show other artists how to earn some income when there had been almost no patrons of the arts for the last ten years. He claimed to be acting "in the name of talent's noble independence." The exhibition lasted until May 1805; it had over forty-thousand visitors, each of whom received a "booklet" explaining David's motives.

*The Sabine Women* marked a turning point, both as a painting and as an exhibition (see page 57). On first sight, it seems to be a return to history painting based on a theme from antiquity. It is a larger and more complex painting than the ones he had done before, with tens of figures and multiple planes. While one would expect it to depict a battle, it features an armistice. The Sabines had attacked the Romans under the walls of Rome to avenge the abduction of their women. Hersilia, the daughter of the Sabine leader Tatius, had since married Romulus, the Roman leader, by whom she had two children. She rushed between the warriors when her father and her husband were about to strike each other....

(1) A pioneer in comparative anatomy, Cuvier reconstructed the soft parts of fossils from their skeletal remains. He identified and named the pterodactyl. (Note of the translator).
(2) E.-J. Delécluze, *op. cit.*, p. 61.

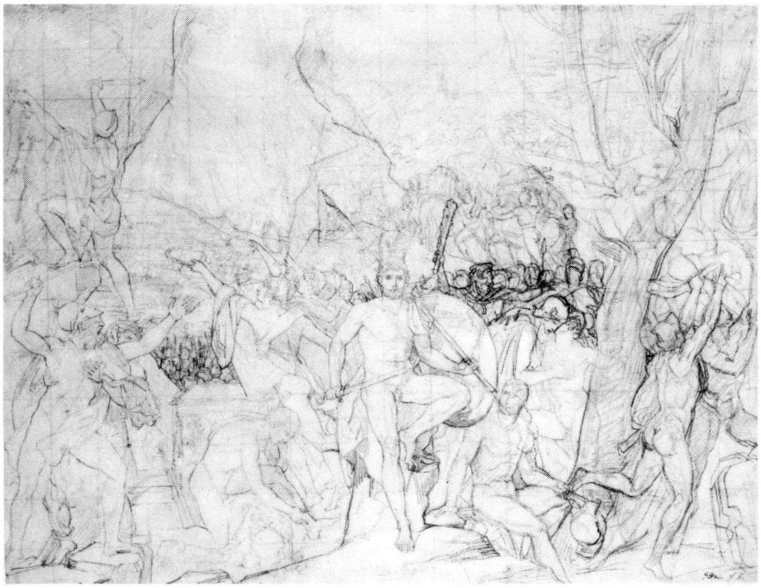

*Leonidas at the Battle of Thermopylae, n.d.*
*Black chalk, squared off in black chalk*
*16″ × 21⅝″ (40.6 × 54.9 cm)*
*The Metropolitan Museum of Art New York. Rogers Fund*

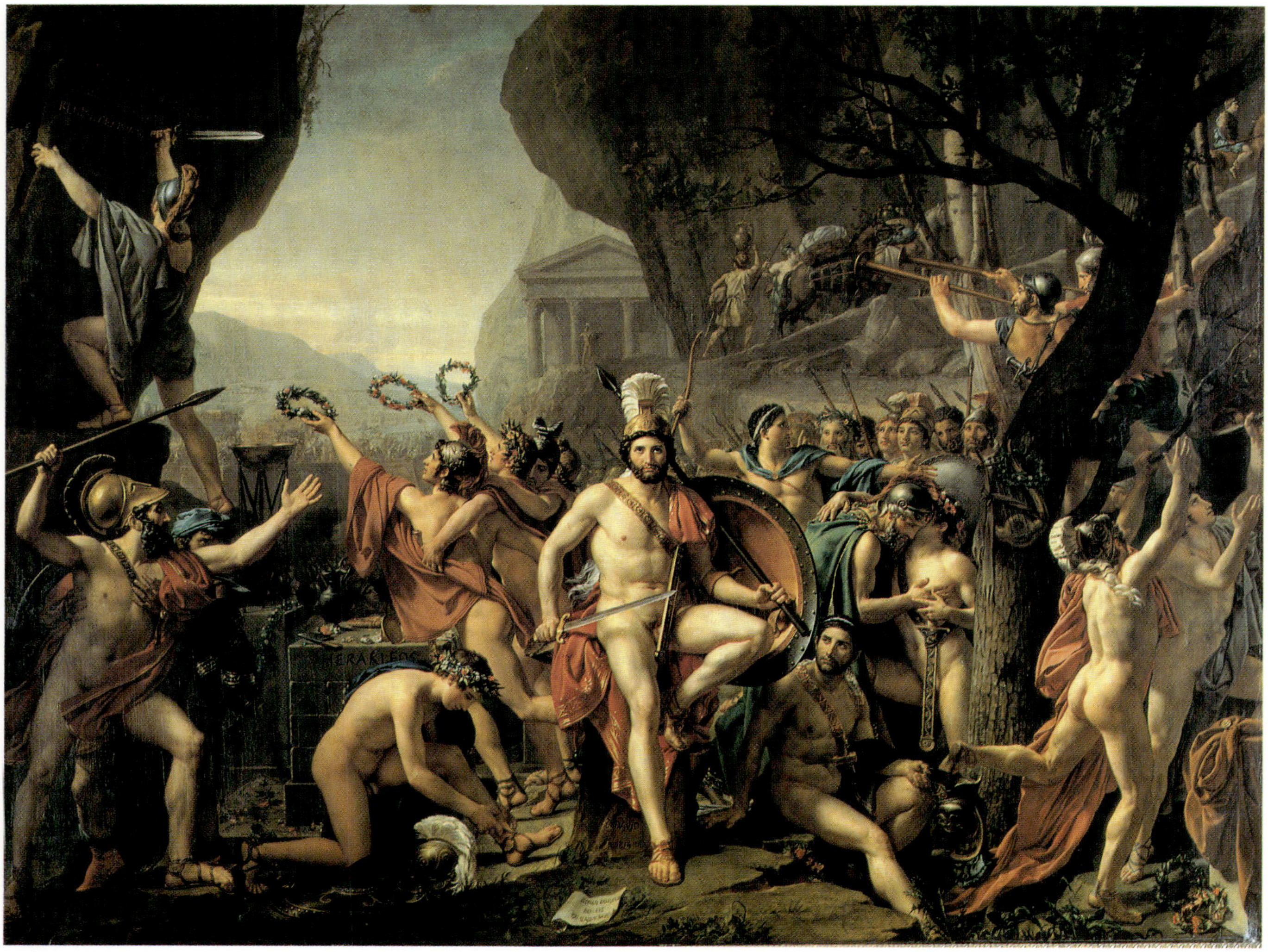

LEONIDAS AT THE BATTLE OF THERMOPYLAE, 1814
Oil on canvas, 12′11½″ × 17′5$\frac{1}{16}$″ (395 × 531 cm)
Musée du Louvre, Paris

David was in jail when he started thinking about this theme and he made the first drawing. He was hesitating between two themes, *The Sabine Women* and *Homer Reading His Verses to the Greeks* (see pages 54 and 56). His "booklet" explains why he preferred *The Sabine Women*:

> Romulus holds back the javelin which he was about to hurl at Tatius. The general of the cavalry puts his sword back into its sheath. Soldiers raise their helmets as a sign of peace. The feelings of conjugal, fatherly, and brotherly love spread through the ranks of both armies. Soon the Romans and Sabines embrace to form one single people.

The theme is reconciliation. This was a relevant message at the time, a call for the reunification of French society, and this was how the painting was received. David's wish to return to Greek principles was not understood as well, although it seemed to go along with the fashion of the time. The most obvious application of these Greek principles was the painting of nude warriors, which was either decried or ridiculed by the public. The politician, Bonaparte, and the writer, Henri Stendhal, both agreed that nude warriors were nonsensical. David had not painted nude bodies for the sake of nudity but to express moral beauty through "simple outlines" and "graceful forms." He claimed that his naïveté had been to believe that he could "portray ancient customs with such exactitude that the Greeks and Romans, had they been able to see the picture, would have felt at home with it." [1]

Nowadays the viewer does not appreciate so much the two theatrical nude warriors who are separated by the beautiful Hersilia. But the entangled shapes, the movement of arms and bodies, the folds of dresses, and the billowing tunics create an animated space that carries the picture. One needs to take one's time, look at *The Sabines* at length, and suddenly the even light and the strong outlines make

(1) J.L.J. David, *op. cit.*

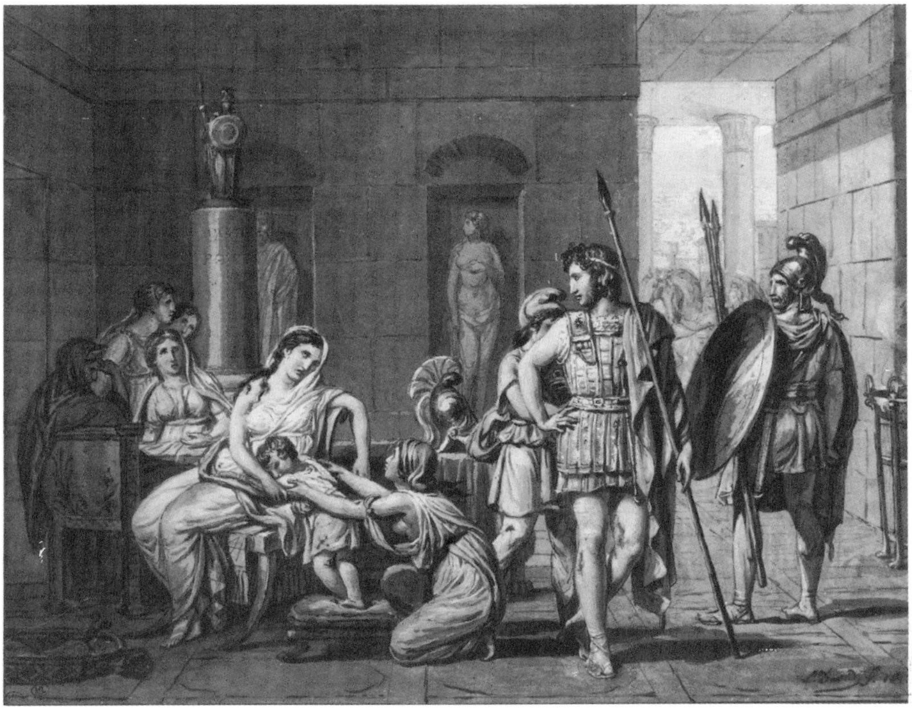

*Hector's Departure, 1812*
*Wash and India ink*
*8 11/16" × 11 7/16"*
*(22 × 29 cm)*
*Musée du Louvre*
*Cabinet des Dessins, Paris*

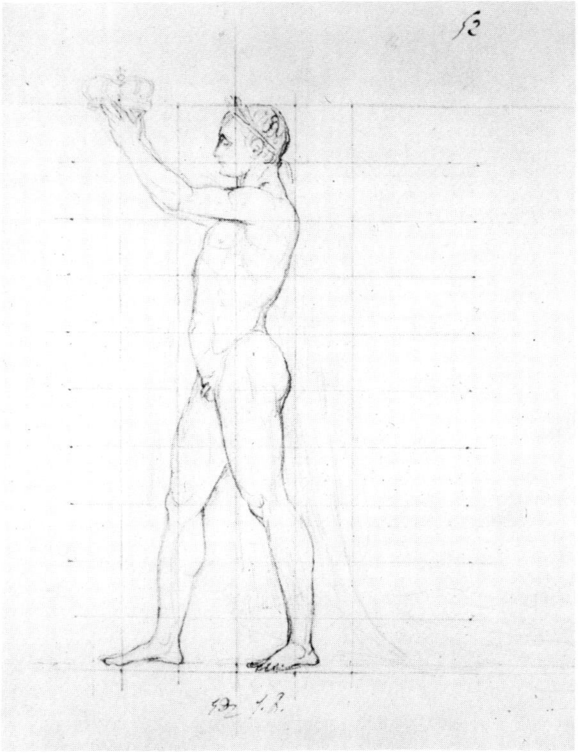

*Study of Napoleon, Nude, Holding a Crown with Both Hands, Sketchbook no. 20, p. 52 recto*
*Black crayon, squared in crayon*
*8¼" × 6⅜" (21 × 16.4 cm)*
*The Fogg Art Museum, Harvard University*
*Cambridge, Massachusetts*
*Bequest of Greenville L. Winthrop*

space rise from the picture. The painting then sheds its story and reveals a rigor which is as effective as a magnetic field would be. The eye follows the movements and colors, it savors the unexpected bundle of hay in the sky — like a sign on the upper right of the painting — as well as the precise outline of Tatius's sandals. It takes note of the romantic look of the young boy pulling a horse on the right or, in the group, a Flemish-style scene with three children playing at Hersilia's feet. The rigid rules of neoclassicism have exploded. The painting overflows with genre scenes, which the rhetoric of history painting only allowed as details: There enters life, settling between the elements of a warlike idiom.

David intended to create a counterpart to *The Sabines* and he made a sketch of *Leonidas at the Battle of Thermopylae* (see page 59). In the meantime, however, he had met Bonaparte, who came to sit in his studio for three hours, in 1797. David had found his hero. The following day he said to his students, "My friends, what a beautiful head he has! It is simple, great, beautiful, like a head from antiquity!"(1) This first meeting resulted in a sketch on canvas, in which David simply outlined a portrait and painted the face in quick brush strokes — this is the most lively portrait of Bonaparte, the young republican general who died on December 2, 1804, when he became the emperor Napoleon (see page 52).

So far, David had only painted dead heroes: Le Peletier, Marat, Barra; or legendary ones: Andromache, the Horatii. Bonaparte, his glory fresh after the Italian campaign, was a living hero, fast becoming more of a hero each day. How was it that the Jacobin who had voted for the death of one king was to accept a new king? Bonaparte flattered David to attach him. The emperor made him his First Painter. It is not certain, however, that David allowed the republican in him to be corrupted by honors, because he was above all an artist. When he was a Jacobin and a member of the Convention, he put himself at the service of the arts, working for the glory of the arts. He followed the same logic under Bonaparte, and later under Napoleon. He saw consistency, where a different definition of political commitment might make one see repudiation. David was then the foremost French painter — and had been for several years. To be given the title of First Painter did not in any way change the place his work occupied, but was merely an official recognition of an existing situation. The government was clever when it sanctioned David's rank in the arts, but it also laid a trap for the artist: It tied him down. This sort of trap has been effective to this day, and many artists have served totalitarian regimes while believing they served the arts. In David's time things were not as clear as they are now, and artists had not yet learned to set themselves apart from power. The Revolution had not had the time to establish the artists' independence. The separation of Art and State was still unthinkable. When David destroyed the old regime of the Academy, he was a part of the government and used its help. Just as God had been overthrown to be replaced

(1) E.-J. Delécluze, *op. cit.*, p. 203.

by Robespierre's Supreme Being, the Academy had been overthrown to be replaced first by Councils and Commissions, and later by the Institut de France. It was already a vicious circle by which the name of the regime was changed — not its nature. David's disillusioned remark is still valid today: "I always thought that we did not have enough virtue to be republicans."

Virtue came from Rome, more precisely the Roman Republic that preceded the Empire in which virtue was lost. The same can be said of Bonaparte, who had virtue until 18 Brumaire. After the Coup, the First Consul, later Emperor, ceased to be virtuous and let himself be carried only by the heroic impetus pictured by David in *Bonaparte Crossing the Great Saint Bernard*, in which Bonaparte was following the example of Hannibal and Charlemagne.[1] This painting is the least symbolic painting by David; the picture

(1) 1801, Château de la Malmaison, Reuil-Malmaison, France.

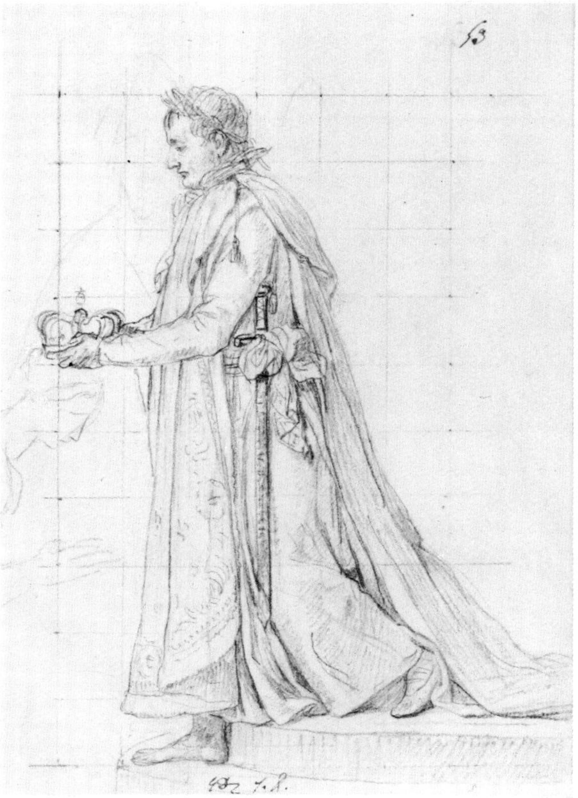

*Napoleon Placing Crown on Josephine's Head*
*Sketchbook no. 20, 1805-1824, p. 53*
*Black crayon, squared in crayon*
*8¼" × 6⅜" (21 × 16 cm)*
*The Fogg Art Museum, Harvard University*
*Cambridge, Massachusetts*
*Bequest of Grenville L. Winthrop*

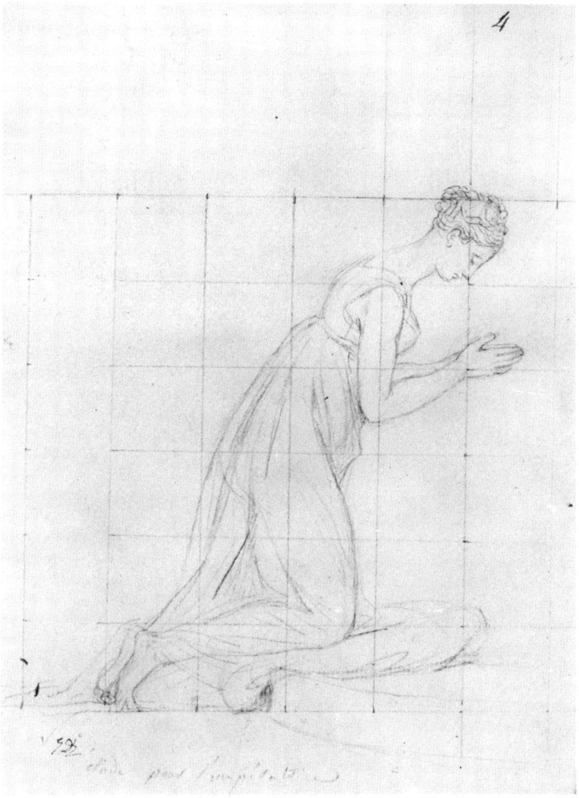

*Study for the Empress Josephine*
*Sketchbook no. 20, 1805-1806, p. 4*
*Graphite, 9⁵⁄₁₆" × 7¼" (23.7 × 17.9 cm)*
*The Fogg Art Museum*
*Harvard University*
*Cambridge, Massachusetts*
*Bequest of Grenville L. Winthrop*

*Study for "The Distribution of the Eagle Standards"*
*Portrait of Cardinal Caprara, ca 1804*
*Black pencil, 9 1/16" × 7 5/16" (23 × 18.5 cm)*
*Musée d'Art et d'Archéologie, Besançon, France*

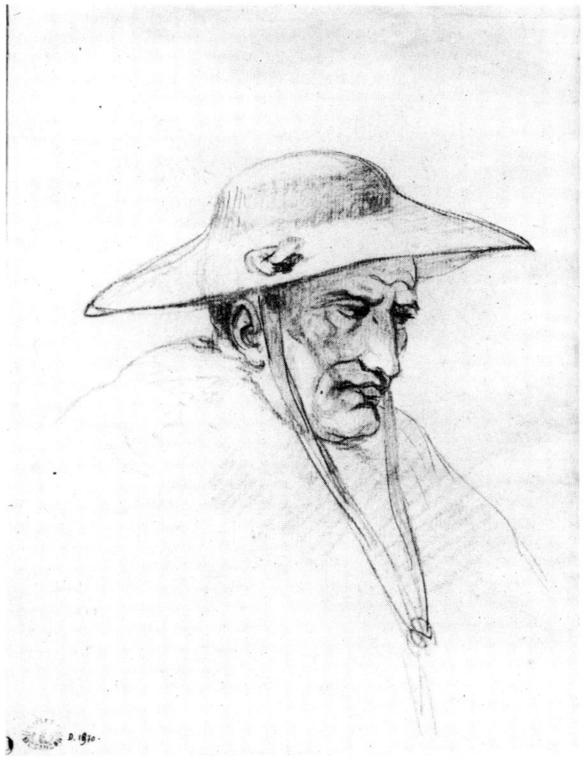

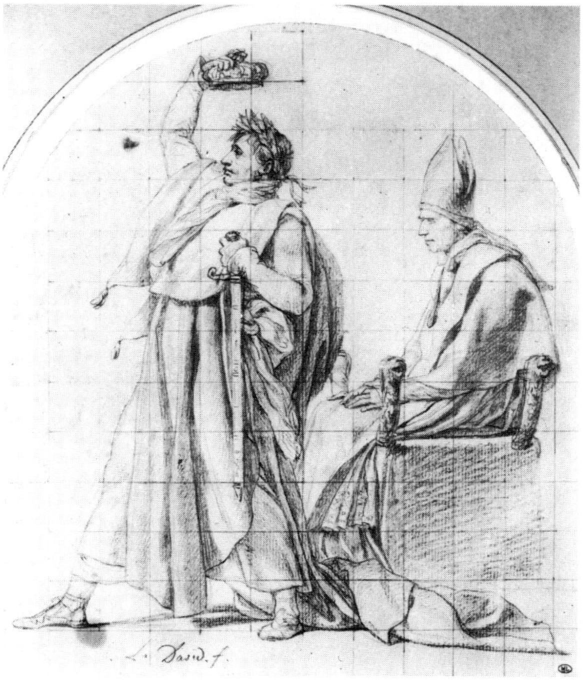

*Napoleon Crowning Himself*
*Study for "The Sacring," ca 1805-1807*
*Black chalk, 11 7/16" × 9 7/8" (29.2 × 25.2 cm)*
*Musée du Louvre*
*Cabinet des Dessins, Paris*

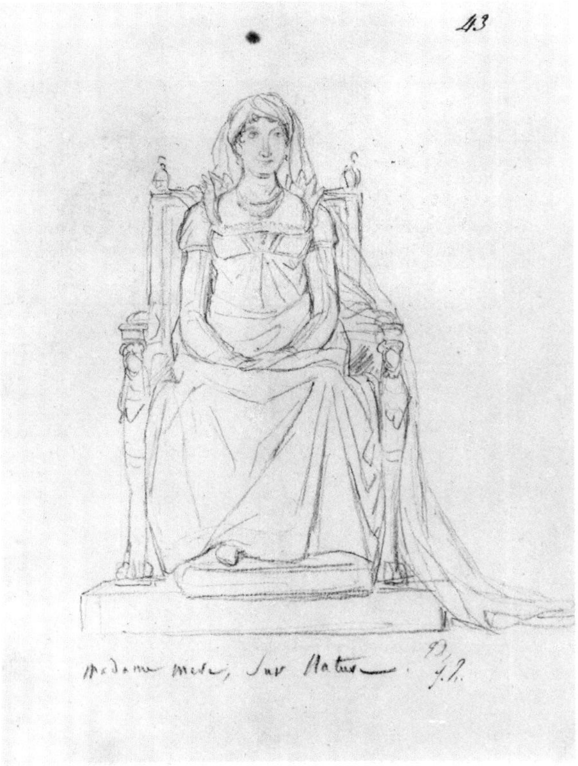

*Marie-Laetizia Bonaparte, Madame Mère*
*Sketchbook no. 20, 1805-1824, p. 43*
*Black chalk, 8 1/4" × 6 5/8" (21 × 16.9 cm)*
*The Fogg Art Museum, Harvard University*
*Cambridge, Massachusetts*
*Bequest of Grenville L. Winthrop*

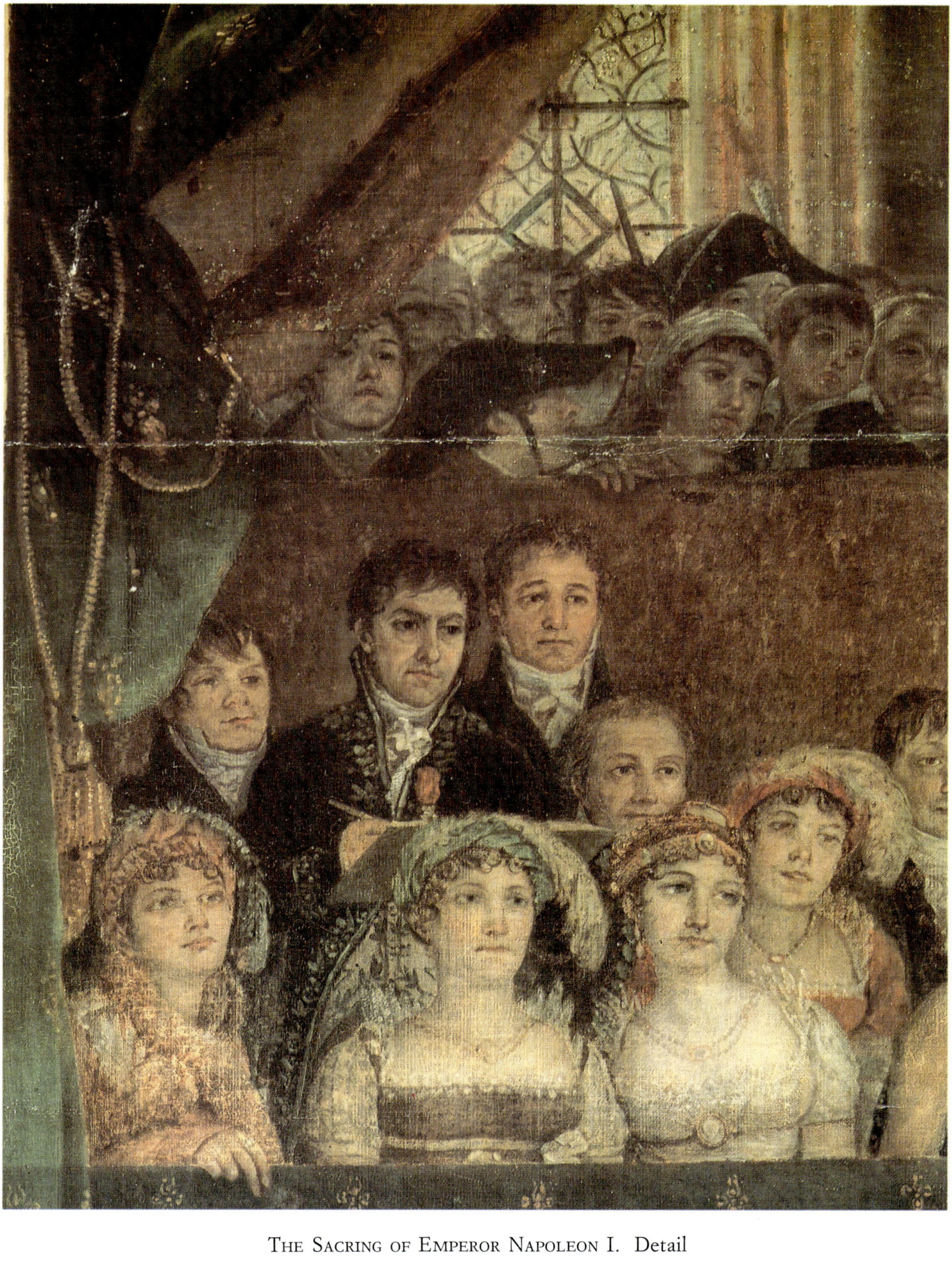

The Sacring of Emperor Napoleon I. Detail

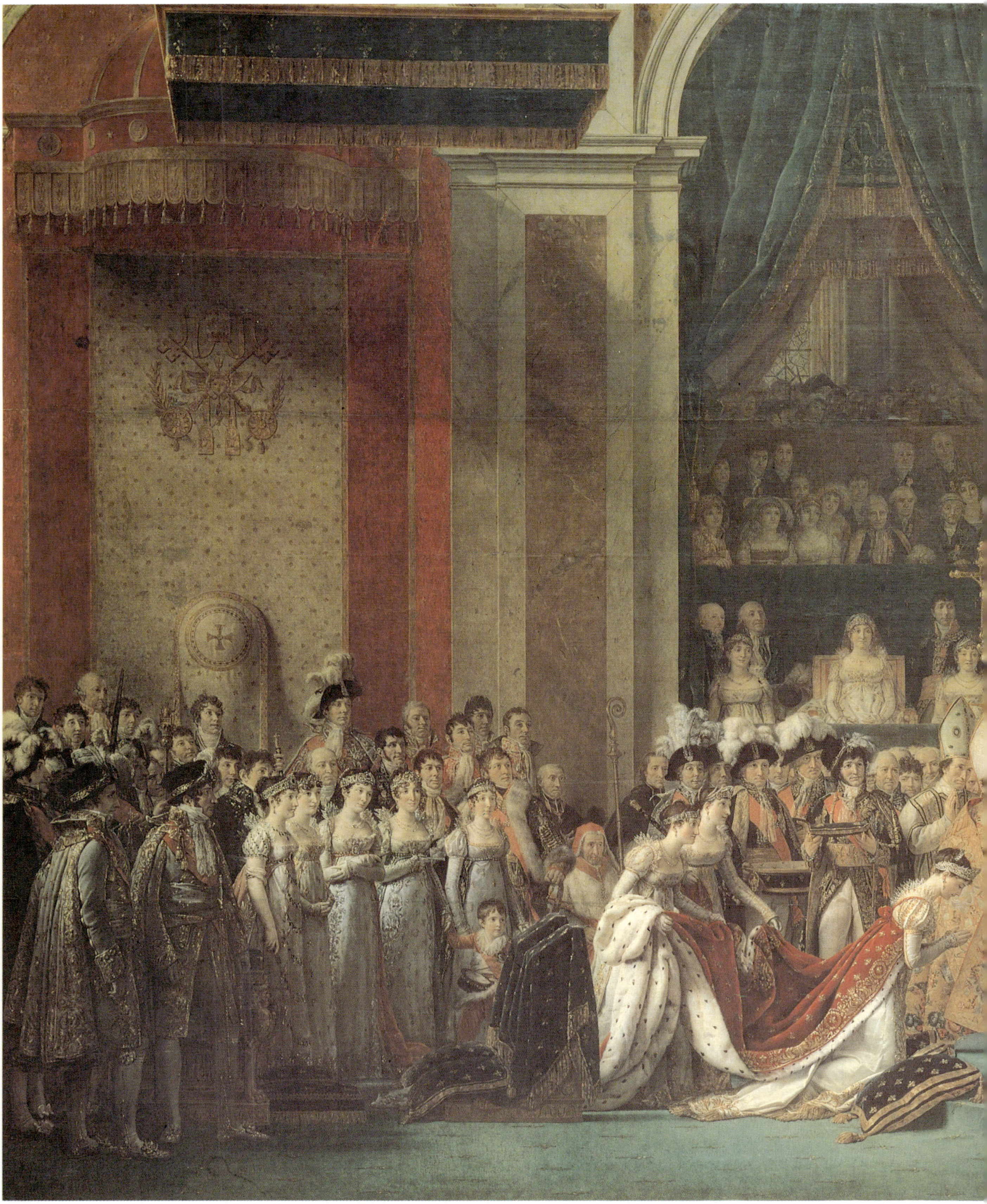

The Sacring of Emperor Napoleon I, 1805-1807
Oil on canvas, 20′4½″ × 32′1½″ (621 × 979 cm)
Musée du Louvre, Paris

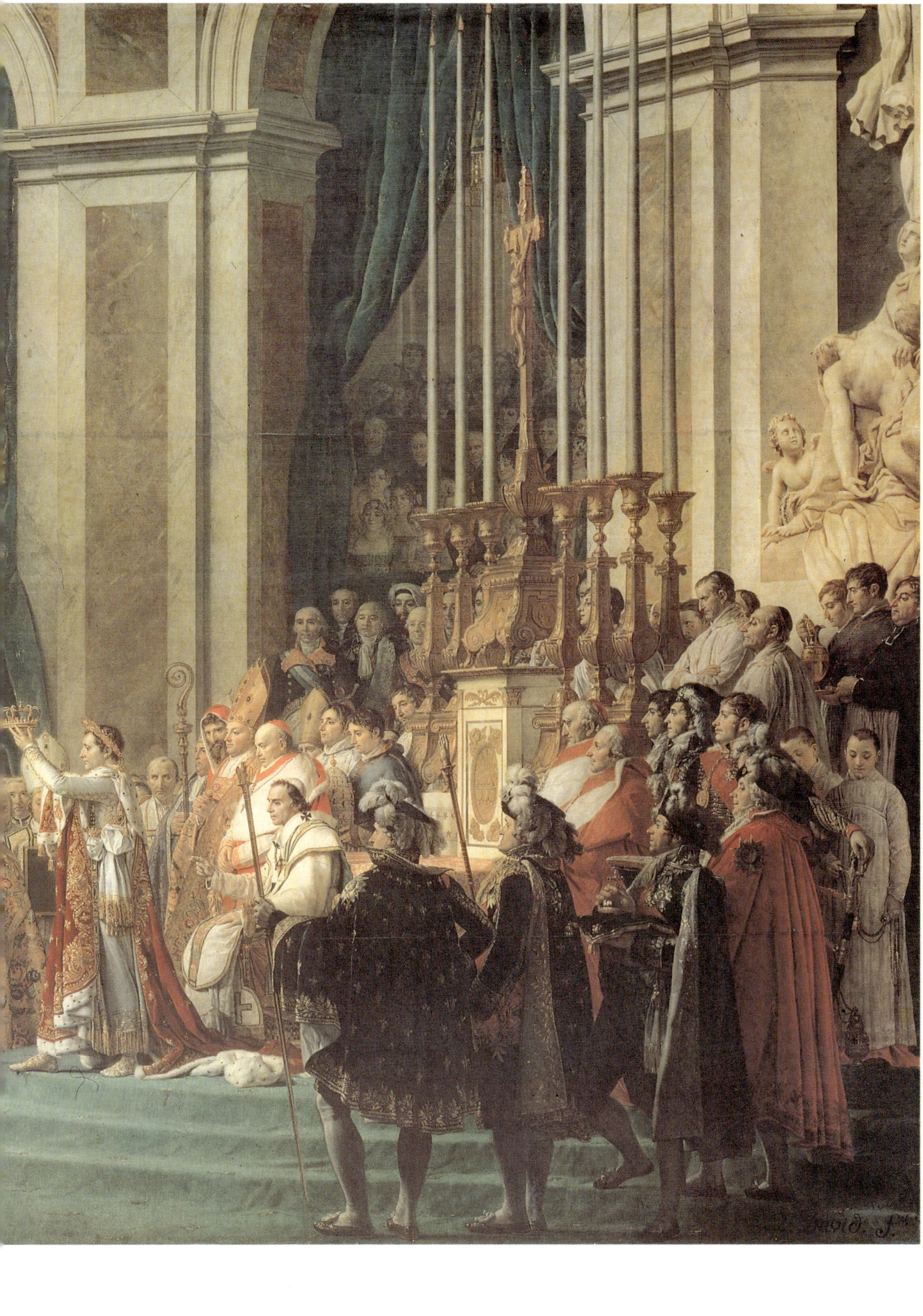

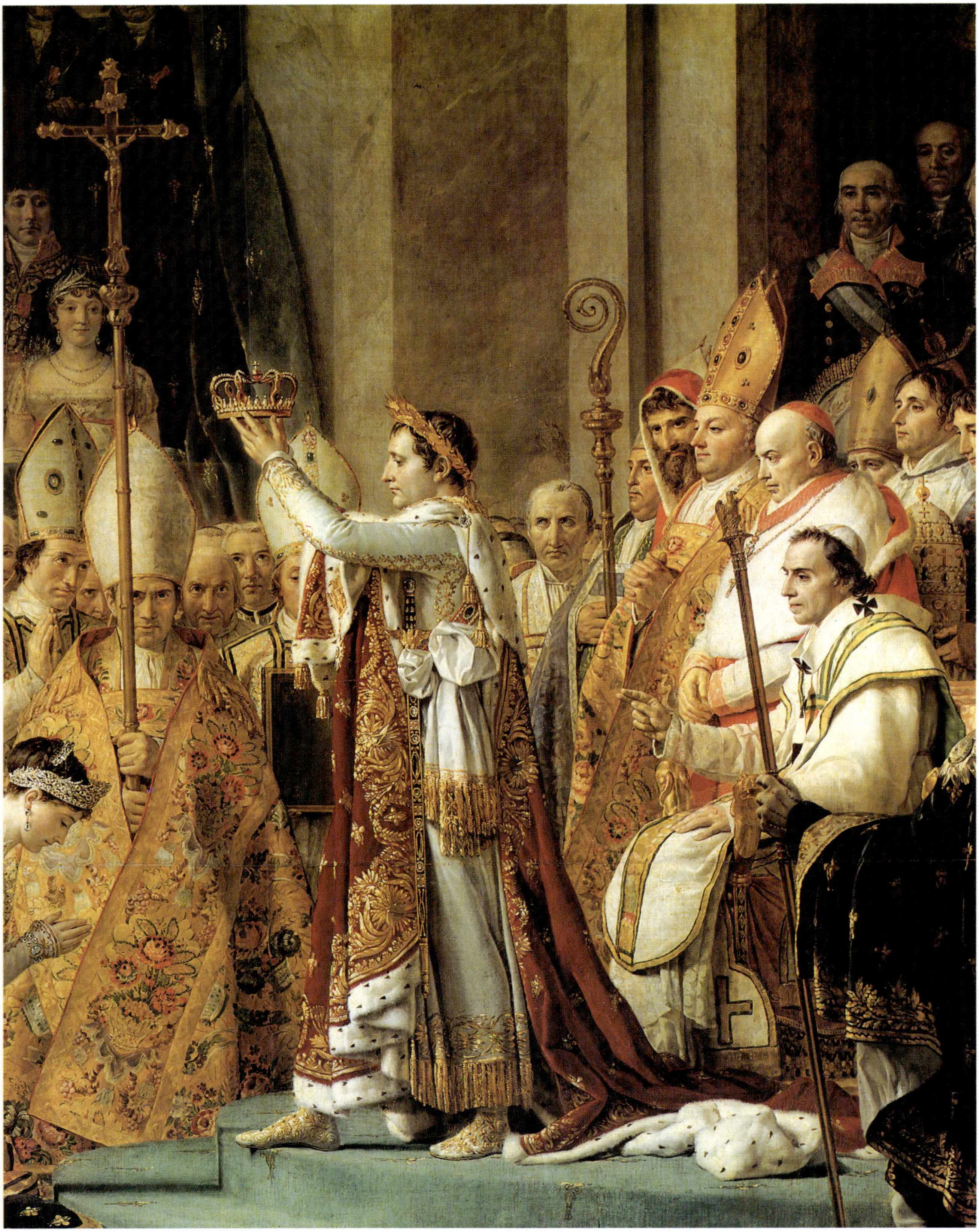

THE SACRING OF EMPEROR NAPOLEON I. Detail
Behind Napoleon, Pope Pius VII, on his left, a bearded Greek
Orthodox bishop and the Cardinals Caprara and Braschi (the latter is wearing a mitre)

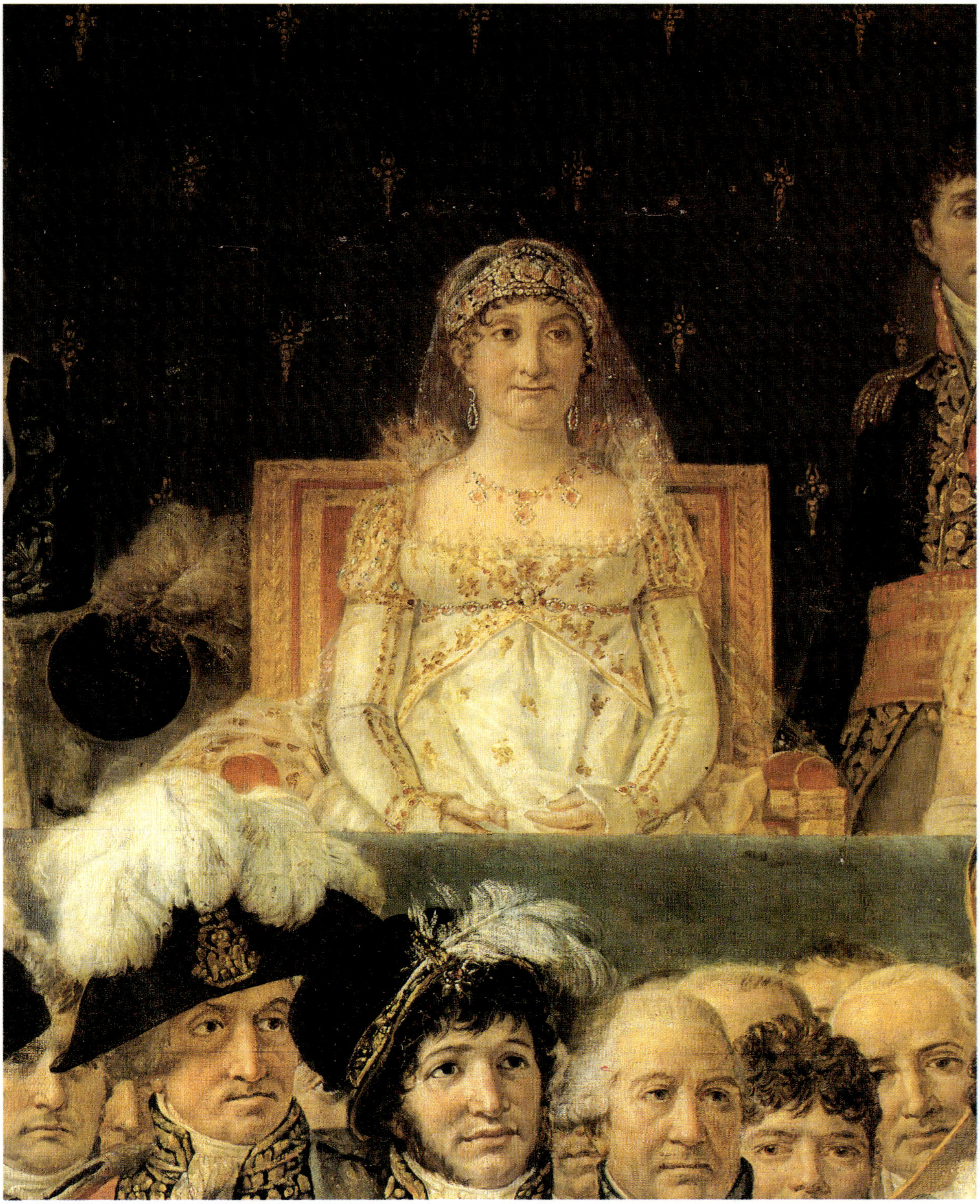

THE SACRING OF EMPEROR NAPOLEON I. Detail
Madame Mère, who was not actually present, nor was Cardinal Caprara

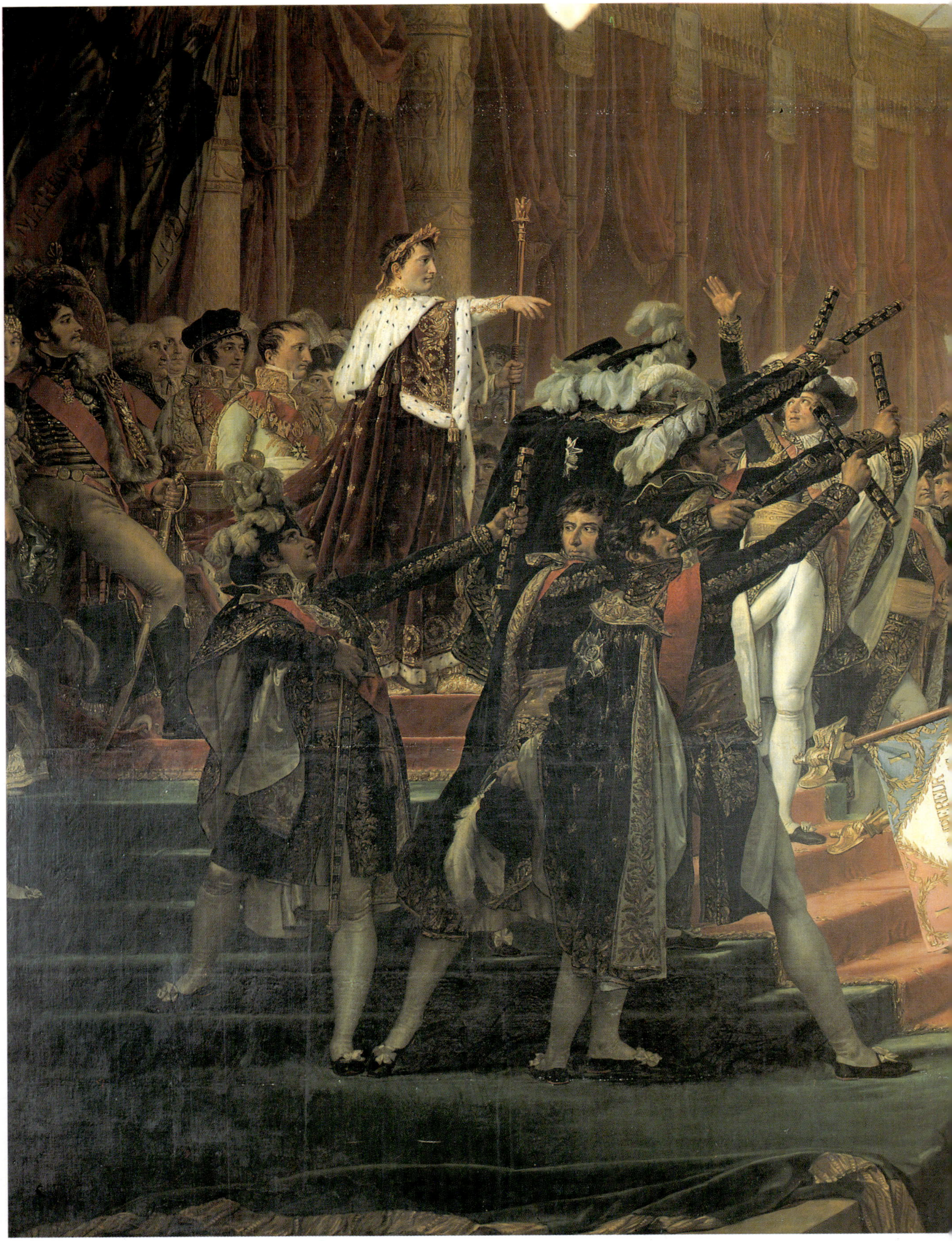

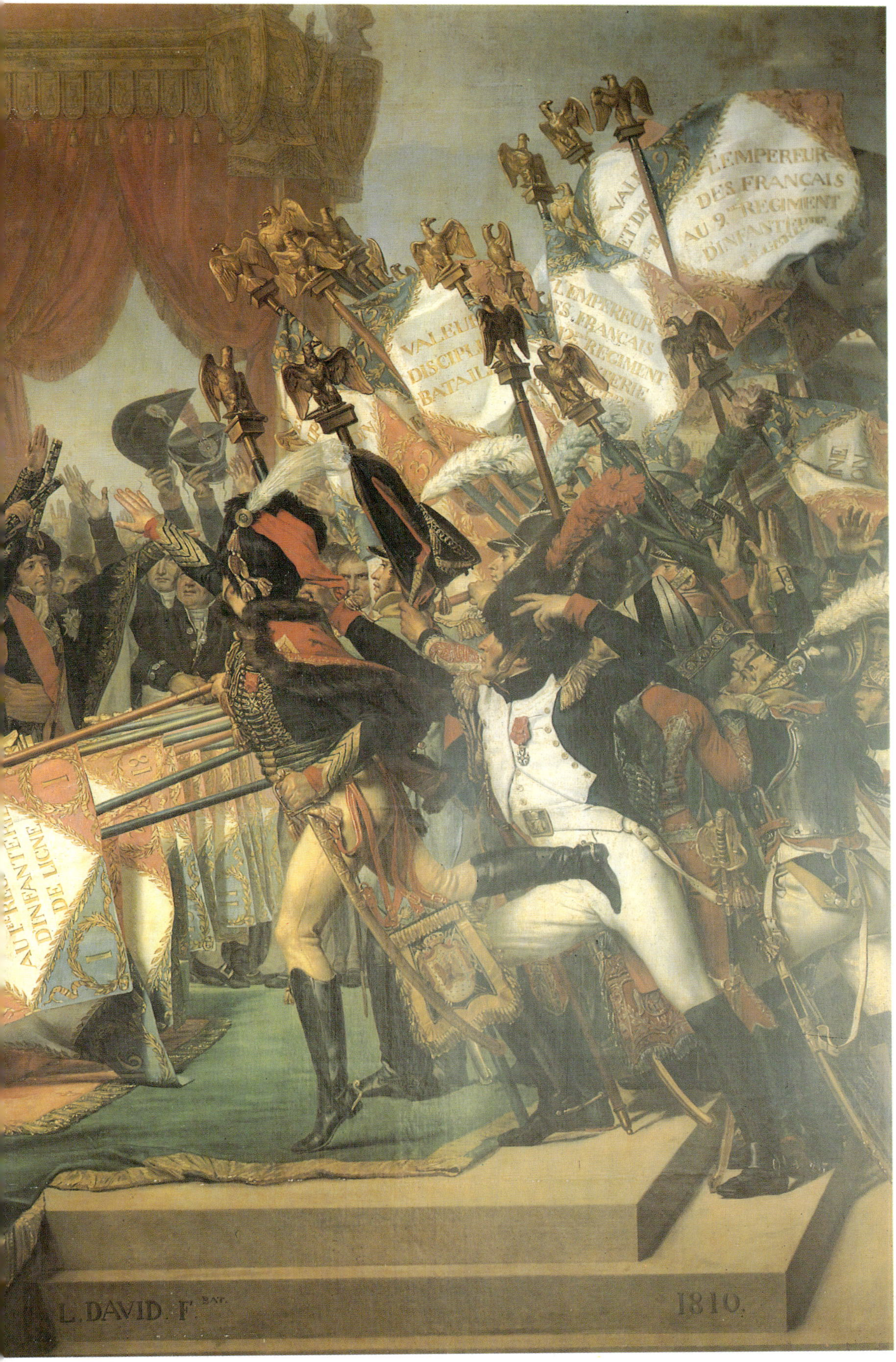


THE DISTRIBUTION OF THE EAGLE STANDARDS
Detail, 1810
Oil on canvas
21′8³⁄₁₆″ × 30′6³⁄₁₆″
(610 × 930 cm)
Musée National du Château de Versailles et des Trianons

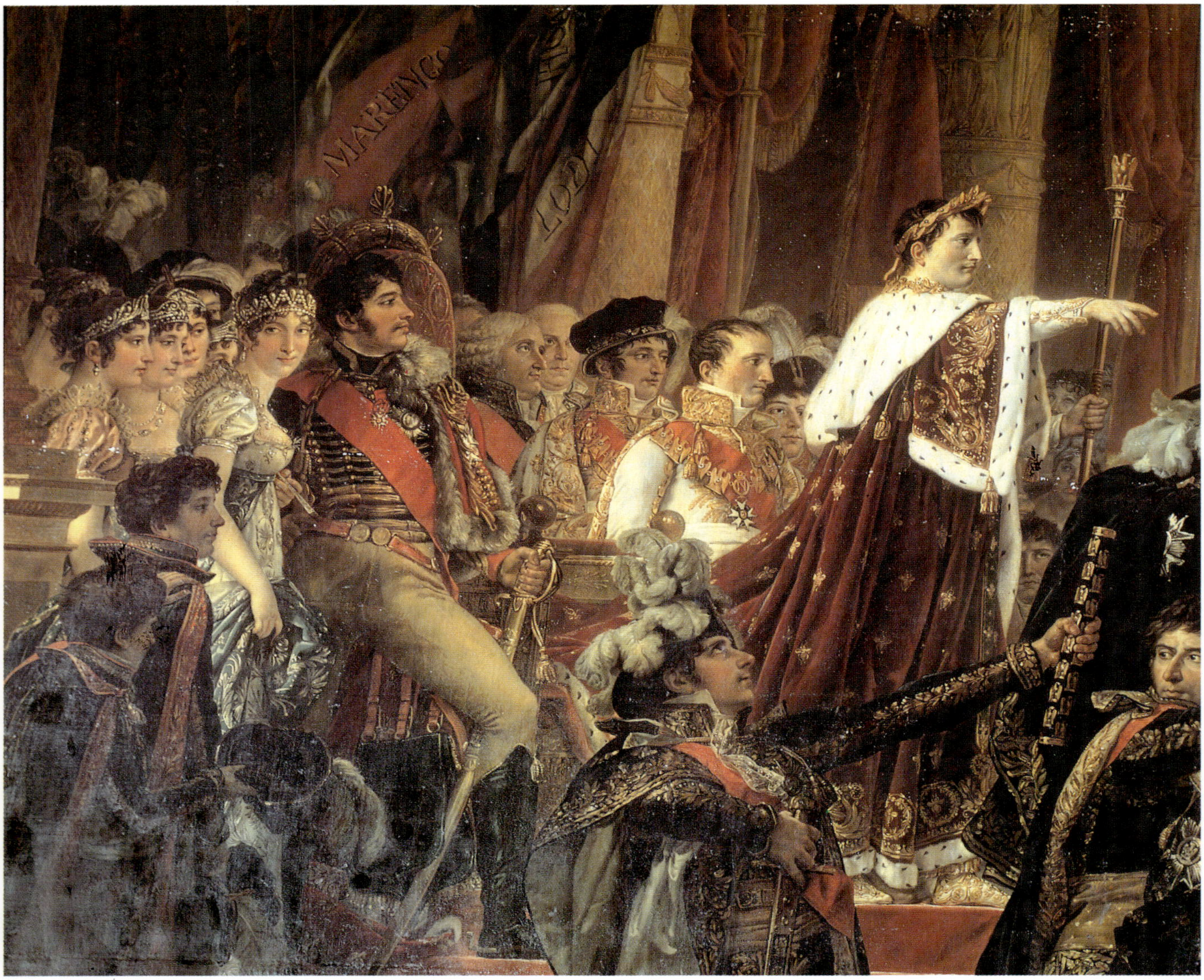


The Distribution of the Eagle Standards
Detail

fits closely with the pictorial purpose. He engraved the name of the conqueror and emperor next to that of Bonaparte, and one may interpret this as a premonition, which he announced without any illusion. There is no need to see only flattery in this inscription, when this grouping of the three names could both please the powerful and criticize. David asked twenty-four-thousand francs for the first version of the painting commissioned by Charles IV of Spain, and twenty-thousand francs for each of the copies that were commissioned later. In contrast, he had never asked any price for his republican paintings.

Between *The Sabines* and *Bonaparte Crossing the Great Saint Bernard* David painted two famous portraits, *Madame de Verninac*(1) and *Madame Récamier* (see page 53). The former is interesting because it features the sister of his future enemy, the painter Eugène Delacroix (who was two years old at the time). David painted Delacroix's sister when she made her formal entrance into society. Delacroix was to paint her as she lay dying, and he inherited her portrait by David. *Madame Récamier* is to David's official portraits what *Marat* is to his history pictures. It may be shocking to bring together the portrait of a martyr and that of a fashionable belle, but as Death had touched Marat with "the tip of his wing," so life had touched Madame Récamier with its social wing.(2)

The portrait of *Madame Récamier* is believed to be unfinished. The final note that David sent her is well known: "Madame, Ladies have their whims, and so do artists. Allow me to satisfy mine. I shall keep your portrait as it is."(3) More finish would have been too much. The painting is so strong because the figure floats in a space that has a presence which rivals that of the woman. The long folds of the dress put some simplicity around the glorious body. The bed makes the woman recline with both modesty and provocation as her body turns partially away and her eyes meet those of the viewer. The shoulders seem to want to be seen from the back, while the neck turns the face forward. Nevertheless, there is more of an offering in the turned body than in the luminous but closed face. The double movement in the body contains a troubling grace which transforms her charm into restraint, and this reticence makes her the more seductive. The space around her suggests a room, giving a sense of depth and filling the eye with a swarming texture. It is both air and time. The scene is placed nowhere, and it is set in a perpetual present. The name of the woman is insignificant next to the significance of the body and face. Look at the arm: The hand at the end of the arm, which offers itself even as it closes. Everything is ambivalent, including the face that belongs to a time but does not age.

How to be the foremost painter of one's time and paint that time? Before, David had to draw from the past that which the present needed; now, he must draw from the present a future which the present needs in order to see itself as it wishes to be. On December 2, 1804, Napoleon crowned himself Emperor in the chancel of Notre-Dame in Paris, after which he crowned Josephine, under the distant and lucid eye of Pope Pius VII. Shortly thereafter he commissioned a painting of the coronation and three other large paintings: *The Enthronement, Arrival at the Town Hall,* and *The Distribution of the Eagle Standards.* Only the first and the last in the series were produced. David immediately set to work. First he chose the scene when Napoleon crowned himself, then he opted for the scene when Josephine was crowned, and he painted *The Sacring of Emperor Napoleon I and the Crowning of Empress Josephine* (20 feet 1/8 inch by 30 feet 6 1/8 inches, or 6.10 meters by 9.30 meters). In November 1807, when it was completed, Napoleon came to admire it for an hour and exclaimed: "How great! What relief! How true! This is not painting; one can walk around in this picture; life is everywhere"(4) (see pages 66-67).

(1) 1799, Musée du Louvre, Paris.
(2) Born in 1777, Madame Récamier was famous for her beauty, her intelligence, and her salon, which became the meeting place of the most brilliant society under the Restoration. (Note of the translator).
(3) E.-J. Delécluze, *op. cit.*, p. 281.
(4) J.L.J. David, *op. cit.*

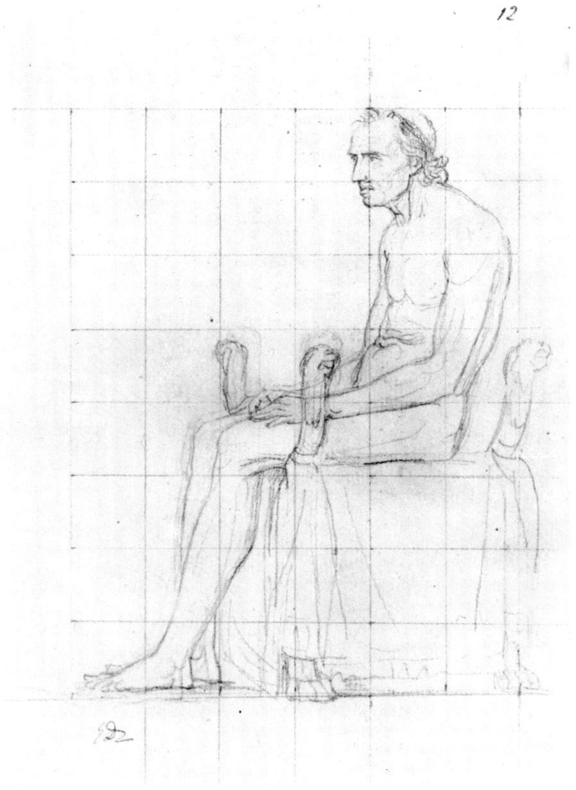

*Study for "Pope Pius VII"*
*Sketchbook no. 14, 1805-1806, p. 12 recto*
*Black crayon over graphite, squared in graphite*
*9 5/16" × 7 1/4" (23.7 × 17.9 cm)*
*The Fogg Art Museum, Harvard University*
*Cambridge, Massachusetts*
*Bequest of Grenville L. Winthrop*

This was a quick assessment, a declaration of victory, ending with a realistic impression: Napoleon perceived correctly that the main effect of the painting, behind the appearances and constraints, was that of space. After which one may look at details and even forget that they are parts of the whole composition. Taken separately each detail is sharp, while in the whole composition the details become blurred in a general movement. There are about one hundred recognizable figures; one may isolate one or another, and observe each attitude and expression. The result is the most extraordinary series of portraits painted in one picture. These are not background figures but individuals carefully observed with a critical eye that turns this apotheosis of a moment into a depiction of the imperial society. David painted the picture that was expected of him, fulfilling the purpose of making everyone immortal. However, he also recorded the deadly trait of this court: The heroes are upstarts who have taken on the manners of the tyrants they had vanquished and reestablished them in caricature form. All the dignitaries of the regime are represented, including those who were not actually present, such as Cardinal Caprara and the Emperor's mother. Above his mother, the faces in the gallery are watching with an avidity relieved by no flourish. David was also present, taking notes. He is not in the picture because he stands for the truth that cannot be depicted. The truth, essentially invisible, is part of a substance also invisible, albeit revealing, that creates the space of the painting.

*The Sacring* was exhibited for an unlimited time at the beginning of 1808, in the great hall of the Louvre. It received the compliments that had to be made to the picture and also the discreet but less flattering comments that could be made about the regime. Flatterers and critics did not notice the social story that developed from one portrait to another. David asked for one-hundred-thousand francs and got into endless difficulties with the imperial administration that refused to pay. At the Salon of 1808, the *Sacring* was hung on the wall opposite *Napoleon at Eylau* by Gros, in which the Emperor and his retinue proceed in the snow, among the dead bodies. A visitor passing between the two paintings is reputed to have said about Napoleon: "Sacring and massacre, there he is in two volumes."

David wished to continue the series of imperial commissions with *Arrival at the Town Hall*, for which he had already made a drawing (see page 76), but he wrote that the Emperor "was pressing [him] to start right away on the theme he preferred, *The Distribution of the Eagle Standards at the Champ-de-Mars*." This new work took a long time, from 1808 to 1810 (see pages 70-71). He had been politically astute when he had chosen to depict the moment when Napoleon crowned Josephine in *The Sacring*. This time, however, he had to redo the left side of *The Distribution* to take Josephine out of the picture, because Napoleon divorced her in 1809. She left an empty space, which was filled by a leg extended

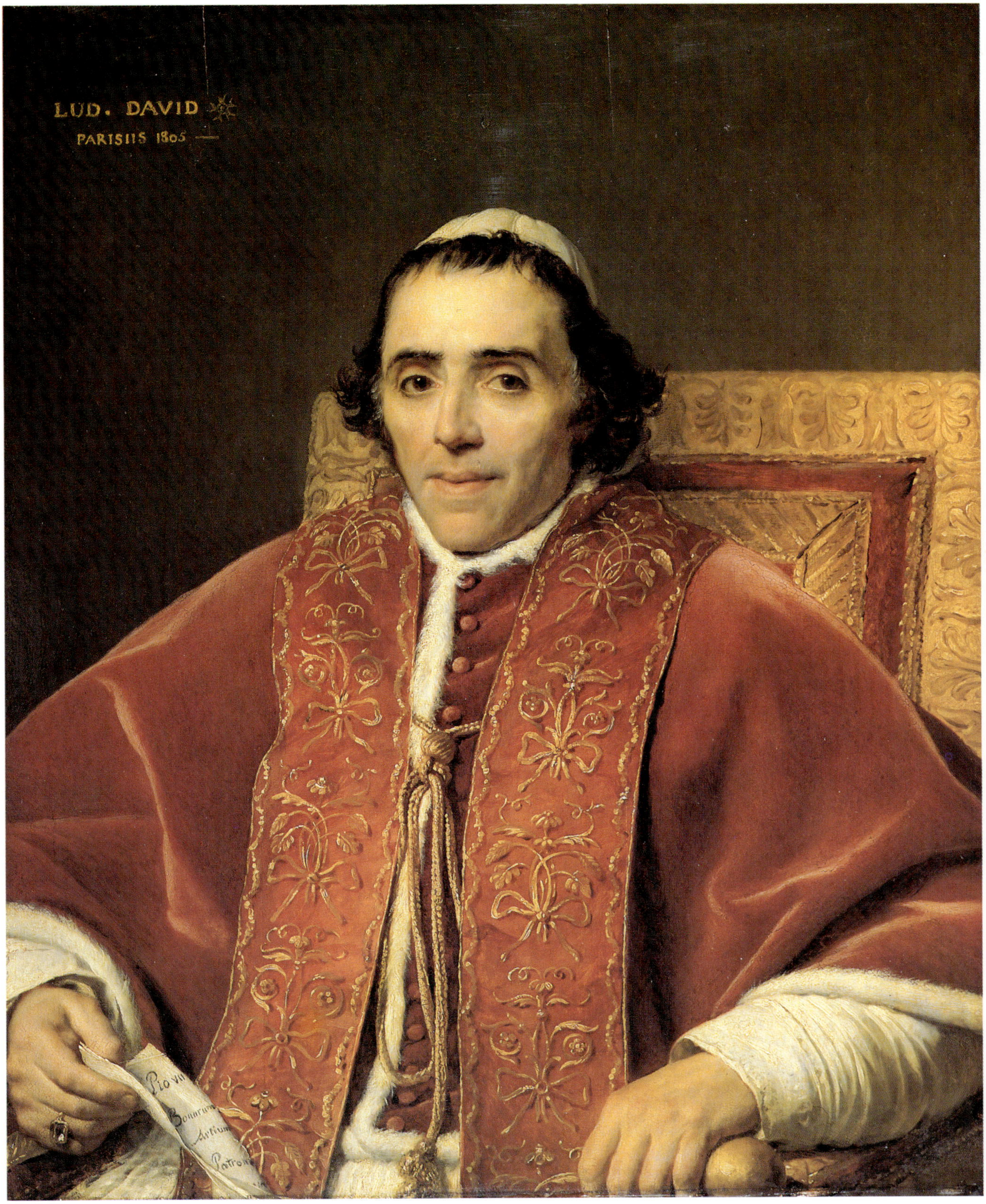


POPE PIUS VII (elected Pope in 1800), 1805. Oil on panel, $33\frac{7}{8}'' \times 27\frac{15}{16}''$ (86 × 71 cm)
Musée du Louvre, Paris

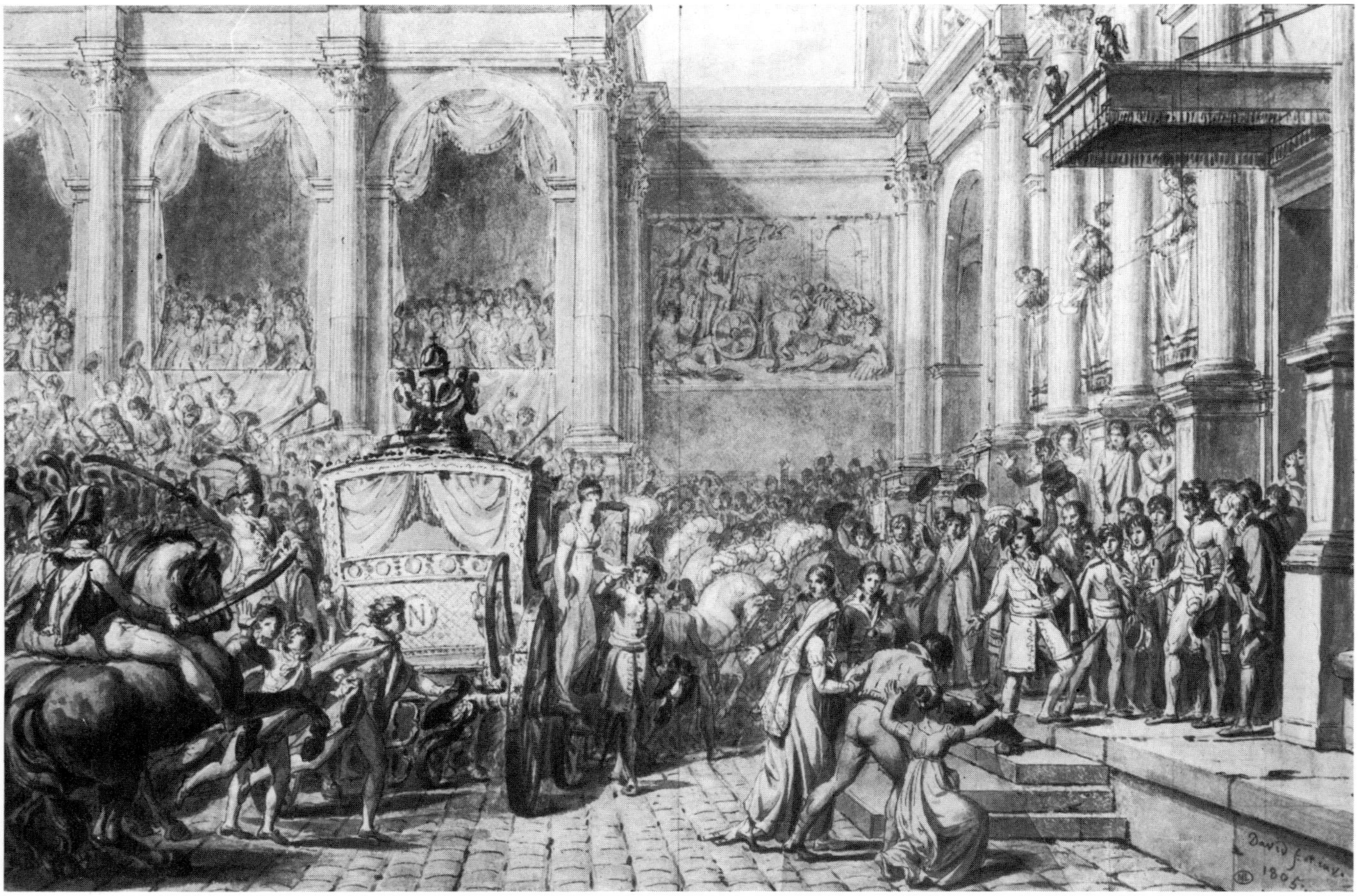

*The Arrival of the Emperor at the Town Hall, 1805*
*Pen drawing with India ink wash, 10¼" × 16⅛" (26 × 41 cm). Musée du Louvre, Cabinet des Dessins, Paris*

forward. Whether it was an ironic touch or persistence, the leg was that of her son, Eugène de Beauharnais, next to his sister, Queen Hortense.

The ceremony took place three days after the Sacring, on December 5. The throne stood on an immense platform fitted out with canopies, porticoes, and steps. The Champ-de-Mars was crowded with representatives of all the districts of the nation and the different military corps. The presidents of the constituencies and the colonels of the military corps were carrying flags and standing on the steps to the throne. At a particular moment, the entire crowd turned to the Emperor, who rose and said: "Soldiers, here are your standards. These eagles will always be your rallying point. Do you swear to sacrifice your life in their defense and to maintain them in the path of glory?" The crowd roared back: "We swear!" (1)

This was David's favorite theme: the oath. The impetus of the oath is such that it is communicated to the whole painting through the attitude of the figures. While the theme of this painting reintroduced virtue, one may wonder whether David did not change its nature by offering it to the new tyrant. The wealth of flags and uniforms gave him an opportunity to create a rich harmony of colors, making

(1) J.L.J. David, *ibid.*

the scene the more vivid. Everybody's attitude and appearance take part wholeheartedly in the oath, with one notable exception: It is the face of Queen Hortense, who looks away and is visibly preoccupied by things outside the canvas, where the artist stood and where the viewer now stands. Queen Hortense takes no part in the oath, but is totally absorbed with something else. Her position introduces an unexpected contradiction, something wild, in a painting otherwise focused entirely on one point.

David had accumulated sketches and drawings to prepare *The Sacring*, and he wished to paint the portrait of the major figures. As a result he made one of his best portraits, *Pius VII*, which he started in December 1804 (see page 75). At first the pope had been reluctant to sit for a painter who had voted for the king's death. Then he met David, whom he charmed. The artist wrote:

> What a dear old man, what a venerable face! How pleasant he is!... He is a real priest.... He is poor as Saint Peter, the gold braidings on his garb are fake! He really lives according to the Gospel.... Pius VII loves the arts. His Holiness put himself entirely at my service.... I must admit that I had long envied the artists who had lived before me for the opportunities that I thought I would never have.... I shall have painted the portrait of an Emperor and even a Pope. (1)

This last sentence leads one to believe that glory has become more significant than virtue, or that the artist is too dependent on glory to be able to resist it in the name of virtue. But this was a time when History was made of historic figures. It would have been impossible to paint history without these figures if the representation of history calls for them.

Almost half of the painting is taken up by the red velvet cape lined with ermine and the red stole brocaded in gold. However, one notices mostly the face, in which life seems to surge. Irony and forbearance lighten his mouth; his eyes are distant, as if they knew too much to pass a judgment. This "man who lives according to the Gospel" is beyond power: He has power but does not derive pleasure from it. One feels that intelligence rather than politics makes him steady. Only his stooped shoulders betray his anxiety. The portrait implies a sensitive attention and a certain egalitarian vision of the world. The artist put a man under this face, not a ruler. In the past, when David started painting, he invented great themes to find history through art; now history itself provided him with great themes, and he could sustain their greatness through his painting. The portrait's power is thus separated from events to be tied only to ideas.

David was rich and famous at the time. He had taught the best painters. Students from all over Europe were coming to his studio. He was leading a simple life entirely devoted to work. One may wonder, however, how accurate this picture is. As he was nearing the age of sixty, he seemed to fit this image, but can a man be totally satisfied? His work and influence were beyond discussion, but the man himself was not without flaws. He also had many enemies: The royalists, who were many and who hated him; the jealous and the young who wanted to get him out of the way to further the development of painting. Stendhal paid a visit to David when the latter was painting a portrait of Stendhal's cousin, Countess Daru. On March 14, 1810, he noted in his diary, "I just saw David painting. He is all paltriness." Stendhal was already a Romantic and David seemed the embodiment of academic art. Later, in 1823, Stendhal recognized that David was a "courageous genius," who responded to "the taste of the people, who were developing a thirst for energy and action." On November 13, 1857, Delacroix — who was younger than Stendhal and a full-fledged Romantic — wrote in his diary that David's work was "grubby, dull, and lifeless." Later, in an entry dated February 22, 1860, he praised David's "singular combination of realism and ideals," and he admitted that "[David] was

(1) E.-J. Delécluze, *op. cit.*, pp. 248-249.

the father of the whole modern school" and that "clearly, everything still derives from him and his principles." Théophile Gautier had the last word: "David's glory was obscured for a while by the dust raised around 1830 in the great battles launched by the Romantics against the Classicists. Nevertheless, he will remain as an unassailable master."

Time has shown that David's work is not inferior to the role it played in his time. As a point of fact, it gained in greatness because it outlasted and surpassed this role. What is unusual is that after David conquered the present by reaching into the past, and after he found his future by painting the present, he returned to the past. He may have been so molded by his education that the present time did not seem significant enough and he may have been seeking in the past a symbolic intensity that could not be questioned. Or was it a search for a virtue made pure by time?

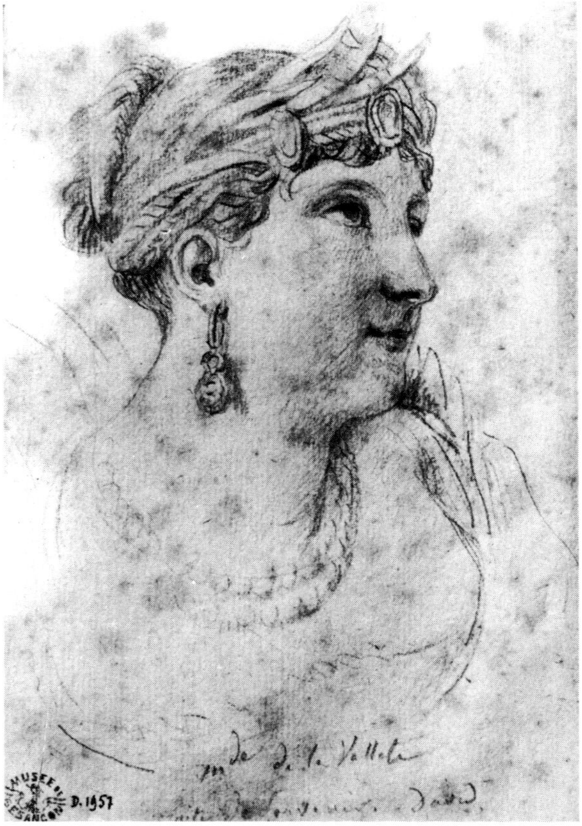

*Madame de la Vallette, ca 1804*
*Black pencil on paper unevenly yellowed*
*6½" × 4¾" (16.5 × 12 cm)*
*Musée d'Art et d'Archéologie*
*Besançon, France*

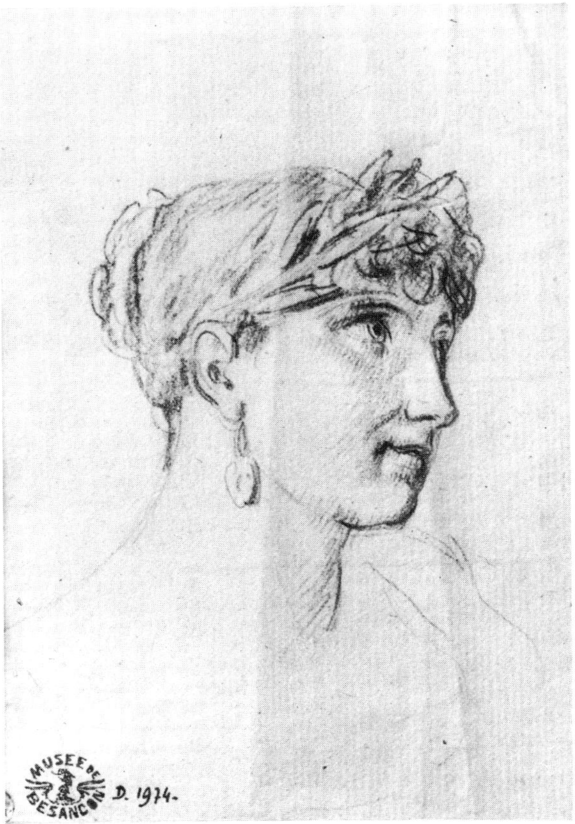

*Madame de la Rochefoucauld, ca 1804*
*Black pencil, broken watermark*
*5" × 3⅛" (12.6 × 9.2 cm)*
*Musée d'Art et d'Archéologie*
*Besançon, France*

In 1809 he painted *Sappho, Phaon and Cupid* for the Russian prince Nicholas Yusupov.(1) This faint echo of *Paris and Helen* of 1788 could have seemed a simple diversion, were it not the first of a whole series. The only contemporary history picture yet to be painted by David was *Napoleon in His Study* (see page 84), which belongs to a beautiful series of portraits of that time, including *Countess Daru,*(2) *Count Français de Nantes,*(3) *Antoine Mongez and His Wife Angélique* (see

(1) The Hermitage, Leningrad.
(2) 1810, Frick Collection, New York. She was the wife of the Quartermaster-General of the Emperor's household. (Note of the translator).
(3) 1812, Musée Jacquemart-André, Paris. Born in 1756, the son of a court solicitor, Français de Nantes was chief customs officer in Nantes when the Revolution broke out. He joined the Jacobins and was elected to the Legislative Assembly. He reluctantly rallied the coup d'état of Brumaire. Under Napoleon he became Director of Hospitals, prefect, Councillor of State, and Count. He was elected deputy under Louis XVIII, and Louis-Philippe made him Peer of France. (Note of the translator).

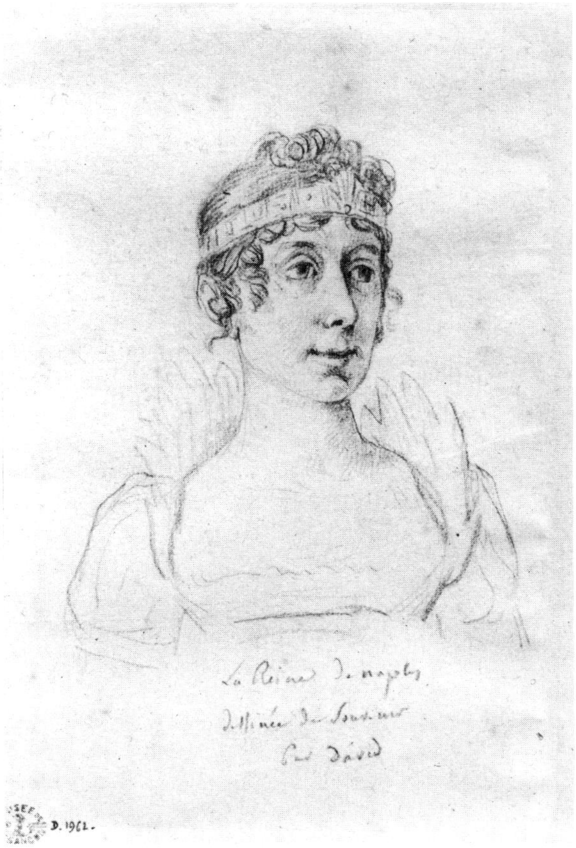

*Portrait of the Queen of Naples, ca 1804*
*Pencil on light blue paper*
*Watermark, 7¾" × 5⅝" (19.7 × 14.3 cm)*
*Musée d'Art et d'Archéologie*
*Besançon, France*

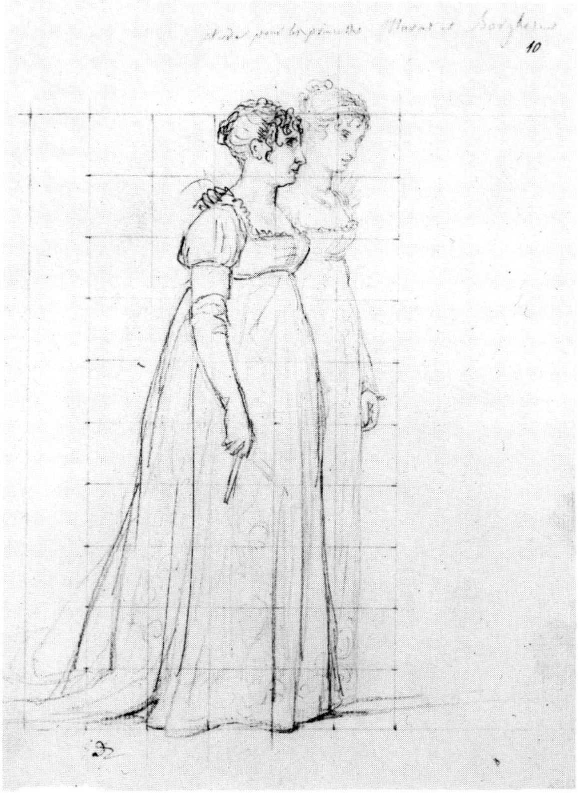

*Study for Caroline Bonaparte*
*the Princess Murat and Pauline Bonaparte*
*the Princess Borghese*
*Sketchbook no. 20, 1805-1806, p. 10 recto*
*Black crayon over graphite*
*squared in graphite on laid paper*
*9⅜" × 7¼" (23.7 × 19.9 cm)*
*The Fogg Art Museum, Harvard University*
*Cambridge, Massachusetts*
*Bequest of Grenville L. Winthrop*

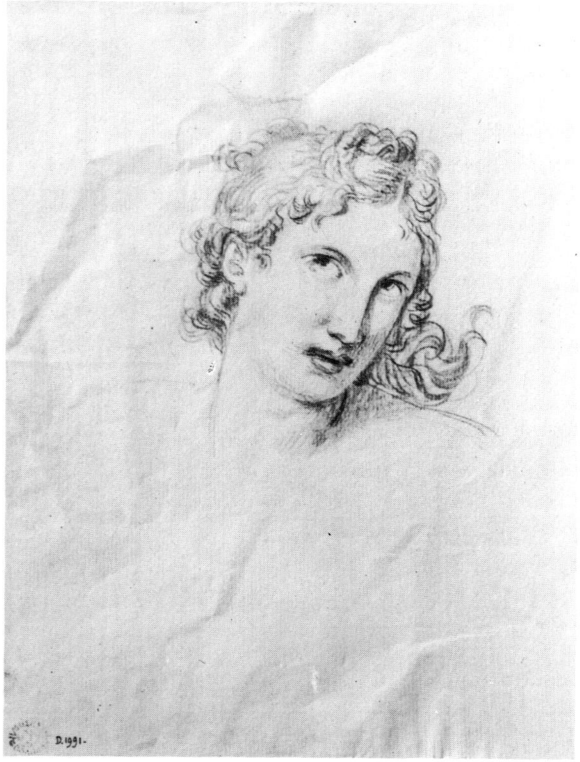

*Head of Young Woman*
*with Curly Hair, ca 1804*
*Pencil, broken watermark*
*9³⁄₁₆" × 7⅞" (23.3 × 18.8 cm)*
*Musée d'Art et d'Archéologie*
*Besançon, France*

page 86),[1] and *Madame David* (see page 81). As he had already done with *The Sabine Women*, he returned to works interrupted by his paintings on Napoleonic history, and in 1813-1814 he completed *Leonidas at the Battle of Thermopylae*, which he had abandoned in 1802 or 1803 (see page 60).

Delécluze wrote that when David returned to *Leonidas*, "He needed to find a rest from royal images and refresh himself in the republican atmosphere around Lacedemonian warriors." He criticized David in a pithy phrase: "[David] finished in prose a painting he had started in verse."[2] He found a lyrical beauty in the young man tying his sandal, the three youths offering crowns, and the old man by the tree embracing his son. He found less imagination in the blind man on the left, and the two soldiers taking down their arms on the right. And he judged Leonidas to be both lyrical and prosaic. Delécluze was

(1) Born in 1747, Mongez was a well-known archeologist and a close friend of David. His wife was a painter and a student of David. (Note of the translator).
(2) E.-J. Delécluze, *op. cit.*, p. 339.

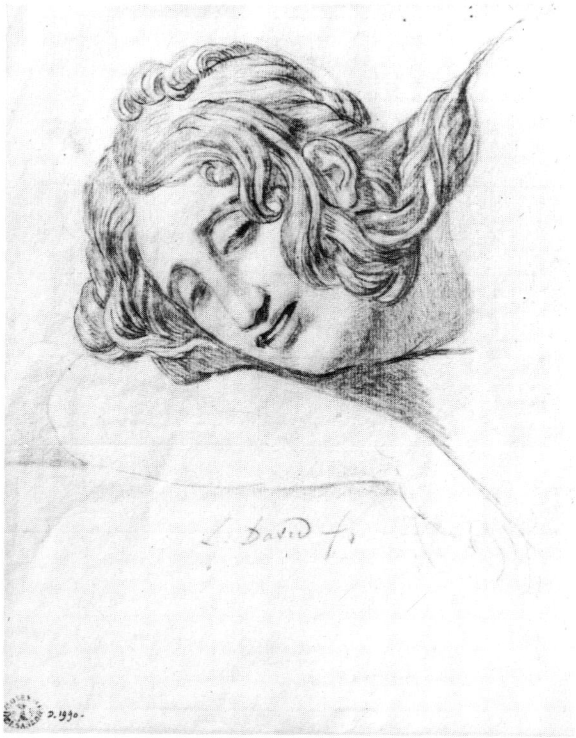

*Study of Young Woman Reclining*
*ca 1804*
*Pencil, watermark*
*9" × 7½" (22.8 × 19 cm)*
*Musée d'Art et d'Archéologie*
*Besançon, France*

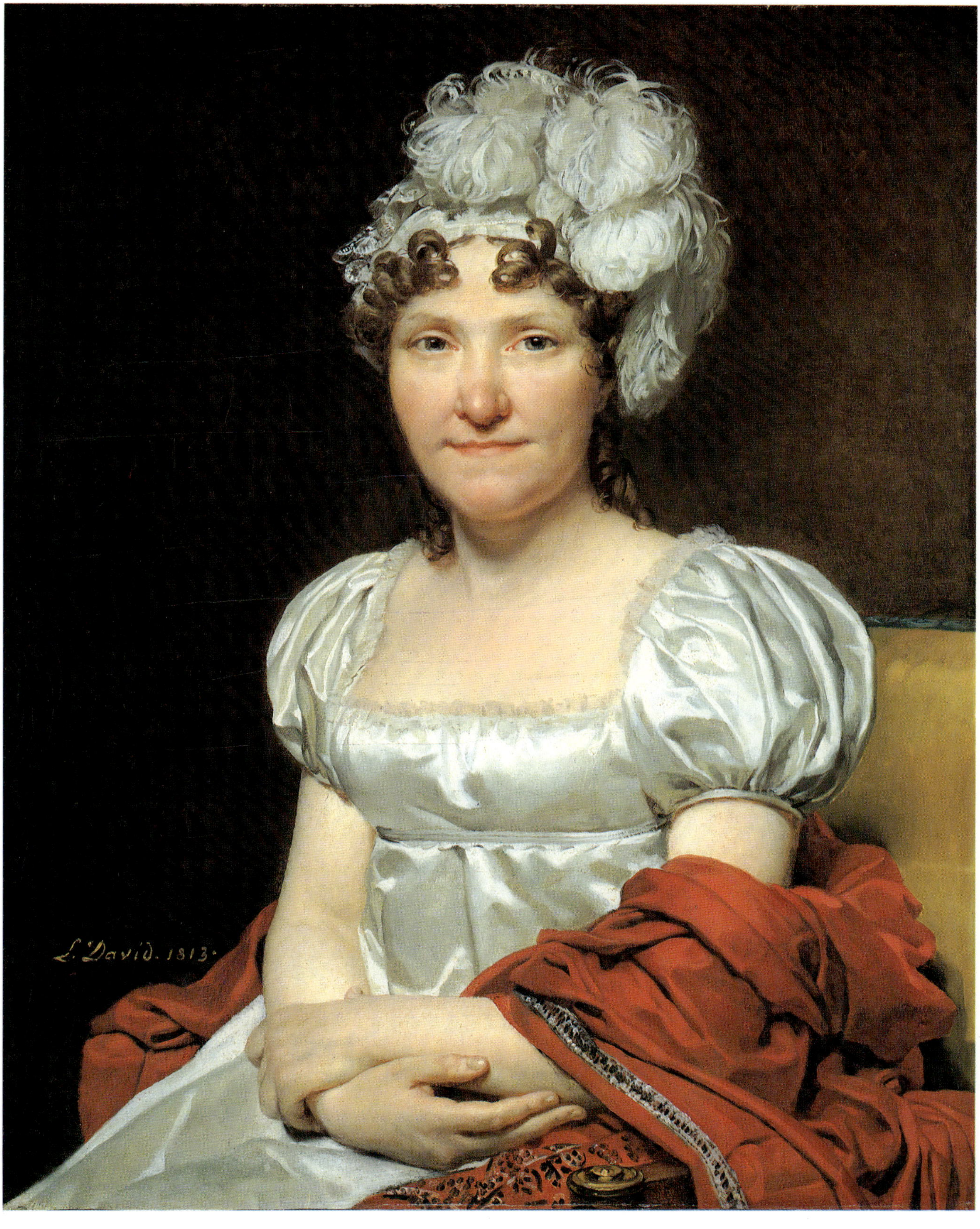

Madame David, 1813. Oil on canvas, 28¾″ × 23⅜″ (72.9 × 59.4 cm)
National Gallery of Art, Washington, D.C. Samuel H. Kress Collection

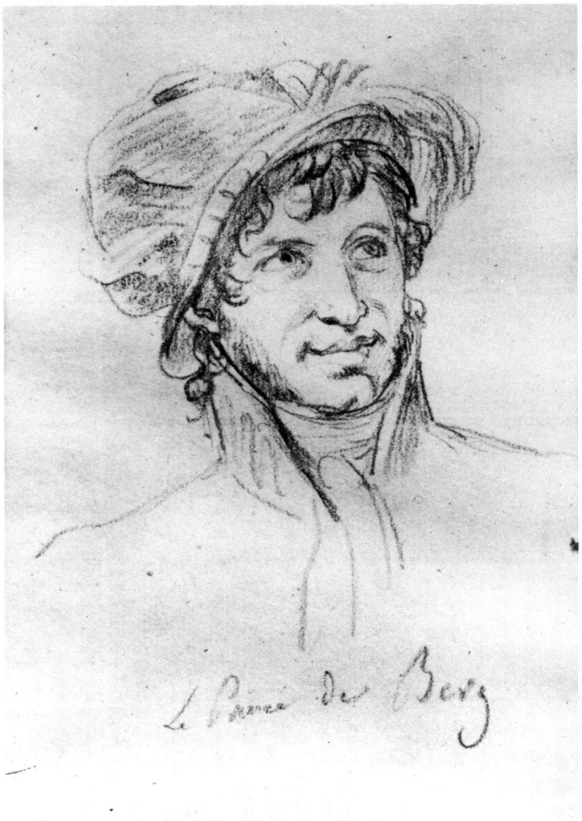


*Murat, Prince of Berg, ca 1808*
*Black pencil, 9″ × 7¼″ (22.8 × 18.4 cm)*
*Musée d'Art et d'Archéologie*
*Besançon, France*

probably wrong, and the David of prose may have painted over parts that Delécluze attributed to the poet in David. He found the realistic touches prosaic, while these very realistic touches achieve this combination mentioned by Delacroix and save the painting from cold rhetoric. Some details may call for ironic comments: the cross-belts masking the sexual organs; or the series of feet at the center, to the left of the hero. Most characteristic in the painting, however, is that the composition fosters the observation of both the whole and the details, as if the artist had given equal importance to the structure and the general movement. David wanted this *Leonidas* to be devoid of any expression of passion. He may have wanted to insure that nothing troubled that which lay beneath the surface: the sublime expectation of death accepted by all.

David felt that the painting was literally Greek because of the care with which he copied attitudes and accessories, which the composition brought

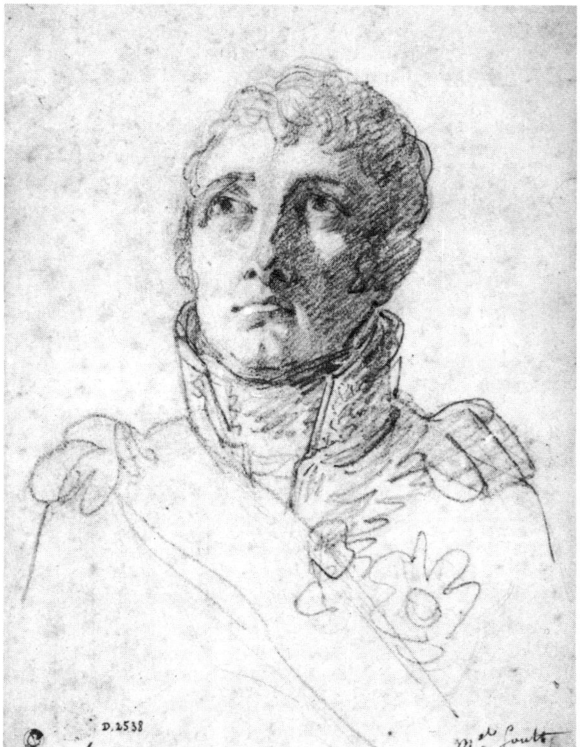

*Marshal Soult, ca 1804*
*Pencil, 7$^{13}/_{16}$″ × 6⅛″ (19.8 × 15.5 cm)*
*Musée d'Art et d'Archéologie*
*Besançon, France*

to life. He used to call it his best work and he may have seen in it his real "sacring," combining heroism and virtue recovered. The viewer knows what lay in store for Leonidas, he is on the side of Fate: He can see that which is still veiled by the thin layer of the present — a thin layer equal to the layer of paints, where light and beauty are contained.

When David completed *Leonidas*, the Empire was ended. At the beginning of April 1814 the Allied Powers were occupying Paris. The royal Bourbon dynasty was restored. In the fall David abstained from taking part in the Salon. *Leonidas* and *The Sabines* were exhibited in his studio. His enemies claimed that his talent was declining. His republican friends called him a genius. The government wanted to reassure everybody and remained silent. Napoleon escaped from Elba and arrived in Paris on March 20, 1815. On April 6, he went to see *Leonidas* and was surprised by the fact that it did not feature any battle. In May, in spite of his friends' advice, David signed

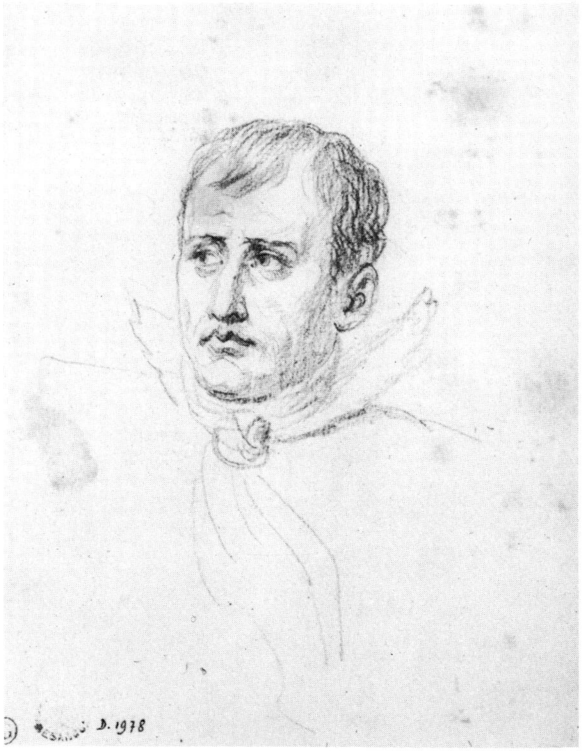

*Portrait of Napoleon, ca 1804*
*Pencil, broken watermark*
*6¼" × 4¾" (16 × 12 cm)*
*Musée d'Art et d'Archéologie*
*Besançon, France*

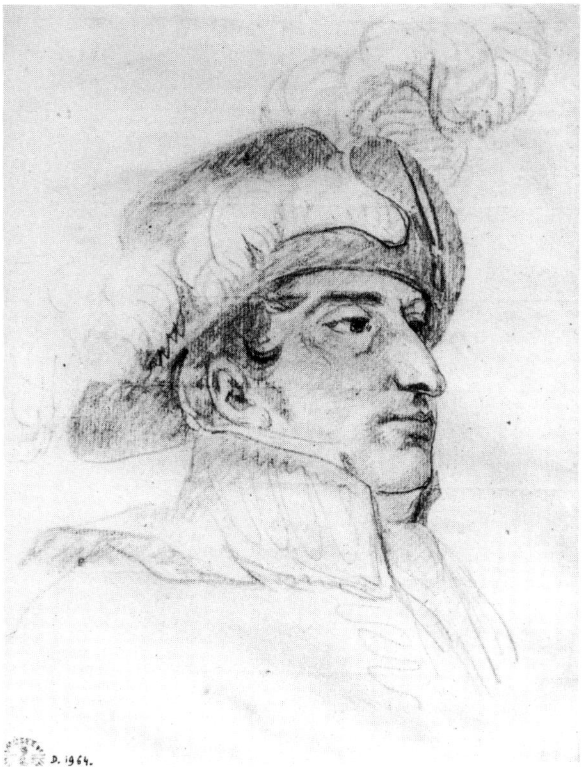

*Portrait of Kellermann, ca 1804*
*Black pencil, watermark, crown*
*9" × 7⅜" (22.9 × 18.8 cm)*
*Musée d'Art et d'Archéologie*
*Besançon, France*

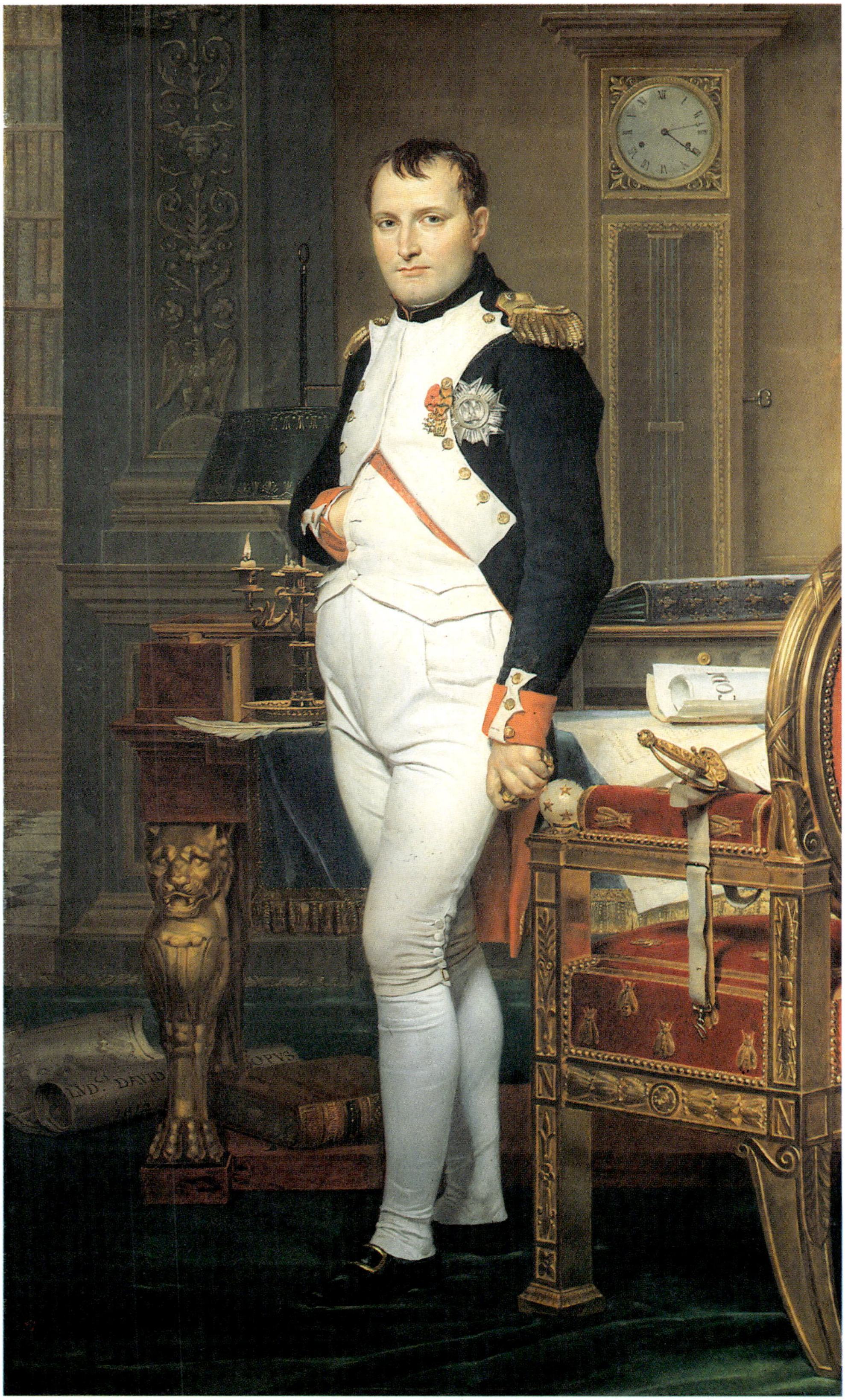

NAPOLEON IN HIS STUDY, 1812. Oil on canvas, 80¼″ × 49¼″ (203 × 125.1 cm)
National Gallery of Art, Washington, D.C. Samuel H. Kress Collection

the "Supplement to the Imperial Constitution," which repudiated the right of the Bourbon dynasty to rule France and excluded the return to the privileges of the Old Regime. On June 15, Napoleon was defeated at the battle of Waterloo.

David left for Switzerland at the end of June 1815. At the end of August he returned to Paris, where he led a discreet life with the support of Gros and some friends. On January 12, 1816, the two Houses voted almost unanimously to banish all who had voted for the death of Louis XVI and signed the Supplement of the Imperial Constitution. Count Decazes, minister of police, informed David that he could benefit from an exception. David answered that he wanted to abide by the law. He arrived in Brussels on January 27. He settled there and refused an offer from the King of Prussia to "live pleasantly" in Berlin and be his Minister of the Arts.

David never changed his mind. He had accepted the Empire because it followed the Revolution, but he rejected the Restoration because it meant a return to times of tyranny. On January 1, 1819, he wrote to his son Jules:

> My colleagues are all returning to France. I could certainly do the same if I were weak enough to ask in writing to be recalled. You know your father and his pride. I could not do such thing. I did what I did knowingly, not out of passion; time will reveal the truth.... Here, I can rest. Years add up, and I feel at peace with my conscience. What more do I need?

On November 2, 1819, he wrote to Gros, who was insisting he come back:

> My dear friend, we shall never understand one another as long as you are convinced that one cannot be happy but in France; I have good reason to think the opposite. Since I came back from Rome ..., I have always been persecuted, tormented in my work by the most odious means. Had the Heavens not endowed me with a steady head and strength, I could have been defeated.

The same year 1819, Count Forbin, David's former student who had become director of the French Museums, persuaded David to allow the French National Collection to recover *Andromache*, *The Sacring*, and *The Distribution of the Eagle Standards*, on condition that it buy *The Sabines* and *Leonidas* for one-hundred-thousand francs. All these paintings had remained in Paris.

David was leading a secluded life, painting and teaching. He stayed aloof from French emigré circles and spent a lot of time at the Théâtre de la Monnaie. He always had a passion for the theater and had been a great friend of François-Joseph Talma, Napoleon's favorite actor. The Belgian painter François-Joseph Navez wrote that "[David] loved working so much that one would have killed him by taking away his palette." He produced many portraits. The most remarkable one was *Portrait of Emmanuel-Joseph Sieyès* (see page 87), whose features and eyes express the same "I survived," which had been his answer when asked what he had done during the Reign of Terror.[1] On the top right David inscribed "Aetatis suae 69,"[2] which was also his own age. The man facing us is disillusioned but not bitter. He is painted with such penetrating sympathy that his thoughts become palpable and stare at us. All at once painting becomes knowledge through the eyes.

(1) Born in 1748, Abbé Sieyès was elected to the States-General. He was a founder of the Jacobins and helped to write the Declaration of the Rights of Man and Citizen and the constitution of 1791. In 1799 he entered the Directory, which he helped Napoleon to topple later that year. After 1816 he lived in exile in Brussels. (Note of the translator).

(2) Sixty-nine years of age.

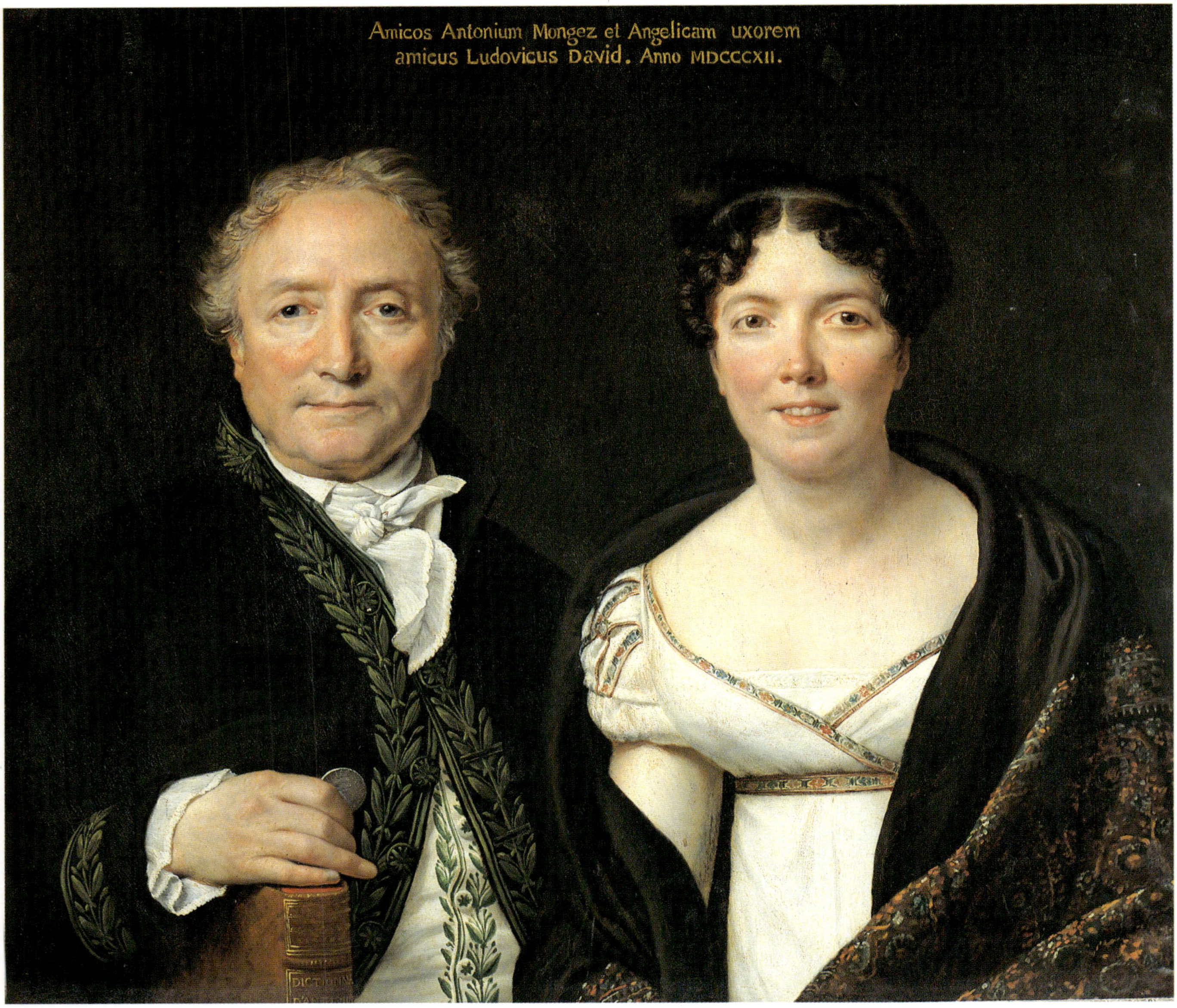


ANTOINE MONGEZ AND HIS WIFE ANGÉLIQUE, 1812
Oil on panel, 29⅛″ × 34¼″ (74 × 87 cm)
Musée du Louvre, Paris

PORTRAIT OF EMMANUEL-JOSEPH SIEYÈS, 1817
Oil on canvas, 37½″ × 28½″ (95.2 × 72.5 cm)
The Fogg Art Museum, Harvard University
Cambridge, Massachusetts

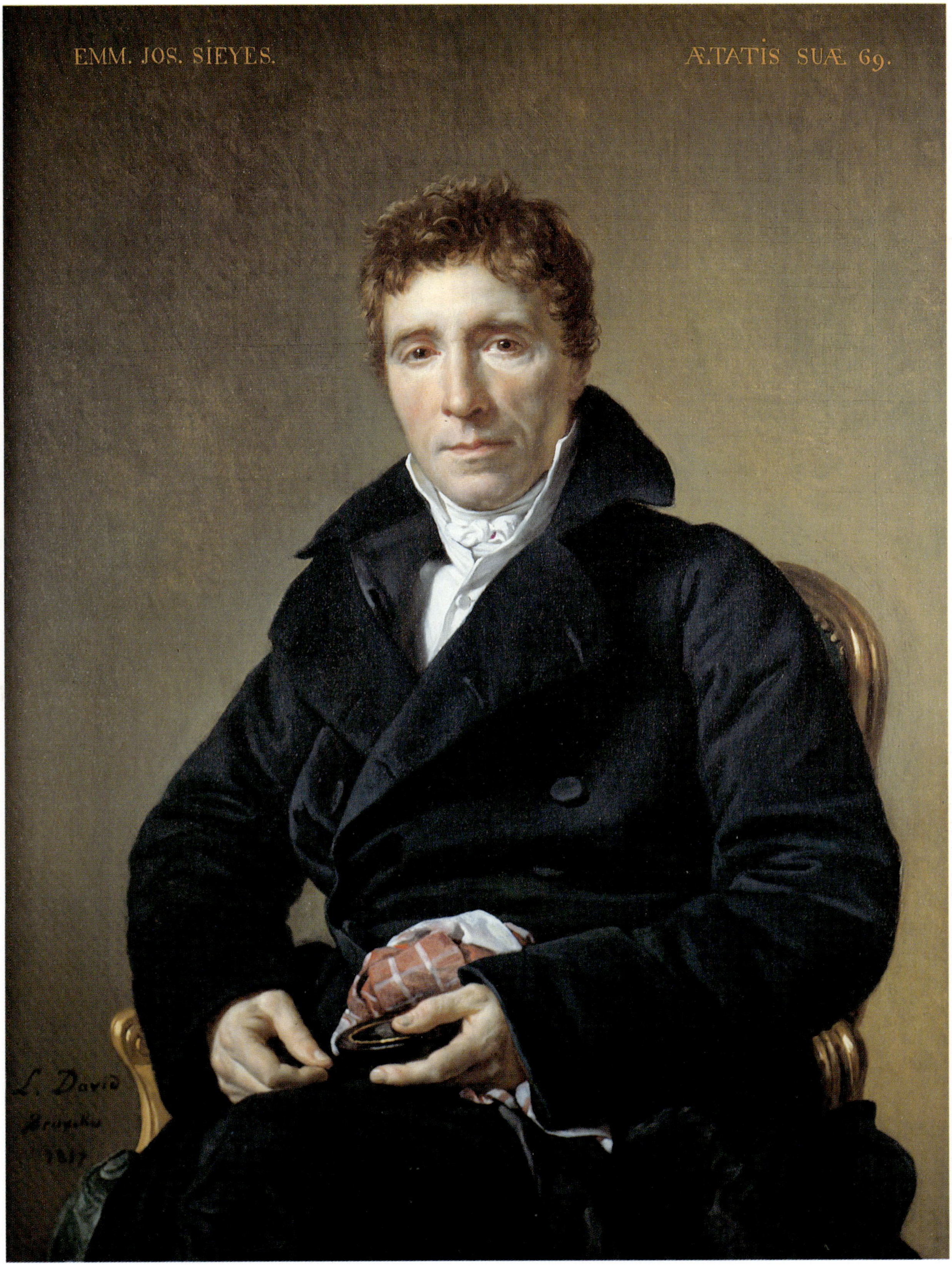
EMM. JOS. SIEYES.
ÆTATIS SUÆ 69.
L. David

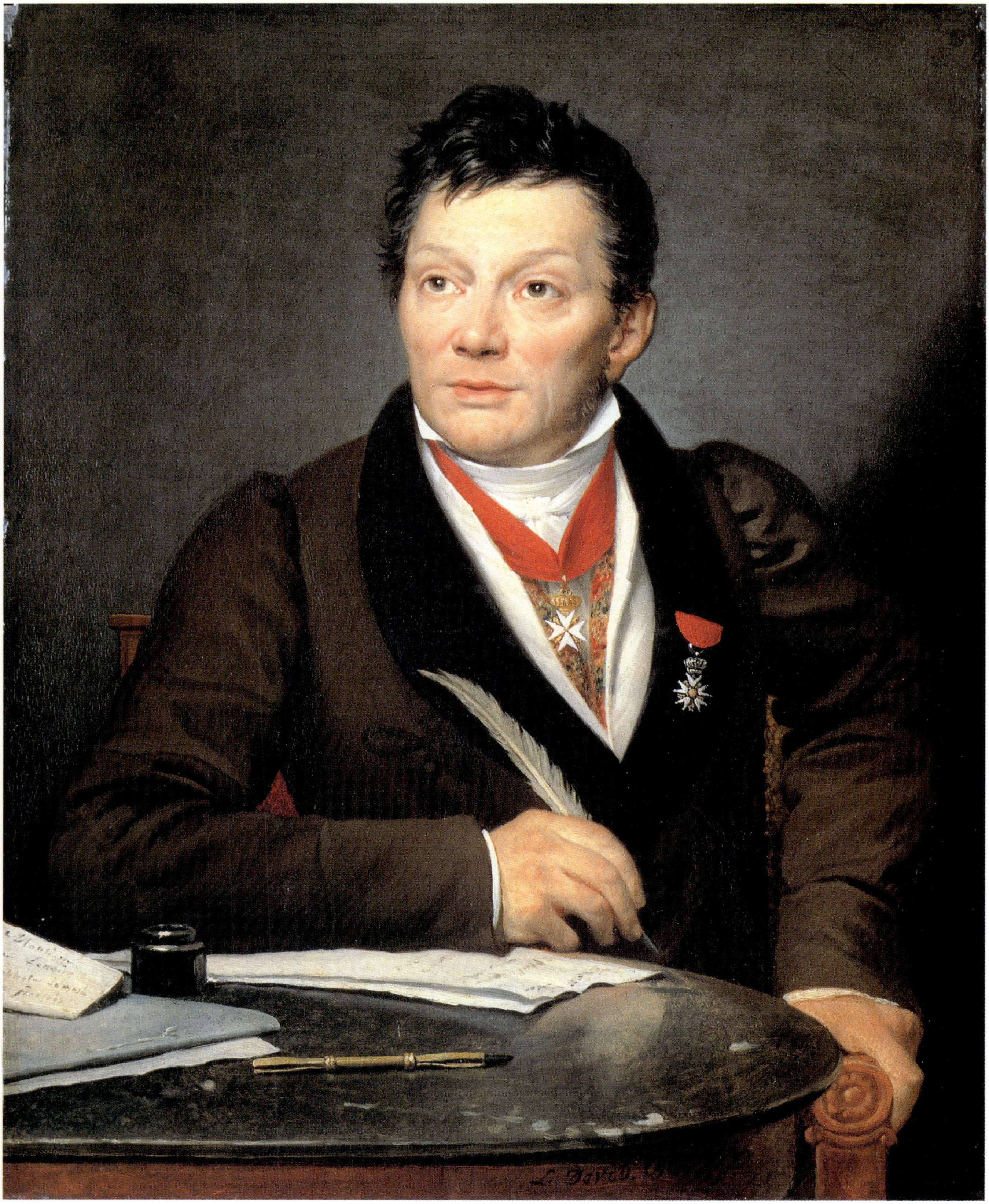

Alexandre Lenoir, 1817. Oil on panel, $29\frac{15}{16}'' \times 24\frac{7}{8}''$ (76 × 62 cm)
Musée du Louvre, Paris

David returned to *Apelles Painting Campaspe in Front of Alexandre*, which he did not complete.[1] He then produced three works in what was to be his last style: *Cupid and Psyche* (see page 90), *Telemachus Bidding Farewell to Eucharis*,[2] and *Mars Disarmed by Venus and the Graces* (see page 91), which he regarded as his final declaration of artistic principles. In an article published on December 8, 1823, he declared to the newspaper "L'Oracle," "This is the last painting I want to make, but I want to outdo myself. I shall inscribe the date of my seventy-fifth year and, afterward, I will not touch a paint brush."

In May 1824, David had a three-room apartment rented in Paris to exhibit his *Mars*. Six thousand visitors came during the first month. The same year, Romanticism and Delacroix triumphed at the Salon with *The Scenes from the Massacre of Scio*.

At first sight, David had never painted anything as formalistic as *Mars*, with its clouds, porticoes, doves, Cupid, and Graces. It seems an academic Restoration. At a second glance, however, the image dissolves in the space of the painting, in the infinite blue sky, the airiness of which penetrates all the shapes.

(1) Musée des Beaux-Arts, Lille, France.
(2) 1822, private collection, France.

*Portrait of Lenoir and His Wife, 1809. Black pencil and lead, 6⅛" × 8½" (15.6 × 21.5 cm)*
*Musée du Louvre, Cabinet des Dessins, Paris*

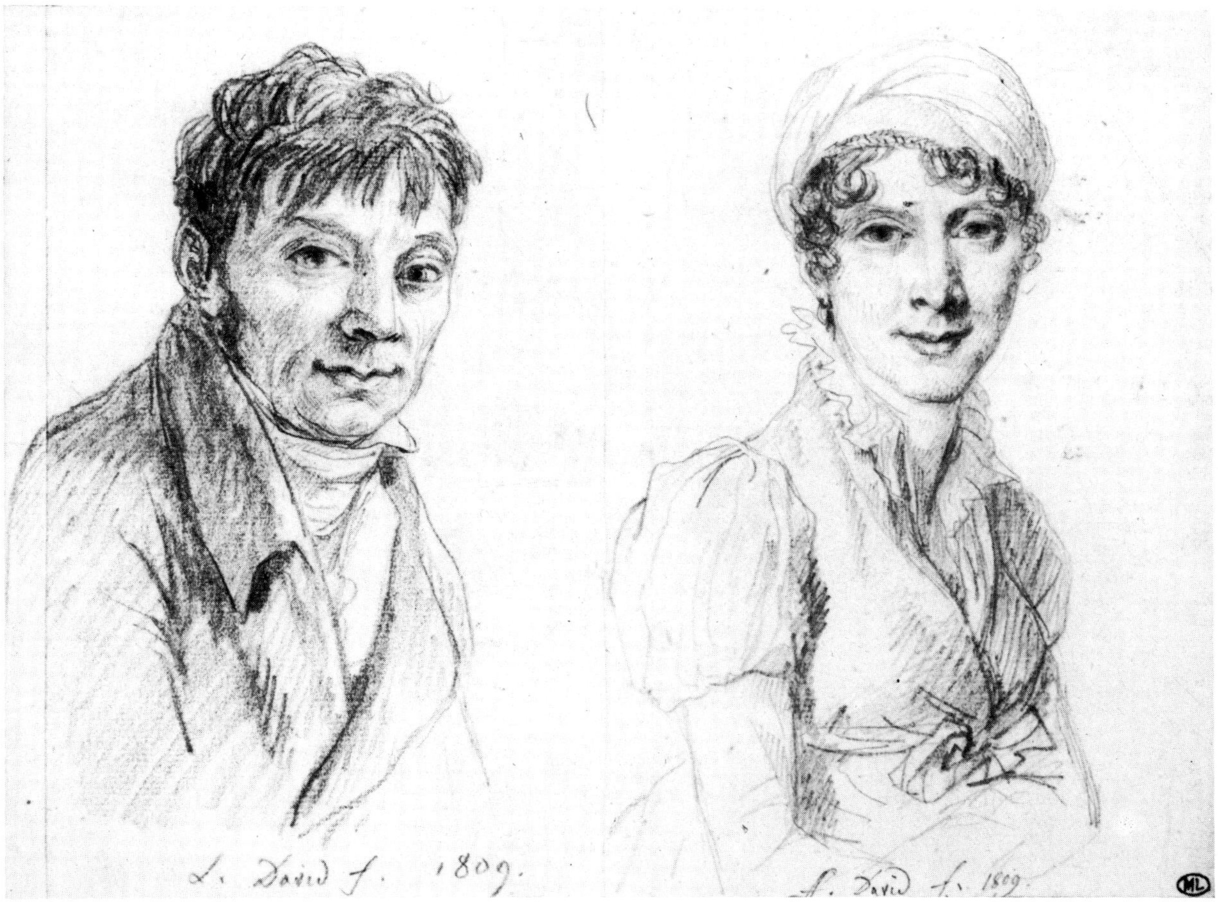

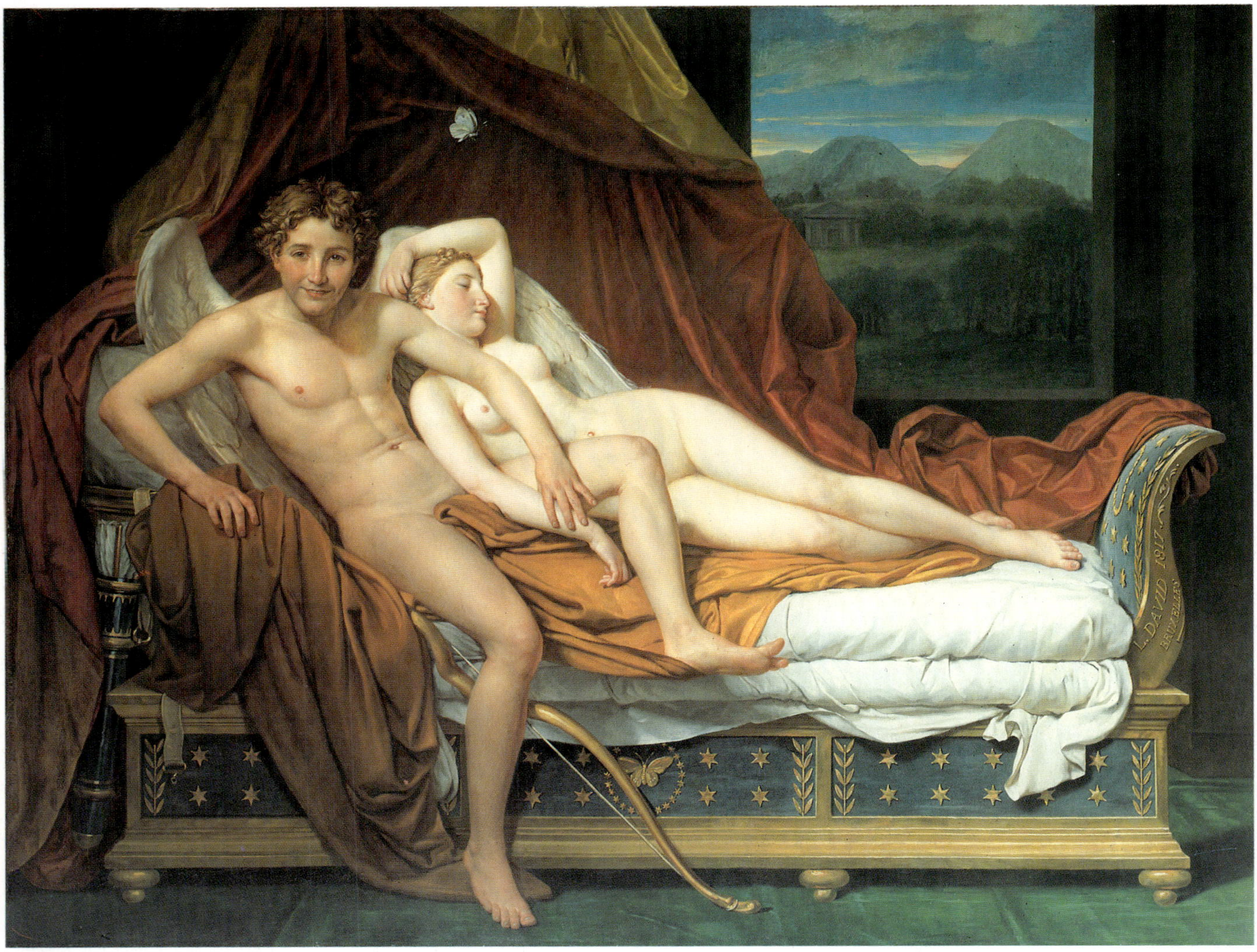


CUPID AND PSYCHE, 1817
Oil on canvas, 7½″ × 95⅛″ (184.2 × 241.6 cm)
The Cleveland Museum of Art
Leonard C. Hanna, Jr. Fund

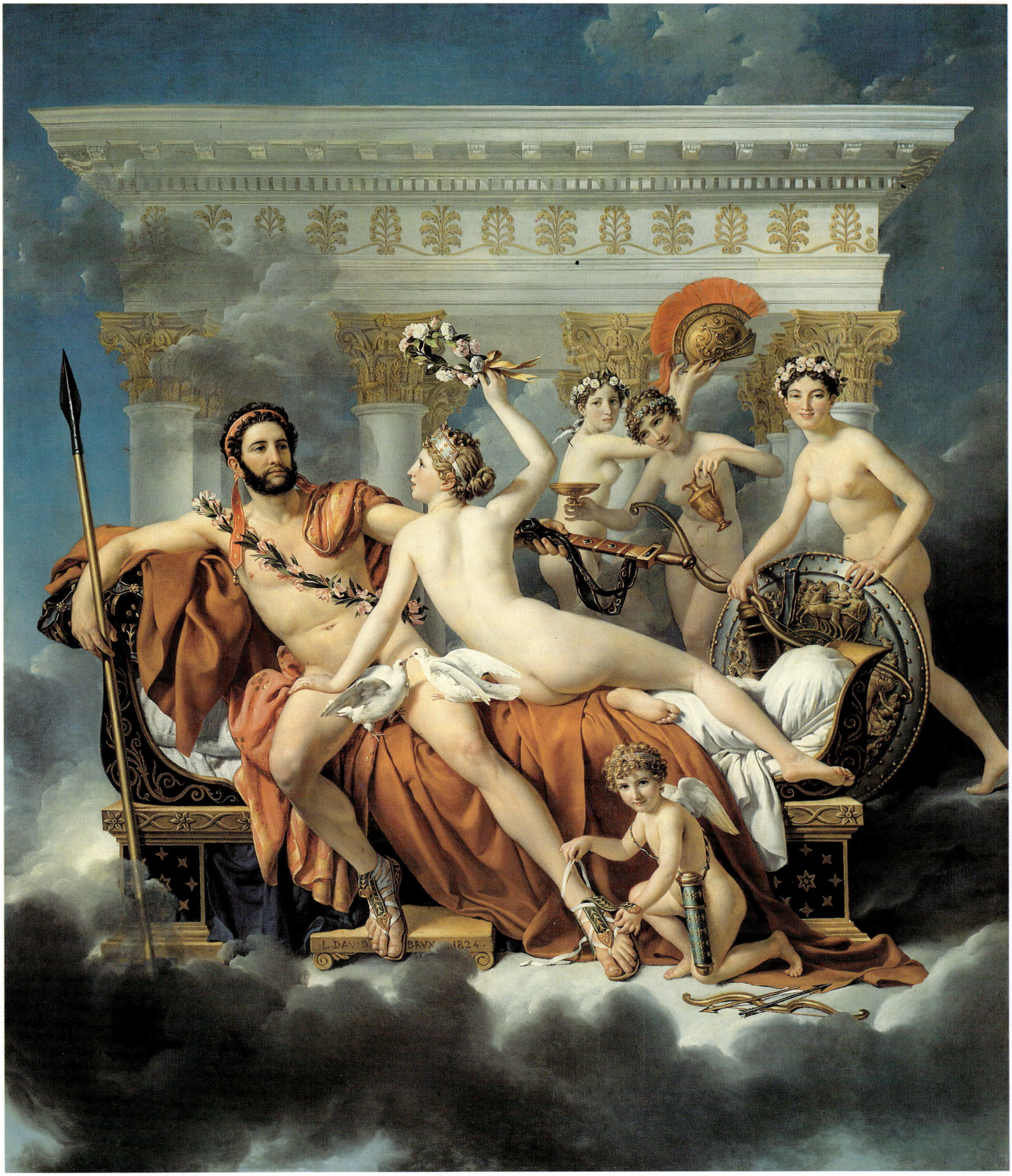


MARS DISARMED BY VENUS AND THE GRACES, 1824. Oil on canvas, 10′1¼″ × 8′8⅜″ (308 × 265 cm)
Musées Royaux des Beaux-Arts de Belgique, Brussels

Lines intertwine, and the outlines bring out the fullness of the bodies. Venus's body is so perfect that, in another context, it would surpass any other. It is also totally realistic. But what is the power of realism in such unrealism? Never before had David achieved such harmony of colors united in a wide movement that helps the meeting of the eye and the painting. One must overlook Cupid and his little wings, and the kissing doves which hide Mars's genitals. Then one can see the energy of the bodies and the gracious curves which structure the space of the painting. This is a representational painting pushed to a brink where the real image and the mind's image overload each other. But the painting foreshadows the artistic vision of Ingres, Théodore Chassériau, Gustave Moreau, the Pre-Raphaelites and the Symbolists. Artists who followed David reduced the excesses seen in *Mars* to an understatement which produces the "sublime pleasure" and the "soothing of the mind" which Henri Matisse claimed to be the function of the arts.

This painting, which David wanted to be his last, brings about a final metamorphosis in his long work on that which is visible. First, he had brought out the reality in history; later, he revealed the history under the reality. David successfully conceived reality and history in his paintings, finding the sense of space which would create a sense of the mind's role. Here he used a different pictorial idiom, but beyond signs and images, the space expressing the artist's inner vision does not change: Its substance creates a unity of the eyes and the mind.

David died in Brussels on December 29, 1825. The French government refused to allow his body to be transferred to Paris. The dead man remained an exile but his work raised him from oblivion and took him out of time. This is his permanent revolution. The bourgeois has divested himself of his own identity — leaving only his artistic vision. And this vision is lasting because it opens onto beauty, which is the end of death.

BERNARD NOËL

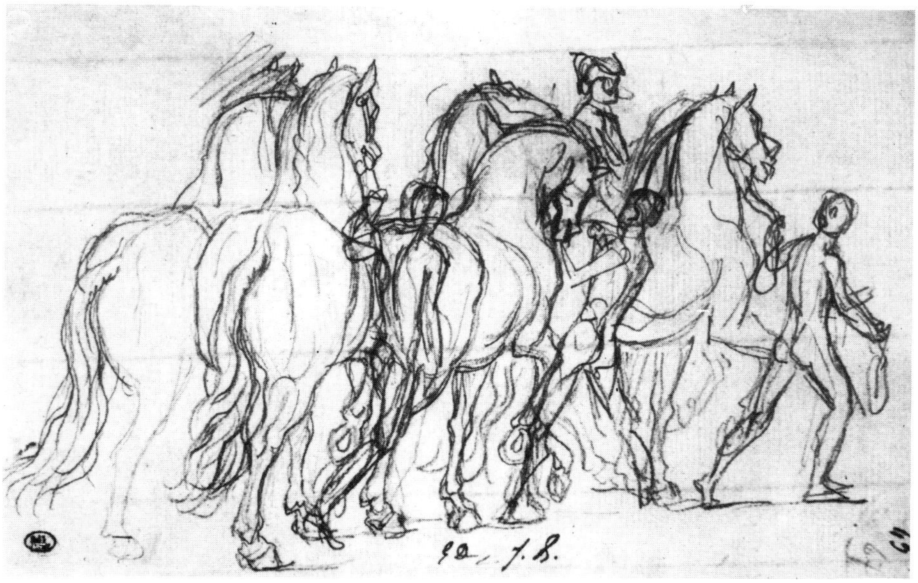

*Horses Held Back by Naked Men*
*1806-1814*
*Lead pencil*
*10¼" × 13⅜"*
*(26 × 34 cm)*
*Musée du Louvre*
*Cabinet des Dessins*
*Paris*

# BIOGRAPHY

1748 Jacques-Louis David was born on August 30, in Paris. His father was a prosperous merchant, his mother was related to a family of architects.

1755 David went to boarding school at Picpus. Later he studied with a private tutor, then attended the Collège de Beauvais and the Collège des Quatre Nations. His mother wanted him to become an architect.

1757 His father died in a duel. His uncles Jacques Buron and Jacques François Desmaisons became his guardians. Buron was a master mason and Desmaisons an architect.

1764 David convinced his guardian to allow him to devote himself to painting. Buron took David to Boucher, who advised him to study with Vien.

1766 He enrolled in Vien's studio at the Academy.

1769 Settled in the house of his godfather, Michel Sedaine. *Portrait of Madame Buron.*

1770 Passed the preliminary examination for the Prix de l'Académie. He did not get an award.

1771 Passed the final examination for the Prix de l'Académie. He got second prize with *Minerva Battling with Mars.*

1772 Failed the competition for the Prix de l'Académie.

1773 Was awarded the Prix de l'Académie for the study of heads and expression.

1774 Was awarded first prize for *Antiochus and Stratonice.*

1775-1780 Stay at the Académie de France in Rome.

1779 Trip to Naples.

1780 Exhibited *Saint Roch* in Rome.

1781 Exhibited the *Portrait of Count Stanislas Potocki* and *Belisarius* at the Salon in Paris. Trip to Flanders.

1782 Married Charlotte Pécoul. *Portrait of Jacques François Desmaisons.*

1783 The Academy accepted his *Andromache Mourning Hector* by unanimous vote. His son, Charles-Louis-Jules, was born.

1784 *Monsieur Pécoul* and *Madame Pécoul.* His second son, Eugène, was born.

1784-1785 Second stay in Rome, where he painted *The Oath of the Horatii.* It caused a sensation at the Salon in Paris.

1786 Birth of his twin daughters, Félicité-Emilie and Pauline-Jeanne.

1787 Exhibited *The Death of Socrates* at the Salon.

1788 Death of his favorite student, Jean-Germain Drouais. *Antoine-Laurent Lavoisier and His Wife.* David was a frequent guest at the salon of Duke d'Orléans.

1789 Exhibited *Paris and Helen* and *Brutus* at the Salon. David became a member of the Club of the Friends of the Constitution, later to be named Club of the Jacobins. As early as September, David demanded a revision of the Academy's bylaws and a review of its role.

1790 Trip to Nantes, in Vendée, to paint an allegory of the revolution there. The Jacobins commissioned him for *The Oath of the Tennis Court.*

1791 On July 17, he signed a petition for the dethronement of the king. The Constituent Assembly voted that *The Oath of the Tennis Court* be paid by the Treasury. The preparatory drawing was exhibited at the Salon, next to *The Oath of the Horatii.*

1791-1792 *Madame Charles-Louis Trudaine.*

1792 Stopped working on *The Oath of the Tennis Court* around March. The painting remained unfinished. On April 15, he organized the first Freedom Day. Elected to the Convention on September 17, where he sat with the Montagnards. Member of the Commission on Public Education and the Commission on the Arts. *Madame Pastoret.*

1793 Voted for the king's execution on January 17. *Le Peletier de Saint-Fargeau.* President of the Jacobins between June 17 and July 14. On July 25 he was elected secretary to the Convention. On September 14, he became a member of the Committee of General Security. *Marat Murdered*, which he presented to the Convention on November 15.

1794 President of the Convention between January 5 and January 20. After his divorce, he kept his two sons with him. His wife and two daughters retired to Saint-Ouen. *Joseph Barra.* On 9 Thermidor (July 27), when Robespierre was overthrown, David was ill and did not attend the Convention. Arrested on August 2 and jailed until December 28.

1795 He was assigned to forced residence at Saint-Ouen, where he stayed with the Sériziat. Imprisoned again on May 29, and freed in August of the same year. On October 26, David received an amnesty.

1795-1780 *The Sabine Women.* The painting was exhibited for five years at the Louvre.

1796 Success at the Salon with *Pierre Sériziat* and *Madame Sériziat* at the Salon, which he had painted the previous year. David and his wife remarried.

1797 First portrait of Bonaparte.

1799 *Madame de Verninac.*

1800 *Madame Récamier.* Bonaparte appointed him Painter of the Government. David declined.

1801 *Bonaparte Crossing the Great Saint Bernard*, commissioned by Charles IV of Spain.

1804 Appointed First Painter of the Emperor. David never took the position. He started work on *Pius VII* at the end of December.

1805 His daughter Emilie married Colonel Meunier.

1805-1808 *The Sacring of Emperor Napoleon I and the Crowning of Empress Josephine*, the first of a series of four paintings commissioned by the Emperor to commemorate his coronation. The painting was exhibited at the Salon in 1808.

1806 His daughter Pauline married General Jeanin.

1808-1810 *The Distribution of the Eagle Standards*, second painting completed in the series about the coronation. It was exhibited at the Salon in 1810.

1809 *Sappho, Phaon and Cupid*, Anacreontic painting commissioned by Prince Yusupov. David was not included in the list of artists commissioned by Denon to paint works commemorating the Emperor's military victories.

1810 *Countess Daru*, portrait of Stendhal's cousin.

1811 *Count Français de Nantes.*

1812 *Napoleon in His Study. Antoine Mongez and His Wife Angélique.*

1813-1814 Completed *Leonidas at the Battle of Thermopylae*, which he had started during the Revolution.

1814 First Restoration of the Bourbon dynasty. David did not show anything at the Salon. He exhibited *Leonidas* and *The Sabine Women* in his studio.

1815 Napoleon returned to Paris on March 15. David remained loyal to the Emperor during the Hundred Days. After Napoleon's defeat at the battle of Waterloo, David left for Switzerland. He returned to Paris at the end of August.

1816 Banished for having voted for the death of Louis XVI and signed the Supplement to the Imperial Constitution. He settled in Brussels and never solicited a pardon. He also refused an invitation from the King of Prussia.

1817 *Cupid and Psyche* commissioned by Count Sommariva. *Portrait of Emmanuel-Joseph Sieyès* at sixty-nine.

1819 The French National Collection recovered *Andromache*, *The Sacring*, and *The Distribution of the Eagle Standards.* It also bought *The Sabine Women* and *Leonidas.*

1821-1824 *Mars Disarmed by Venus and the Graces*, which he regarded as his final declaration of artistic principles. The painting was exhibited in Paris in May, in an apartment he had rented for that purpose.

1822 *Telemachus Bidding Farewell to Eucharis* commissioned by Count Schoenborn.

1824 He was run over by a coach. His health began to deteriorate.

1825 He suffered a stroke in July. David died in Brussels on December 29. The French government refused to allow his body to be transferred to Paris. The two posthumous sales of the content of his studio, in 1826 and 1835 respectively, were a failure.

# BIBLIOGRAPHY


## CATALOGUE RAISONNÉ

Wildenstein, D. and G. *Documents complémentaires au catalogue de l'œuvre de Louis David.* Paris, 1973.

## WORKS ON DAVID AND HIS TIME

Adhémar, Jean and Cassou, Jean. *David, naissance du génie d'un peintre.* Paris, 1983.

ANON., *Description du tableau exposé au Musée Napoléon, représentant le Sacre de leurs Majestés, peint par M. David, peintre de leurs Majestés.* Paris: Gauthier, 1808.

ANON., *Notice sur la vie et les ouvrages de M. J.L. David.* Paris, 1824.

ANON., *Notice sur le Marat de Louis David.* Paris: Imprimerie Jouaust, 1867.

BAUDELAIRE, C. *Curiosités esthétiques.* Paris, 1846.

BLEYL, M. *Das klassizistische Porträt, Gestaltungsanalyse am Beispiel J.-L. Davids.* Rev. ed. of the author's doctoral thesis, Ruhr Universität Bochum, 1908. Francfort: Lang, 1982.

BORDES, Ph. *Le Serment du Jeu de Paume de Jacques-Louis David. Le peintre, son milieu et son temps de 1789 à 1792.* Paris: Editions de la Réunion des Musées Nationaux, 1983.

BROOKNER, A. *Jacques-Louis David.* London: Harper & Row, 1980.

CANTINELLI, R. *Jacques-Louis David.* Brussels: Van Œst, 1930.

CHAUSSARD, P. *Notices sur la vie et les ouvrages de M. Jacques-Louis David.* Paris, 1843.

CHÉNIER, André. *Le Jeu de Paume. A Louis David.* Paris, 1791.

COEKELBERGHS, D. and VOLLE, N. *Catalogue. Autour du néo-classicisme en Belgique.* Ixelles (Brussels, Belgium): Musée communal, 1985.

COUPIN, M.P.A. *Essai sur J.L. David peintre d'histoire.* Paris, 1827.

CROW, Th.E. *Painters and Public Life in Eighteenth-Century Paris.* New Haven, London, 1985.

DAVID, J.L. Jules. *Le Peintre Louis David 1748-1825. Souvenirs et documents inédits.* Paris: Havard, 1880, 2 vol.

DAVID, J.L. Jules. *Notice sur le Marat de Louis David, suivie de la liste des tableaux dressée par lui-même.* Paris, 1867.

DELÉCLUZE, E.-J. *Journal de Delécluze 1824-1828.* Introduction and notes by Robert Baschet. Paris: Grasset, 1948.

DELÉCLUZE, E.-J. *Louis David, son école et son temps. Souvenirs.* Paris: Didier, 1855. 2nd ed. with preface and notes by J.-P. Mouilleseaux. Paris: Macula, 1983.

DIDEROT, Denis. *Salons.* Ed. by Jean Seznec and Jean Adhémar. Oxford: Clarendon Press, 1957-1967.

DOWD, D.L. *Pageant-Master of the Republic. Jacques-Louis David and the French Revolution.* Lincoln, Nebraska: University of Nebraska, 1948.

FLORISOONE, M. *Jacques-Louis David.* Catalogue of the exhibition held for the second centenary anniversary of his birth. Musée de l'Orangerie, Paris, 1948.

GONZALEZ PALACIOS, Alvar. *David e la pittura napoleonia.* Milan: Fabbri, 1967.

HAUTECŒUR, L. *Louis David.* Paris: La Table Ronde, 1954.

HERBERT, Robert L. *David, Voltaire, Brutus and the French Revolution. An Essay in Art and Politics.* London: Allen Lane, 1972.

HOLMA, K. *David, son évolution et son style.* Paris: Sorlot, 1940.

HOWARD, Seymour. *Sacrifice of the Hero: The Roman Years. A Classical Frieze by Jacques-Louis David.* Sacramento, California: E.B. Crocker Art Gallery, 1975.

HUMBERT, Agnès. *Louis David peintre et conventionnel. Essai de critique marxiste.* Paris: Editions Sociales Internationales, 1936. 2nd ed., Paris: Hier et Aujourd'hui, 1947.

IRWIN, David. *Winckelmann, Writings on Art.* London: Phaidon, 1972.

LEITH, J.A. *The Idea of Art as Propaganda in France 1750-1789. A Study in the History of Ideas.* Toronto, 1965.

LENOIR, A. *David. Souvenirs historiques.* Paris, 1835.

LEVEY, Michael. *Rococo to Revolution.* London: Thames and Hudson, 1966.

LINDSAY, Jack. *Death of the Hero. French Painting from David to Delacroix.* London: Studio, 1960.

LOISEL-LEGRAND, C. *Catalogue. Autour de David et Delacroix.* Besançon: Musée des Beaux-Arts, 1982.

MARET, Jacques. *David.* Monaco: Documents d'Art, 1943.

MIETTE DE VILLARS. *Mémoires de David, peintre et député de la Convention.* Paris, 1850.

NANTEUIL, Luc de. *Jacques-Louis David.* Paris: Cercle d'Art, 1987.

OLEANDER, W. *"Pour transmettre à la postérité": French Painting and Revolution, 1774-1795.* Unpublished doctoral thesis, New York University, 1983.

ROSENAU, H. *The Painter Jacques-Louis David.* London, 1948.

ROSENTHAL, Léon. *Louis David.* Paris: Librairie de l'Art ancien et moderne, undated.

SAHUT, M.-C. and VOLLE, N. *Catalogue. Diderot et l'art de Boucher à David, les Salons: 1757-1781.* Paris: Hôtel de la Monnaie, 1985.

SAHUT, M.-C. and MICHEL, R. *David, l'art et le politique.* Paris: Gallimard, 1988.

SCHNAPPER, Antoine. *David témoin de son temps.* Fribourg: Office du Livre, 1980. *David.* Trans. by Helga Harrison. New York: Alpine Fine Arts Collection, 1982.

STOLPE, Elmar. *Klassizismus und Krieg. Über den Historienmaler Jacques-Louis David.* Francfort, New York: Campus, 1985.

THOMÉ DE GAMOND, A. *Vie de David, premier peintre de Napoléon.* Brussels, 1826.

TRAEGER, J. *Der Tod des Marat. Revolution des Menschenbildes.* Munich: Prestel, 1986.

VALENTINER, W. R., *Jacques David and the French Revolution.* New York, 1929.

VERBRAEKEN, R. *Jacques-Louis David jugé par ses contemporains et par la postérité.* Paris: Léonce Laget, 1973.

WINCKELMANN, Johann Joachim. *Gedanken über die Nachahnung der griechischen Werke in der Malerei und Bildhauerkunst.* Dresden, 1755.

WINCKELMANN, Johann Joachim. *Geschichte der Kunst des Altentums.* English translation, *A History of Ancient Art,* 1763.

*We wish to thank the owners of the pictures reproduced herein.*

## MUSEUMS

BELGIUM : Musées Royaux des Beaux-Arts de Belgique, *Brussels.*

FRANCE : Musée Calvet, *Avignon* - Musée d'Art et d'Archéologie, *Besançon* - Musée Thomas Henry, *Cherbourg* - Musée des Beaux-Arts, *Lille* - Musée Fabre, *Montpellier* - École Nationale supérieure des Beaux-Arts, *Paris* - Cabinet des Dessins, Musée du Louvre, *Paris* - Musée du Louvre, *Paris* - Musée National du Château de *Versailles* et des Trianons.

POLAND : Muzeum Narodowe, *Warsaw.*

U.S.A. : The Fogg Art Museum, Harvard University, *Cambridge*, Massachusetts - The Art Institute, *Chicago* - The *Cleveland* Museum of Art, Ohio - The Metropolitan Museum of Art, *New York* - Smith College Museum of Art, *Northampton*, Massachusetts - National Gallery of Art, *Washington*, D.C.

## PHOTOGRAPHS

Charles Choffet, *Besançon* - Frédéric Jaulmes, *Montpellier* - Giraudon, *Paris* - Hubert Josse, *Paris* - Service Photographique de la Réunion des Musées Nationaux, *Paris* - Photo Savary, *Tourlaville*, Manche - H. Edelstein, *Northampton*, Massachusetts - Herbert P. Vose, *Wellesley Hills*, Massachusetts.

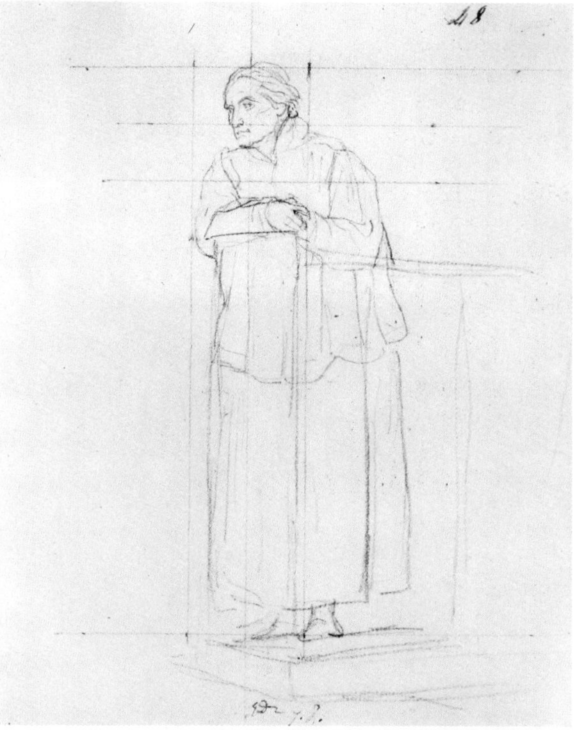

*Unidentified Cleric Leaning on a Rail*
*Sketchbook no. 14, 1805-1806, p. 48 recto*
*Pencil, 9⁵⁄₁₆" × 7¼" (23.7 × 17.9 cm)*
*The Fogg Art Museum, Harvard University*
*Cambridge, Massachusetts*
*Bequest of Grenville L. Winthrop*

# ILLUSTRATIONS